SpringBoard®

English Language Development

California Edition

Grade
8

CollegeBoard

ABOUT THE COLLEGE BOARD

The College Board is a mission-driven not-for-profit organization that connects students to college success and opportunity. Founded in 1900, the College Board was created to expand access to higher education. Today, the membership association is made up of more than 6,000 of the world's leading educational institutions and is dedicated to promoting excellence and equity in education. Each year, the College Board helps more than seven million students prepare for a successful transition to college through programs and services in college readiness and college success—including the SAT® and the Advanced Placement Program®. The organization also serves the education community through research and advocacy on behalf of students, educators and schools. For further information, visit www.collegeboard.com.

ISBN: 978-1-4573-0478-1
ISBN: 1-4573-0478-3

1 2 3 4 5 6 7 8   16 17 18 19 20 21 22
Printed in the United States of America

ACKNOWLEDGMENTS

The College Board gratefully acknowledges the outstanding work of the classroom teachers, reviewers, and writers who have been integral to the development of this program. The end product is testimony to their expertise, understanding of student learning needs, and dedication to rigorous English language arts instruction that is accessible to all students.

Patty M. Blome
English Language Arts teacher
Mar Vista Academy
San Diego, California

Shinay Bowman
English Language Arts Coach
King Middle School
San Bernardino, California

Michelle Callahan-Dumont
English Teacher
Sunnyside High School
Tucson, Arizona

Michael Gudex
English Language Arts Teacher
Sun Valley Magnet School
Sun Valley, California

Maria Larios-Horton
Director of Multilingual and
Migrant Education Programs
Santa Maria Joint Union High School
District
Santa Maria, California

Eden Orlando
English Learner Resource Teacher
Mission Bay High School
San Diego, California

Dr. Virginia Rojas
Language Education
Consultant

Jody Talkington
English Language Learner Specialist
Oakland International High School
Oakland, California

SPRINGBOARD ENGLISH LANGUAGE DEVELOPMENT

Lori O'Dea
Executive Director
Content Development

Doug Waugh
Executive Director
Product Management

JoEllen Victoreen
English Language Arts
Instructional Manager

Sarah Balistreri
English Language Arts Editor

Jennifer Duva
English Language Arts Editor

Rebecca Grudzina
English Language Arts Editor

Melissa Ragan
English Language
Development Editor

Spencer Gonçalves
Assistant ELA Editor

Jessica Pippin
Assistant ELA Editor

Contents

Unit 1 The Challenge of Heroism: Evaluating Narratives to Define "Hero"

Part One: Short Story: "The Drummer Boy of Shiloh" by Ray Bradbury

Part Two: Epic Poem: from the *Odyssey* by Homer, translation by Tony Kline

Part Three: Poem: "O Captain! My Captain!" by Walt Whitman

Unit 2 The Challenge of Utopia: Analyzing and Evaluating Literary and Informational Texts

Unit 3   The Challenge to Make a Difference: Evaluating and Presenting Arguments

Part One: Novel: from *The Boy in the Striped Pajamas* by John Boyne

Part Two: Speech: from Elie Wiesel's Nobel Peace Prize Acceptance Speech by Elie Wiesel

Part Three: Speech: Address by Cesar Chavez, President United Farm Workers of America, AFL-CIO by Cesar Chavez

Unit 4   The Challenge of Comedy: Critiquing and Creating Comedy

To the Student

Dear Student,

In the United States, the number of students whose first language is one other than English has grown. More and more students like you face the challenge of achieving academic success while continuing to develop their English skills.

While this is a big challenge, SpringBoard believes you can do it!

We designed this course to help you. Research shows that students who understand how English works, and who practice English in meaningful interactions can make huge gains. These gains lead to success in middle school courses as well as in high school, and eventually in the college and career choices you'll make.

In SpringBoard English Language Development, you will build your language in four key ways. You will:

- Study language that helps you understand English language arts.
- Learn academic vocabulary, so you can express yourself in any class.
- Identify the meaning of language that you may encounter in the texts you'll read.
- Use skills that will help you figure out the meaning of unknown or multiple meaning words when you read on your own.

The primary goal of SpringBoard English Language Development is to build your English language, and we hope that you will make this your goal, too.

Another goal is for you to become a stronger reader who can make meaning from even the most challenging texts that you read. In SpringBoard English Language Development, you will spend more time with each text, returning to it while engaging in interactive activities with your classmates. Your teacher will lead you in close reading sessions, during which you will zoom in on complex parts of a text to increase your understanding.

In addition to the language and reading goals, SpringBoard English Language Development wants you to speak and listen to your peers about the texts you're reading, their themes, and, of course, your own ideas. Most importantly, while you are in discussions with your classmates, you will learn how to support your opinions and ideas with evidence, add details, and produce the effect you want by choosing just the right words. In addition to frequent academic conversations, you will also have the opportunity to plan, prepare for, practice, and deliver presentations and performances.

Every day in SpringBoard English Language Development you will be writing. Sometimes you will be jotting down notes after a conversation or annotating a text as you read. Sometimes you will be adding words and phrases to a graphic organizer. Other times you will be completing sentences or writing your own sentences. You will be writing short summaries and explanations. You will also be crafting longer arguments, as well as creating narratives of your own. You will do all of these kinds of writing with the collaboration and support of your peers and your teacher. Working together, you will inspire and help each other to achieve the best results.

A final goal for SpringBoard English Language Development is for you to achieve something beyond the classroom— beyond the ELD classroom, that is. All the work you will be doing—building your language, analyzing complex texts, expressing and defending your ideas in discussions, writing arguments, explanations, and stories, and presenting your work to your peers—will help you to achieve success in another class: SpringBoard English Language Arts. What you learn in the ELD class will prepare you with the language resources you need to achieve at the highest levels.

The challenge is yours and we hope you will accept the challenge!

Sincerely,

SpringBoard

California English Language Development Standards

Part I: Interacting in Meaningful Ways

Communicative Modes	Standard Code	Emerging	Expanding	Bridging
Collaborative	PI.8.1	**Exchanging information/ideas** Engage in conversational exchanges and express ideas on familiar topics by asking and answering *yes–no* and *wh-* questions and responding using simple phrases.	**Exchanging information/ideas** Contribute to class, group, and partner discussions by following turn-taking rules, asking relevant questions, affirming others, adding relevant information, and paraphrasing key ideas.	**Exchanging information/ideas** Contribute to class, group, and partner discussions by following turn-taking rules, asking relevant questions, affirming others, adding relevant information and evidence, paraphrasing key ideas, building on responses, and providing useful feedback.
	PI.8.2	**Interacting via written English** Engage in short written exchanges with peers and collaborate on simple written texts on familiar topics, using technology when appropriate.	**Interacting via written English** Engage in longer written exchanges with peers and collaborate on more detailed written texts on a variety of topics, using technology when appropriate.	**Interacting via written English** Engage in extended written exchanges with peers and collaborate on complex written texts on a variety of topics, using technology when appropriate.
	PI.8.3	**Supporting opinions and persuading others** Negotiate with or persuade others in conversations (e.g., to gain and hold the floor or to ask for clarification) using learned phrases (e.g., *I think . . . Would you please repeat that?*) and open responses.	**Supporting opinions and persuading others** Negotiate with or persuade others in conversations (e.g., to provide counter-arguments) using learned phrases (*I agree with X, but . . .*) and open responses.	**Supporting opinions and persuading others** Negotiate with or persuade others in conversations using an appropriate register (e.g., to acknowledge new information and justify views) using a variety of learned phrases, indirect reported speech (e.g., *I heard you say X, and that's a good point. I still think Y, though, because . . .*) and open responses.
	PI.8.4	**Adapting language choices** Adjust language choices according to social setting (e.g., classroom, break time) and audience (e.g., peers, teacher).	**Adapting language choices** Adjust language choices according to purpose (e.g., explaining, persuading, entertaining), task, and audience.	**Adapting language choices** Adjust language choices according to task (e.g., facilitating a science experiment, providing peer feedback on a writing assignment), purpose, and audience.

Communicative Modes	Standard Code	Emerging	Expanding	Bridging
Interpretive	PI.8.5	**Listening actively** Demonstrate active listening in oral presentation activities by asking and answering basic questions with prompting and substantial support.	**Listening actively** Demonstrate active listening in oral presentation activities by asking and answering detailed questions with occasional prompting and moderate support.	**Listening actively** Demonstrate active listening in oral presentation activities by asking and answering detailed questions with minimal prompting and support.
	PI.8.6a	**Reading/viewing closely** Explain ideas, phenomena, processes, and text relationships (e.g., compare/contrast, cause/effect, problem/solution) based on close reading of a variety of grade-appropriate texts and viewing of multimedia with substantial support.	**Reading/viewing closely** Explain ideas, phenomena, processes, and text relationships (e.g., compare/contrast, cause/effect, problem/solution) based on close reading of a variety of grade-appropriate texts and viewing of multimedia with moderate support.	**Reading/viewing closely** Explain ideas, phenomena, processes, and text relationships (e.g., compare/contrast, cause/effect, problem/solution) based on close reading of a variety of grade-level texts and viewing of multimedia with light support.
	PI.8.6b	**Reading/viewing closely** Express inferences and conclusions drawn based on close reading of grade-appropriate texts and viewing of multimedia using some frequently used verbs (e.g., *shows that, based on*).	**Reading/viewing closely** Express inferences and conclusions drawn based on close reading of grade-appropriate texts and viewing of multimedia using a variety of verbs (e.g., *suggests that, leads to*).	**Reading/viewing closely** Express inferences and conclusions drawn based on close reading of grade-level texts and viewing of multimedia using a variety of precise academic verbs (e.g., *indicates that, influences*).
	PI.8.6c	**Reading/viewing closely** Use knowledge of morphology (e.g., affixes, roots, and base words), context, reference materials, and visual cues to determine the meanings of unknown and multiple-meaning words on familiar topics.	**Reading/viewing closely** Use knowledge of morphology (e.g., affixes, roots, and base words), context, reference materials, and visual cues to determine the meanings of unknown and multiple-meaning words on familiar and new topics.	**Reading/viewing closely** Use knowledge of morphology (e.g., affixes, roots, and base words), context, reference materials, and visual cues to determine the meanings, including figurative and connotative meanings, of unknown and multiple-meaning words on a variety of new topics.

Communicative Modes	Standard Code	Emerging	Expanding	Bridging
Interpretive	PI.8.7	**Evaluating language choices** Explain how well writers and speakers use language to support ideas and arguments with detailed evidence (e.g., identifying the precise vocabulary used to present evidence, or the phrasing used to signal a shift in meaning) when provided with substantial support.	**Evaluating language choices** Explain how well writers and speakers use specific language to present ideas or support arguments and provide detailed evidence (e.g., showing the clarity of the phrasing used to present an argument) when provided with moderate support.	**Evaluating language choices** Explain how well writers and speakers use specific language resources to present ideas or support arguments and provide detailed evidence (e.g., identifying the specific language used to present ideas and claims that are well supported and distinguishing them from those that are not) when provided with light support.
	PI.8.8	**Analyzing language choices** Explain how phrasing or different common words with similar meanings (e.g., choosing to use the word persistent versus the term *hard worker*) produce different effects on the audience.	**Analyzing language choices** Explain how phrasing or different words with similar meanings (e.g., describing a character as *stubborn* versus *persistent*) or figurative language (e.g., *Let me throw some light onto the topic.*) produce shades of meaning and different effects on the audience.	**Analyzing language choices** Explain how phrasing or different words with similar meanings (e.g., *cunning* versus *smart*, *stammer* versus *say*) or figurative language (e.g., *Let me throw some light onto the topic.*) produce shades of meaning, nuances, and different effects on the audience.
Productive	PI.8.9	**Presenting** Plan and deliver brief informative oral presentations on concrete topics.	**Presenting** Plan and deliver longer oral presentations on a variety of topics using details and evidence to support ideas.	**Presenting** Plan and deliver longer oral presentations on a variety of concrete and abstract topics using reasoning and evidence to support ideas and using a growing understanding of register.
	PI.8.10a	**Writing** Write short literary and informational texts (e.g., an argument about whether the government should fund research using stem cells) collaboratively (e.g., with peers) and independently.	**Writing** Write longer literary and informational texts (e.g., an argument about whether the government should fund research using stem cells) collaboratively (e.g., with peers) and independently using appropriate text organization.	**Writing** Write longer and more detailed literary and informational texts (e.g., an argument about whether the government should fund research using stem cells) collaboratively (e.g., with peers) and independently using appropriate text organization and growing understanding of register.

Communicative Modes	Standard Code	Emerging	Expanding	Bridging
Productive	PI.8.10b	**Writing** Write brief summaries of texts and experiences using complete sentences and key words (e.g., from notes or graphic organizers).	**Writing** Write increasingly concise summaries of texts and experiences using complete sentences and key words (e.g., from notes or graphic organizers).	**Writing** Write clear and coherent summaries of texts and experiences using complete and concise sentences and key words (e.g., from notes or graphic organizers).
	PI.8.11a	**Justifying/arguing** Justify opinions by providing some textual evidence or relevant background knowledge with substantial support.	**Justifying/arguing** Justify opinions or persuade others by providing relevant textual evidence or relevant background knowledge with moderate support.	**Justifying/arguing** Justify opinions or persuade others by providing detailed and relevant textual evidence or relevant background knowledge with light support.
	PI.8.11b	**Justifying/arguing** Express attitude and opinions or temper statements with familiar modal expressions (e.g., *can, may*).	**Justifying/arguing** Express attitude and opinions or temper statements with a variety of familiar modal expressions (e.g., *possibly/likely, could/would*).	**Justifying/arguing** Express attitude and opinions or temper statements with nuanced modal expressions (e.g., *potentially/certainly/absolutely, should/might*).
	PI.8.12a	**Selecting language resources** Use a select number of general academic words (e.g., *specific, contrast*) and domain-specific words (e.g., *scene, cell, fraction*) to create some precision while speaking and writing.	**Selecting language resources** Use a growing set of academic words (e.g., *specific, contrast, significant, function*), domain-specific words (e.g., *scene, irony, suspense, analogy, cell membrane, fraction*), synonyms, and antonyms to create precision and shades of meaning while speaking and writing.	**Selecting language resources** Use an expanded set of general academic words (e.g., *specific, contrast, significant, function, adequate, analysis*), domain-specific words (e.g., *scene, irony, suspense, analogy, cell membrane, fraction*), synonyms, antonyms, and figurative language to create precision and shades of meaning while speaking and writing.
	PI.8.12b	**Selecting language resources** Use knowledge of morphology to appropriately select affixes in basic ways (e.g., *She likes X. He walked to school.*).	**Selecting language resources** Use knowledge of morphology to appropriately select affixes in a growing number of ways to manipulate language (e.g., *She likes walking to school. That's impossible.*).	**Selecting language resources** Use knowledge of morphology to appropriately select affixes in a variety of ways to manipulate language (e.g., *changing destroy ⟶ destruction, probably ⟶ probability, reluctant ⟶ reluctantly*).

Part II: Learning About How English Works

Language Processes	Standard Code	Emerging	Expanding	Bridging
Structuring Cohesive Texts	PII.8.1	**Understanding text structure** Apply understanding of how different text types are organized to express ideas (e.g., how narratives are organized sequentially) to comprehending texts and to writing brief arguments, informative/explanatory texts and narratives.	**Understanding text structure** Apply understanding of the organizational features of different text types (e.g., how narratives are organized by an event sequence that unfolds naturally versus how arguments are organized around reasons and evidence) to comprehending texts and to writing increasingly clear and coherent arguments, informative/explanatory texts and narratives.	**Understanding text structure** Apply understanding of the organizational structure of different text types (e.g., how narratives are organized by an event sequence that unfolds naturally versus how arguments are organized around reasons and evidence) to comprehending texts and to writing clear and cohesive arguments, informative/explanatory texts and narratives.
	PII.8.2a	**Understanding cohesion** Apply knowledge of familiar language resources for referring to make texts more cohesive (e.g., how pronouns refer back to nouns in text) to comprehending and writing brief texts.	**Understanding cohesion** Apply knowledge of familiar language resources for referring to make texts more cohesive (e.g., how pronouns refer back to nouns in text, how using synonyms helps avoid repetition) to comprehending and writing texts with increasing cohesion.	**Understanding cohesion** Apply knowledge of familiar language resources for referring to make texts more cohesive (e.g., how pronouns, synonyms, or nominalizations are used to refer backward in a text) to comprehending texts and writing cohesive texts.
	PII.8.2b	**Understanding cohesion** Apply basic understanding of how ideas, events, or reasons are linked throughout a text using everyday connecting words or phrases (e.g., *at the end, next*) to comprehending and writing brief texts.	**Understanding cohesion** Apply growing understanding of how ideas, events, or reasons are linked throughout a text using a variety of connecting words or phrases (e.g., *for example, as a result, on the other hand*) to comprehending and writing texts with increasing cohesion.	**Understanding cohesion** Apply increasing understanding of how ideas, events, or reasons are linked throughout a text using an increasing variety of academic connecting and transitional words or phrases (e.g., *for instance, in addition, consequently*) to comprehending and writing texts with increasing cohesion.

Language Processes	Standard Code	Emerging	Expanding	Bridging
Expanding and Enriching Ideas	PII.8.3	**Using verbs and verb phrases** Use a variety of verbs in different tenses (e.g., present, past, future) and aspects (e.g., simple, progressive) appropriate for the text type and discipline (e.g., simple past and past progressive for recounting an experience) on familiar topics.	**Using verbs and verb phrases** Use a variety of verbs in different tenses (e.g., present, past, future) and aspects (e.g., simple, progressive, perfect) appropriate for the task, text type, and discipline (e.g., the present perfect to describe previously made claims or conclusions) on an increasing variety of topics.	**Using verbs and verb phrases** Use a variety of verbs in different tenses (e.g., present, past, future), aspects (e.g., simple, progressive, perfect), voices (active and passive), and moods (e.g., declarative, interrogative, subjunctive) appropriate for the task, text type, and discipline (e.g., the passive voice in simple past to describe the methods of a scientific experiment) on a variety of topics.
	PII.8.4	**Using nouns and noun phrases** Expand noun phrases in basic ways (e.g., adding a sensory adjective to a noun) in order to enrich the meaning of sentences and add details about ideas, people, things, etc.	**Using nouns and noun phrases** Expand noun phrases in a growing number of ways (e.g., adding prepositional or adjective phrases) in order to enrich the meaning of sentences and add details about ideas, people, things, etc.	**Using nouns and noun phrases** Expand noun phrases in an increasing variety of ways (e.g., embedding relative or complement clauses) in order to enrich the meaning of sentences and add details about ideas, people, things, etc.
	PII.8.5	**Modifying to add details** Expand sentences with simple adverbials (e.g., adverbs, adverb phrases, prepositional phrases) to provide details (e.g., time, manner, place, cause) about a familiar activity or process.	**Modifying to add details** Expand sentences with adverbials (e.g., adverbs, adverb phrases, prepositional phrases) to provide details (e.g., time, manner, place, cause) about a familiar or new activity or process.	**Modifying to add details** Expand sentences with increasingly complex adverbials (e.g., adverbs, adverb phrases and clauses, prepositional phrases) to provide details (e.g., time, manner, place, cause) about a variety of familiar and new activities and processes.

Language Processes	Standard Code	Emerging	Expanding	Bridging
Connecting and Condensing Ideas	PII.8.6	**Connecting ideas** Combine clauses in a few basic ways to make connections between and join ideas (e.g., creating compound sentences using *and, but, so*; creating complex sentences using *because*).	**Connecting ideas** Combine clauses in an increasing variety of ways (e.g., creating compound and complex sentences) to make connections between and join ideas, for example, to express a reason (e.g., *He stayed at home on Sunday to study for Monday's exam.*) or to make a concession (e.g., *She studied all night even though she wasn't feeling well.*).	**Connecting ideas** Combine clauses in a wide variety of ways (e.g., creating compound and complex sentences, and compound- complex sentences) to make connections between and join ideas, for example, to show the relationship between multiple events or ideas (e.g., *After eating lunch, the students worked in groups while their teacher walked around the room.*) or to evaluate an argument (e.g., *The author claims X, although there is a lack of evidence to support this claim.*).
	PII.8.7	**Condensing ideas** Condense ideas in simple ways (e.g., by compounding verbs, adding prepositional phrases, or through simple embedded clauses or other ways of condensing as in, This is a story about a girl. The girl changed the world. ····⟩ This is a story about a girl *who changed the world.*) to create precise and detailed sentences.	**Condensing ideas** Condense ideas in an increasing variety of ways (e.g., through various types of embedded clauses and other ways of condensing, as in, Organic vegetables are food. They're made without chemical fertilizers. They're made without chemical insecticides. ····⟩ Organic vegetables are foods *that are made without chemical fertilizers or insecticides.*) to create precise and detailed sentences.	**Condensing ideas** Condense ideas in a variety of ways (e.g., through various types of embedded clauses, ways of condensing, and nominalization as in, They *destroyed* the rainforest. Lots of animals *died.* ····⟩ The *destruction* of the rainforest led to the *death* of many animals.) to create precise and detailed sentences.
Foundational Literacy Skills: **Literacy in an Alphabetic Writing System** • Print concepts • Phonological awareness • Phonics and word recognition • Fluency	PIII.8	**See Appendix A [of the California ELD Standards] for information on teaching reading foundational skills to English learners of various profiles based on age, native language, native language writing system, schooling experience, and literacy experience and proficiency. Some considerations are:** • Native language and literacy (e.g., phoneme awareness or print concept skills in native language) should be assessed for potential transference to English language and literacy. • Similarities between native language and English should be highlighted (e.g., phonemes or letters that are the same in both languages). • Differences between native language and English should be highlighted (e.g., some phonemes in English may not exist in the student's native language; native language syntax may be different from English syntax).		

California Common Core State Standards

Reading Standards for Literature

Key Ideas and Details	RL.8.1	Cite the textual evidence that most strongly supports an analysis of what the text says explicitly as well as inferences drawn from the text.
	RL.8.2	Determine a theme or central idea of a text and analyze its development over the course of the text, including its relationship to the characters, setting, and plot; provide an objective summary of the text.
	RL.8.3	Analyze how particular lines of dialogue or incidents in a story or drama propel the action, reveal aspects of a character, or provoke a decision.
Craft and Structure	RL.8.4	Determine the meaning of words and phrases as they are used in a text, including figurative and connotative meanings; analyze the impact of specific word choices on meaning and tone, including analogies or allusions to other texts. **(See grade 8 Language standards 4–6 for additional expectations.) CA**
	RL.8.5	Compare and contrast the structure of two or more texts and analyze how the differing structure of each text contributes to its meaning and style.
	RL.8.6	Analyze how differences in the points of view of the characters and the audience or reader (e.g., created through the use of dramatic irony) create such effects as suspense or humor.
Integration of Knowledge and Ideas	RL.8.7	Analyze the extent to which a filmed or live production of a story or drama stays faithful to or departs from the text or script, evaluating the choices made by the director or actors.
	RL.8.8	(Not applicable to literature)
	RL.8.9	Analyze how a modern work of fiction draws on themes, patterns of events, or character types from myths, traditional stories, or religious works such as the Bible, including describing how the material is rendered new.
Range of Reading and Text Complexity	RL.8.10	By the end of the year, read and comprehend literature, including stories, dramas, and poems, at the high end of grades 6–8 text complexity band independently and proficiently.

Reading Standards for Informational Text

Key Ideas and Details	RI.8.1	Cite the textual evidence that most strongly supports an analysis of what the text says explicitly as well as inferences drawn from the text.
	RI.8.2	Determine a central idea of a text and analyze its development over the course of the text, including its relationship to supporting ideas; provide an objective summary of the text.
	RI.8.3	Analyze how a text makes connections among and distinctions between individuals, ideas, or events (e.g., through comparisons, analogies, or categories).
Craft and Structure	RI.8.4	Determine the meaning of words and phrases as they are used in a text, including figurative, connotative, and technical meanings; analyze the impact of specific word choices on meaning and tone, including analogies or allusions to other texts. **(See grade 8 Language standards 4–6 for additional expectations.) CA**
	RI.8.5	Analyze in detail the structure of a specific paragraph in a text, including the role of particular sentences in developing and refining a key concept.
	RI.8.5a	**Analyze the use of text features (e.g., graphics, headers, captions) in consumer materials. CA**
	RI.8.6	Determine an author's point of view or purpose in a text and analyze how the author acknowledges and responds to conflicting evidence or viewpoints.
Integration of Knowledge and Ideas	RI.8.7	Evaluate the advantages and disadvantages of using different mediums (e.g., print or digital text, video, multimedia) to present a particular topic or idea.
	RI.8.8	Delineate and evaluate the argument and specific claims in a text, assessing whether the reasoning is sound and the evidence is relevant and sufficient; recognize when irrelevant evidence is introduced.
	RI.8.9	Analyze a case in which two or more texts provide conflicting information on the same topic and identify where the texts disagree on matters of fact or interpretation.
Range of Reading and Text Complexity	RI.8.10	By the end of the year, read and comprehend literary nonfiction at the high end of the grades 6–8 text complexity band independently and proficiently.

Writing Standards

Text Types and Purposes	W.8.1	Write arguments to support claims with clear reasons and relevant evidence.
	W.8.1a	Introduce claim(s), acknowledge and distinguish the claim(s) from alternate or opposing claims, and organize the reasons and evidence logically.
	W.8.1b	Support claim(s) with logical reasoning and relevant evidence, using accurate, credible sources and demonstrating an understanding of the topic or text.
	W.8.1c	Use words, phrases, and clauses to create cohesion and clarify the relationships among claim(s), counterclaims, reasons, and evidence.
	W.8.1d	Establish and maintain a formal style.
	W.8.1e	Provide a concluding statement or section that follows from and supports the argument presented.
	W.8.2	Write informative/explanatory texts, **including career development documents (e.g., simple business letters and job applications),** to examine a topic and convey ideas, concepts, and information through the selection, organization, and analysis of relevant content. **CA**
	W.8.2a	Introduce a topic **or thesis statement** clearly, previewing what is to follow; organize ideas, concepts, and information into broader categories; include formatting (e.g., headings), graphics (e.g., charts, tables), and multimedia when useful to aiding comprehension. **CA**
	W.8.2b	Develop the topic with relevant, well-chosen facts, definitions, concrete details, quotations, or other information and examples.
	W.8.2c	Use appropriate and varied transitions to create cohesion and clarify the relationships among ideas and concepts.
	W.8.2d	Use precise language and domain-specific vocabulary to inform about or explain the topic.
	W.8.2e	Establish and maintain a formal style.
	W.8.2f	Provide a concluding statement or section that follows from and supports the information or explanation presented.
	W.8.3	Write narratives to develop real or imagined experiences or events using effective technique, relevant descriptive details, and well-structured event sequences.
	W.8.3a	Engage and orient the reader by establishing a context and point of view and introducing a narrator and/or characters; organize an event sequence that unfolds naturally and logically.

Writing Standards

Text Types and Purposes	W.8.3b	Use narrative techniques, such as dialogue, pacing, description, and reflection, to develop experiences, events, and/or characters.
	W.8.3c	Use a variety of transition words, phrases, and clauses to convey sequence, signal shifts from one time frame or setting to another, and show the relationships among experiences and events.
	W.8.3d	Use precise words and phrases, relevant descriptive details, and sensory language to capture the action and convey experiences and events.
	W.8.3e	Provide a conclusion that follows from and reflects on the narrated experiences or events.
Production and Distribution of Writing	W.8.4	Produce clear and coherent writing in which the development, organization, and style are appropriate to task, purpose, and audience. (Grade-specific expectations for writing types are defined in standards 1–3 above.)
	W.8.5	With some guidance and support from peers and adults, develop and strengthen writing as needed by planning, revising, editing, rewriting, or trying a new approach, focusing on how well purpose and audience have been addressed. (Editing for conventions should demonstrate command of Language standards 1–3 up to and including grade 8.)
	W.8.6	Use technology, including the Internet, to produce and publish writing and present the relationships between information and ideas efficiently as well as to interact and collaborate with others.
Research to Build and Present Knowledge	W.8.7	Conduct short research projects to answer a question (including a self-generated question), drawing on several sources and generating additional related, focused questions that allow for multiple avenues of exploration.
	W.8.8	Gather relevant information from multiple print and digital sources, using search terms effectively; assess the credibility and accuracy of each source; and quote or paraphrase the data and conclusions of others while avoiding plagiarism and following a standard format for citation.
	W.8.9	Draw evidence from literary or informational texts to support analysis, reflection, and research.
	W.8.9a	Apply grade 8 Reading standards to literature (e.g., "Analyze how a modern work of fiction draws on themes, patterns of events, or character types from myths, traditional stories, or religious works such as the Bible, including describing how the material is rendered new").
	W.8.9b	Apply grade 8 Reading standards to literary nonfiction (e.g., "Delineate and evaluate the argument and specific claims in a text, assessing whether the reasoning is sound and the evidence is relevant and sufficient; recognize when irrelevant evidence is introduced").
Range of Writing	W.8.10	Write routinely over extended time frames (time for research, reflection, and revision) and shorter time frames (a single sitting or a day or two) for a range of discipline-specific tasks, purposes, and audiences.

Speaking and Listening Standards

Comprehension and Collaboration	SL.8.1	Engage effectively in a range of collaborative discussions (one-on-one, in groups, and teacher-led) with diverse partners on grade 8 topics, texts, and issues, building on others' ideas and expressing their own clearly.
	SL.8.1a	Come to discussions prepared, having read or researched material under study; explicitly draw on that preparation by referring to evidence on the topic, text, or issue to probe and reflect on ideas under discussion.
	SL.8.1b	Follow rules for collegial discussions and decision-making, track progress toward specific goals and deadlines, and define individual roles as needed.
	SL.8.1c	Pose questions that connect the ideas of several speakers and respond to others' questions and comments with relevant evidence, observations, and ideas.
	SL.8.1d	Acknowledge new information expressed by others, and, when warranted, qualify or justify their own views in light of the evidence presented.
	SL.8.2	Analyze the purpose of information presented in diverse media and formats (e.g., visually, quantitatively, orally) and evaluate the motives (e.g., social, commercial, political) behind its presentation.
	SL.8.3	Delineate a speaker's argument and specific claims, evaluating the soundness of the reasoning and relevance and sufficiency of the evidence and identifying when irrelevant evidence is introduced.
Presentation of Knowledge and Ideas	SL.8.4	Present claims and findings (e.g., argument, narrative, response to literature presentations), emphasizing salient points in a focused, coherent manner with relevant evidence, sound valid reasoning, and well-chosen details; use appropriate eye contact, adequate volume, and clear pronunciation. CA
	SL.8.4a	Plan and present a narrative that: establishes a context and point of view, presents a logical sequence, uses narrative techniques (e.g., dialogue, pacing, description, sensory language), uses a variety of transitions, and provides a conclusion that reflects the experience. CA
	SL.8.5	Integrate multimedia and visual displays into presentations to clarify information, strengthen claims and evidence, and add interest.
	SL.8.6	Adapt speech to a variety of contexts and tasks, demonstrating command of formal English when indicated or appropriate. (See grade 8 Language standards 1 and 3 for specific expectations.)

Language Standards

Conventions of Standard English	L.8.1	Demonstrate command of the conventions of standard English grammar and usage when writing or speaking.
	L.8.1a	Explain the function of verbals (gerunds, participles, infinitives) in general and their function in particular sentences.
	L.8.1b	Form and use verbs in the active and passive voice.
	L.8.1c	Form and use verbs in the indicative, imperative, interrogative, conditional, and subjunctive mood.
	L.8.1d	Recognize and correct inappropriate shifts in verb voice and mood.
	L.8.2	Demonstrate command of the conventions of standard English capitalization, punctuation, and spelling when writing.
	L.8.2a	Use punctuation (comma, ellipsis, dash) to indicate a pause or break.
	L.8.2b	Use an ellipsis to indicate an omission.
	L.8.2c	Spell correctly.
Knowledge of Language	L.8.3	Use knowledge of language and its conventions when writing, speaking, reading, or listening.
	L.8.3a	Use verbs in the active and passive voice and in the conditional and subjunctive mood to achieve particular effects (e.g., emphasizing the actor or the action; expressing uncertainty or describing a state contrary to fact).
Vocabulary Acquisition and Use	L.8.4	Determine or clarify the meaning of unknown and multiple-meaning words or phrases based on grade 8 reading and content, choosing flexibly from a range of strategies.
	L.8.4a	Use context (e.g., the overall meaning of a sentence or paragraph; a word's position or function in a sentence) as a clue to the meaning of a word or phrase.
	L.8.4b	Use common, grade-appropriate Greek or Latin affixes and roots as clues to the meaning of a word (e.g., precede, recede, secede).
	L.8.4c	Consult general and specialized reference materials (e.g., dictionaries, glossaries, thesauruses), both print and digital, to find the pronunciation of a word or determine or clarify its precise meaning or its part of speech **or trace the etymology of words. CA**
	L.8.4d	Verify the preliminary determination of the meaning of a word or phrase (e.g., by checking the inferred meaning in context or in a dictionary).

Language Standards

Vocabulary Acquisition and Use	L.8.5	Demonstrate understanding of figurative language, word relationships, and nuances in word meanings.
	L.8.5a	Interpret figures of speech (e.g. verbal irony, puns) in context.
	L.8.5b	Use the relationship between particular words to better understand each of the words.
	L.8.5c	Distinguish among the connotations (associations) of words with similar denotations (definitions) (e.g., bullheaded, willful, firm, persistent, resolute).
	L.8.6	Acquire and use accurately grade-appropriate general academic and domain-specific words and phrases; gather vocabulary knowledge when considering a word or phrase important to comprehension or expression.

THE CHALLENGE OF HEROISM:
Evaluating Narratives to Define "Hero"

Visual Prompt: What do you picture when you hear the word *hero*? What words and images immediately come to mind?

Unit Overview

This unit focuses on the challenges of heroism. Because this word is used every day—in television shows, movies, video games, books, the news, school, and conversations—we rarely take time to actually think about what it means. In this unit, you will read and write to develop a more complex understanding of this important societal and cultural concept.

**ACTIVITY
1.1**

 LANGUAGE RESOURCES

Selecting Language Resources

 WORD CONNECTIONS

Cognates

The English word ***protagonist*** and the Spanish word ***protagonista*** are cognates. They both mean "the main actor" and come from the Greek roots ***protos***, meaning "first," and ***agonistes***, meaning "actor" or "competitor."

Learning Targets

- Develop language resources to use while speaking and writing about a short story.
- Use an expanded set of words to speak and write precisely.
- Adjust language choices to suit the academic setting.

The chart presents words and phrases you will use in discussion and writing. Think about each word or phrase. Circle Q, H, or T to indicate how well you know it. Work with a partner, asking your partner to explain each word or phrase. Listen closely to the explanation, and then write your partner's name in the In Our Own Words column along with his or her condensed idea.

Rating	Q	H	T
	I have seen this word, but I have **questions** about its meaning.	I have **heard** this word but do not know it well.	I know this word so well that I could **teach** it to someone else.

Word or Phrase	Definition	In Our Own Words
setting Rating Q H T	the place and time in which a story happens, or where and when a story takes place	
conflict Rating Q H T	the main problem or struggle that a character faces	
protagonist Rating Q H T	the hero or main character in a story	
pacing Rating Q H T	how fast the events of the story are described; fast pacing covers a large amount of time quickly while slow pacing slows the time down to give more details	
narrative Rating Q H T	a type of writing that tells a story or describes a sequence of events in an incident	
call Rating Q H T	a prompting to take an action or go somewhere	
action Rating Q H T	the events that take place in a work of art	
stage Rating Q H T	a part of a journey; a phase of development	

Academic and Social Language Preview

Learning Target

- Develop a growing set of academic and social vocabulary to use in reading, speaking, and writing.

VOCABULARY PREVIEW

dawn: (noun) the time when the sun rises; the beginning of something new

lead: (noun) a gray metal that is used to make pencils, bullets, and other objects

murmur: (verb) to speak in a quiet voice

mute: (adjective) to be silent, speechless, or unwilling to talk

polish: (noun) a substance that is rubbed or painted on to make something shiny or smooth

riveted: (verb) to hold or fasten together with metal pins or bolts

solemn: (adjective) to be serious or formal; to be sad; to be sincere or truthful

steady: (adjective) in a continuous or dependable way; remaining the same or not changing

Vocabulary Practice

Use the definitions in the Vocabulary Preview or a dictionary to support your work.

Practice 1. Circle the word or phrase whose meaning is closest to the meaning of the vocabulary word.

Vocabulary Word	Words or Phrases to Choose From
solemn	casual colorful serious
mute	talkative active silent
riveted	fastened attracted unmoved
murmur	shout grumble whisper
dawn	sunset sunrise noon

WORD CONNECTIONS

Multiple Meaning Words

Polish can mean the substance used to make something shiny, as in nail **polish**.
It can also describe the shiny surface itself: *The wax brought back the car's original* **polish**.

Practice 2. Complete each sentence, paying attention to the **bold** vocabulary word.

1. Dawn is not my favorite time of day; **therefore,**

_____

2. **Although** the runner's legs felt like lead at the beginning of the race, she

_____

Practice 3. Choose the right word in the pair that fits the sentence.

1. The canoe was **tied/riveted** to the top of the car with a rope.
2. The shoemaker used **lead/polish** to make the old boots look shiny and new.
3. He was so shy and quiet that some of the neighbors thought he might be **solemn/mute**.

Practice 4. Circle all the things or events below that would be described as **solemn**.

a football game   a church wedding

adults at a funeral   a shopping mall

the oath witnesses take to tell the truth   a noisy restaurant

                                             people at candlelight vigil

Interpret the Text Using Close Reading

Learning Target
Apply understanding of how short stories are structured to comprehend a text.

Read and Annotate
Read "The Drummer Boy of Shiloh" and annotate the text as you read.
- Use the My Notes area to write questions or ideas you have about the story.
- Underline words and phrases that show how the protagonist feels at different parts of the story.
- Put a star next to the protagonist's call.
- Circle unknown words.

Short Story

"The Drummer Boy of Shiloh"

by Ray Bradbury

1 In the April night, more than once, blossoms fell from the orchard trees and lit with rustling taps on the drumskin. At midnight a peach stone left miraculously on a branch through winter flicked by a bird fell swift and unseen struck once like panic, which jerked the boy upright. In silence he listened to his own heart **ruffle** away away—at last gone from his ears and back in his chest again.

2 After that, he turned the drum on its side, where its great lunar face peered at him whenever he opened his eyes.

3 His face, alert or at rest, was solemn. It was indeed a solemn night for a boy just turned fourteen in the peach field near the Owl Creek not far from the church at Shiloh.[1]

4 "…thirty-one, thirty-two, thirty-three…"

5 Unable to see, he stopped counting.

6 Beyond the thirty-three familiar shadows, forty thousand men, exhausted by nervous expectation, unable to sleep for **romantic** dreams of battles yet unfought, lay crazily askew in their uniforms. A mile yet farther on, another army was strewn **helter-skelter**, turning slow, basting themselves with the thought of what they would do when the time came: a leap, a yell, a blind plunge their strategy, raw youth their protection and **benediction**.

7 Now and again the boy heard a vast wind come up, that gently stirred the air. But he knew what it was—the army here, the army there, whispering to itself in the dark. Some men talking to others, others murmuring to themselves, and all so quiet it was like a natural element arisen from South or North with the motion of the earth toward dawn.

---

[1] **Shiloh** (n.): site of a Civil War battle in 1862; now a national military park in southwest Tennessee

My Notes

ruffle: to flutter or move in a slow, wavy pattern

romantic: fondly imaginary

helter-skelter: in a confused or disorderly way
benediction: a prayer or blessing

Is he part of the army? He's only 14!

Interpret the Text Using Close Reading

bindled: held together in a sack

immortality: the ability to live forever

My Notes

8 What the men whispered the boy could only guess, and he guessed that it was: "Me, I'm the one, I'm the one of all the rest who won't die. I'll live through it. I'll go home. The band will play. And I'll be there to hear it."

9 Yes, thought the boy, that's all very well for them, they can give as good as they get!

10 For with the careless bones of the young men harvested by the night and **bindled** around campfires were the similarly strewn steel bones of their rifles, with bayonets fixed like eternal lightning lost in the orchard grass.

11 Me, thought the boy, I got only a drum, two sticks to beat it and no shield.

12 There wasn't a man-boy on the ground tonight who did not have a shield he cast, riveted or carved himself on his way to his first attack, compounded of remote but nonetheless firm and fiery family devotion, flag-blown patriotism and cocksure **immortality** strengthened by the touchstone of very real gunpowder; ramrod, Minié ball[2] and flint. But without these last the boy felt his family move yet farther off away in the dark, as if one of those great prairie-burning trains had chanted them away never to return—leaving him with this drum which was worse than a toy in the game to be played tomorrow or some day much too soon.

13 The boy turned on his side. A moth brushed his face, but it was peach blossom. A peach blossom flicked him, but it was a moth. Nothing stayed put. Nothing had a name. Nothing was as it once was.

14 If he lay very still when the dawn came up and the soldiers put on their bravery with their caps, perhaps they might go away, the war with them, and not notice him lying small here, no more than a toy himself.

15 "Well … now," said a voice.

16 The boy shut up his eyes to hide inside himself, but it was too late. Someone, walking by in the night, stood over him.

17 "Well," said the voice quietly, "here's a soldier crying before the fight. Good. Get it over. Won't be time once it all starts."

18 And the voice was about to move on when the boy, startled, touched the drum at his elbow. The man above, hearing this, stopped. The boy could feel his eyes, sense him slowly bending near. A hand must have come down out of the night, for there was a little rat-tat as the fingernails brushed and the man's breath fanned his face.

19 "Why, it's the drummer boy, isn't it?"

20 The boy nodded not knowing if his nod was seen. "Sir, is that you?" he said.

21 "I assume it is." The man's knees cracked as he bent still closer.

22 He smelled as all fathers should smell, of salt sweat, ginger, tobacco, horse, and boot leather, and the earth he walked upon. He had many eyes. No, not eyes—brass buttons that watched the boy.

23 He could only be, and was, the general.

24 "What's your name, boy?" he asked.

25 "Joby," whispered the boy, starting to sit up.

---

[2] **Minié ball:** a type of rifle bullet that became prominent during the Civil War

26 "All right Joby, don't stir." A hand pressed his chest gently and the boy relaxed. "How long you been with us, Joby?"

27 "Three weeks, sir."

28 "Run off from home or joined legitimately, boy?"

29 Silence.

30 ". . . Fool question," said the general. "Do you shave yet, boy? Even more of a … fool. There's your cheek, fell right off the tree overhead. And the others here not much older. Raw, raw, the lot of you. You ready for tomorrow or the next day, Joby?"

31 "I think so, sir."

32 "You want to cry some more, go on ahead. I did the same last night."

33 "You, sir?"

34 "It's the truth. Thinking of everything ahead. Both sides figuring the other side will just give up, and soon, and the war done in weeks, and us all home. Well, that's not how it's going to be. And maybe that's why I cried."

35 Yes, sir," said Joby.

36 The general must have taken out a cigar now, for the dark was suddenly filled with the smell of tobacco unlit as yet, but chewed as the man thought what next to say.

37 "It's going to be a crazy time," said the general. "Counting both sides, there's a hundred thousand men, give or take a few thousand out there tonight, not one as can spit a sparrow off a tree, or knows a horse clod from a Minié ball. Stand up, bare the breast, ask to be a target, thank them and sit down, that's us, that's them. We should turn tail and train four months, they should do the same. But here we are, taken with spring fever and thinking it blood lust, taking our sulfur with cannons instead of with molasses, as it should be, going to be a hero, going to live forever. And I can see all of them over there nodding agreement, save the other way around. It's wrong, boy, it's wrong as a head put on hindside front and a man marching backward through life…More innocents will get shot out of pure … enthusiasm than ever got shot before. Owl Creek was full of boys splashing around in the noonday sun just a few hours ago. I fear it will be full of boys again, just floating, at sundown tomorrow, not caring where the tide takes them."

38 The general stopped and made a little pile of winter leaves and twigs in the darkness, as if he might at any moment strike fire to them to see his way through the coming days when the sun might not show its face because of what was happening here and just beyond.

39 The boy watched the hand stirring the leaves and opened his lips to say something, but did not say it. The general heard the boy's breath and spoke himself.

40 "Why am I telling you this? That's what you wanted to ask, eh? Well, when you got a bunch of wild horses on a loose rein somewhere somehow you got to bring order, rein them in. These lads, fresh out of the milkshed, don't know what I know, and I can't tell them: men actually die in war. So each is his own army. I got to make one army of them. And for that, boy, I need you."

41 "Me!" The boy's lips barely twitched.

My Notes

Interpret the Text Using Close Reading

My Notes

42 "Now, boy," said the general quietly, "you are the heart of the army. Think of that. You're the heart of the army. Listen, now."

43 And, lying there, Joby listened. And the general spoke on.

44 If he, Joby, beat slow tomorrow, the heart would beat slow in the men. They would lag by the wayside. They would drowse in the fields on their muskets. They would sleep for ever, after that, in those same fields—their hearts slowed by a drummer boy and stopped by enemy lead.

45 But if he beat a sure, steady, ever faster rhythm, then, then their knees would come up in a long line down over that hill, one knee after the other, like a wave on the ocean shore! Had he seen the ocean ever? Seen the waves rolling in like a well-ordered cavalry charge to the sand? Well, that was it that's what he wanted, that's what was needed! Joby was his right hand and his left. He gave the orders, but Joby set the pace!

resolute: determined

46 So bring the right knee up and the right foot out and the left knee up and the left foot out. One following the other in good time, in brisk time. Move the blood up the body and made the head proud and the spine stiff and the jaw **resolute**. Focus the eye and set the teeth, flare the nostrils and tighten the hands, put steel armor all over the men, for blood moving fast in them does indeed make men feel as if they'd put on steel. He must keep at it, at it! Long and steady, steady and long! The men, even though shot or torn, those wounds got in hot blood—in blood he'd helped stir—would feel less pain. If their blood was cold, it would be more than slaughter, it would be murderous nightmare and pain best not told and no one to guess.

slack: to diminish or fade away

47 The general spoke and stopped, letting his breath **slack** off. Then after a moment, he said, "So there you are, that's it. Will you do that, boy? Do you know now you're general of the army when the general's left behind?"

48 The boy nodded mutely.

49 "You'll run them through for me then boy?"

50 "Yes, sir."

51 "Good. And maybe, many nights from tonight, many years from now, when you're as old or far much older than me, when they ask you what you did in this awful time, you will tell them—one part humble and one part proud—'I was the drummer boy at the battle of Owl Creek,' or the Tennessee River, or maybe they'll just name it after the church there. 'I was the drummer boy at Shiloh.' Who will ever hear those words and not know you, boy, or what you thought this night, or what you'll think tomorrow or the next day when we must get up on our legs and move!"

52 The general stood up. "Well then … Bless you, boy. Good night."

53 "Good night, sir." And tobacco, brass, boot polish, salt sweat and leather, the man moved away through the grass.

54 Joby lay for a moment, staring but unable to see where the man had gone. He swallowed. He wiped his eyes. He cleared his throat. He settled himself. Then, at last, very slowly and firmly, he turned the drum so that it faced up toward the sky.

55 He lay next to it, his arm around it, feeling the tremor, the touch, the muted thunder as, all the rest of the April night in the year 1862, near the Tennessee River, not far from the Owl Creek, very close to the church named Shiloh, the peach blossoms fell on the drum.

Interacting in Meaningful Ways:
Academic Collaboration

Learning Targets

- Ask and answer questions about a short story in collaborative conversations, demonstrating active listening, and drawing upon an expanding pool of language resources for discussing literature.

- Express and support opinions of a short story in conversation.

Turn to your partner or small group to discuss each question about "The Drummer Boy of Shiloh." After you have discussed a question, write notes about your answer before going on to the next question.

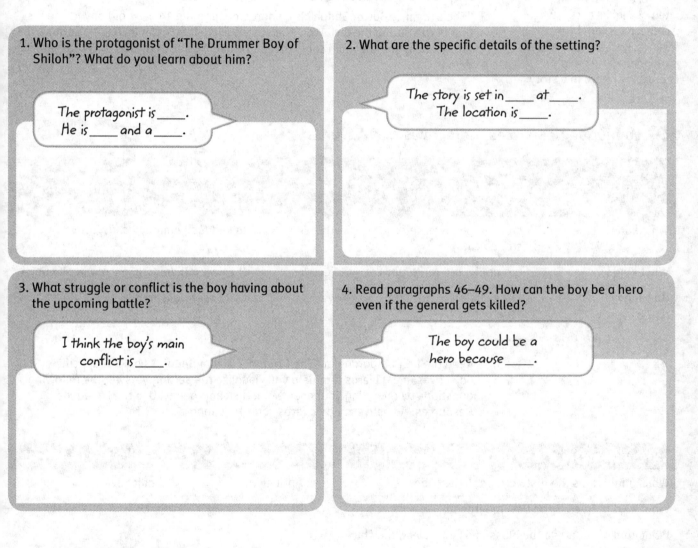

1. Who is the protagonist of "The Drummer Boy of Shiloh"? What do you learn about him?

> The protagonist is ____.
> He is ____ and a ____.

2. What are the specific details of the setting?

> The story is set in ____ at ____.
> The location is ____.

3. What struggle or conflict is the boy having about the upcoming battle?

> I think the boy's main conflict is ____.

4. Read paragraphs 46–49. How can the boy be a hero even if the general gets killed?

> The boy could be a hero because ____.

Asking Questions

Joby's perspective changes over the course of this story. Discuss questions you have about this shift and what Joby's perspective is at the end. Write one question to share with the whole class.

_____

_____

HEW How English Works: Adjectives and Adverbs

Language Resources

exposition: the details of a story that introduce the setting, characters, and main conflict

conflict: a struggle between opposing forces, either internal or external. An internal conflict occurs when a character is torn by two feelings, decisions, or values.

protagonist: the main character or hero in a story

Learning Targets

- Use adjectives and adverbs to comprehend and write a text.
- Explain in conversation how different word choices help readers to visualize a story's details.
- Write a short narrative description using adjectives and adverbs effectively.

Adjectives and Adverbs

"The Drummer Boy of Shiloh" is a short story about a 14-year-old boy facing his first battle during the Civil War. The story's exposition establishes the setting, the protagonist, and the main conflict, using adjectives and adverbs to create specific details.

Language Resources: Adjectives and Adverbs

Adjectives Modify or describe nouns by telling *which one*, *what kind* or *how many*		Adverbs Modify or describe verbs, adjectives or other adverbs by telling *how*, *when*, *where*	
Which one?	*green* apple, *wrecked* car, *striped* cat	Verbs	talked *fast*, jumped *easily*, drove *yesterday*
What kind?	*tart* apple, *old* car, *tabby* cat	Adjectives	the *very* tall unicorn, my *rather* shy uncle
How many?	*three* apples, *many* cars, *several* cats	Adverbs	cried *especially* loudly

Read the first paragraph of "The Drummer Boy of Shiloh." Look for specific adjectives and adverbs that help you visualize the setting. Answer the following questions by recording your answers in the chart below. Use the Language Resources: Adjectives and Adverbs chart for support.

Questions from "The Drummer Boy of Shiloh"	Answer	Adjective or Adverb
Which night does the first paragraph describe?	an April night	adjective
What kind of trees is the boy underneath?		
What kind of sound do the blossoms make when they hit the drumskin?		
How is the peach stone left on the branch?		
How does the stone fall?		
How is the boy jerked?		

Quick Conversation

- Share your work with a partner. Discuss your responses. How do these words help you visualize the setting? What do they make you see and feel? Record notes from your discussion.

> The adjective _____ helps me see _____.

> In my opinion, the word _____ makes the setting the most vivid.

> I think the adverb _____ helps me understand _____.

Write a Short Narrative Description

After analyzing the descriptive language in "The Drummer Boy of Shiloh," you have enough information to write a description of the story's setting. Write a short narrative description of the story's setting using some descriptive language from the text as well as new adjectives and adverbs.

_____

_____

_____

_____

_____

_____

_____

_____

_____

_____

_____

_____

_____

_____

Interacting in Meaningful Ways: Analyze Clauses

Language Resources
Pacing: How fast the time moves in a story
Mood: the overall emotion that the reader feels when reading a scene or an entire work

Learning Targets

- Analyze and explain in conversation and writing how combining clauses produces effects on the reader.

- Evaluate and explain in conversation and writing how effectively the author uses pacing.

- Express and justify opinions in conversation and writing by providing text evidence and using nuanced modal expressions and phrases.

Using Clauses to Establish Pacing

Ray Bradbury uses pacing in "The Drummer Boy of Shiloh" to show how a character is feeling and to set different moods for the reader. One way a writer creates pacing is by creating sentences of different lengths. A paragraph with several short sentences is like a quick drumbeat with a fast pace and might emphasize action or energy. A paragraph with long sentences made by combining clauses and phrases slows the pace down. A slower pace might emphasize a character's thoughts or set a mood of reflection for the reader.

Language Resources

Clause	A group of words that contains a subject and a verb
Phrase	A group of words that does not contain a subject, a verb, or both
Combined clause	A sentence that contains two or more clauses

Read the last two paragraphs of "The Drummer Boy of Shiloh." Answer the questions in the chart for each paragraph. Then analyze each paragraph to understand why Bradbury chose to write each paragraph the way he did. What effect does the pacing have on the story and the mood?

	Paragraph 54	Paragraph 55
Short or Combined Clauses?		
Pacing: Fast or Slow?		
Joby's Feelings/Actions		
Mood Created		
Author's Purpose in Choosing Pacing		

Quick Conversation

• Share your work with a partner. Take turns explaining your analysis of the pacing in the two paragraphs. Discuss whether your partner agrees or disagrees with your analysis. Record notes from your discussion.

> In my opinion, the pacing in paragraph 54 emphasizes _____.

> I agree with your analysis, and _____.

> The effect of the pacing in paragraph 55 is _____.

> I disagree with your analysis because _____.

Write a Short Argument

After analyzing the pacing in "The Drummer Boy of Shiloh," you have enough information to write a short argument. Write a short argument about paragraph 54 in which you identify the pacing, explain what effect the pacing creates, and why the author chose to use this pacing. Then state your opinion of how effective it is, and give a reason why. Before writing, read the model short argument provided. Try structuring your argument in the same way.

_____

_____

_____

_____

_____

_____

_____

_____

_____

_____

MODEL: SHORT ARGUMENT

Ray Bradbury uses slow pacing in the last paragraph to emphasize the long night ahead for Joby. The slow pacing is created by one long sentence of combined clauses that describes the historical setting and April night before the battle. In my opinion, this slow pacing is effective because it helps the reader feel what Joby must be feeling while he waits for dawn.

Interacting in Meaningful Ways: Writing a Narrative

Language Resources

narrative: a story that opens with a central conflict and describes a sequence of events

Hero's Journey archetype: a plot pattern that shows the development of a hero

Beginning of the Adventure stage: the hero begins the adventure, leaving safety to go into an unknown and dangerous world

Learning Targets

- Express and justify opinions about the Hero's Journey in conversation and writing.

- Write a narrative using the Hero's Journey archetype text structure.

- Use knowledge about the character/hero and the Beginning of the Adventure stage to determine and write character details and plot events.

- Combine clauses and use sentence length to create mood.

Review your annotations and notes on "The Drummer Boy of Shiloh" and use them to complete the graphic organizer.

Setting	Character/Hero Actions	Plot Events
What are specific details about the setting? What is the time of day, place, month, and weather?	How does Joby feel as he gets ready for battle? What does he do, say, or think?	What events happen in the story? How does Joby react to the events?

Quick Conversation

Share your work with your partner. Compare your ideas about the setting, character, and events.

Next, read aloud the last two sentences of paragraph 51:

> 'I was the drummer boy at Shiloh.' Who will ever hear those words and not know you, boy, or what you thought this night, or what you'll think tomorrow or the next day when we must get up on our legs and move.

Discuss the sentences. According to the Hero's Journey archetype, what will Joby do the next morning during the battle? Will he respond with courage? Will he keep his promise to the general? Record notes from your discussion.

I think that Joby will _____ the next morning.

I disagree because _____.

I think Joby will feel _____ when the battle starts because _____.

My opinion is that _____.

Planning a Narrative

Use the graphic organizer to plan your narrative, following the Hero's Journey archetype text structure. Think about the setting, what Joby will do, and what will happen during this stage. Make notes in the graphic organizer below by answering the questions.

Setting Details	Character/Hero Actions	Plot Events
What does morning on the battlefield look, sound, and feel like?	How does Joby feel as the day begins? What does he do, say, or think?	What events happen next? How does the battle start? What happens once it starts?

Narrative Writing Prompt

Write a draft of your narrative. Be sure to:

- Establish the setting (give details that show the time, place, weather, etc.).
- Describe the hero's actions and feelings.
- Develop the story with events that show the hero beginning the adventure.
- Combine clauses and use sentence length to create pacing and mood in the story.

_____

_____

_____

_____

_____

_____

_____

_____

_____

_____

_____

_____

_____

_____

Selecting Language Resources

Roots and Affixes

The word **diction** comes from the Latin root *dict*, which means "to say." This root also gives us the words **dictionary**, a book that explains how to say or pronounce words; **dictator**, a person who has the final "say;" and **predict**, to say or tell something before it happens.

Learning Targets

● Develop language resources to use while speaking and writing about epics.

● Use an expanded set of words to speak and write precisely.

● Adjust language choices to suit the academic setting.

The chart presents words and phrases you will use in discussion and writing. Think about each word or phrase. Circle Q, H, or T to indicate how well you know it. Work with a partner, asking your partner to explain each word or phrase. Listen closely to the explanation, and then write your partner's name in the In Our Own Words column along with his or her condensed idea.

Rating	Q	H	T
	I have seen this word or phrase, but I have **questions** about its meaning.	I have **heard** this word or phrase but do not know it well.	I know this word or phrase so well that I could **teach** it to someone else.

Word or Phrase	Definition	In Our Own Words
epic Rating Q H T	a long poem that tells the story about the deeds of a hero or gods	
point of view Rating Q H T	the perspective from which a story is told	
archetype Rating Q H T	a character, symbol, story pattern, or other element that is common to human experiences across cultures	
diction Rating Q H T	the specific words a writer uses	
imagery Rating Q H T	word pictures that describe how something looks, sounds, feels, tastes, or smells	

Academic and Social Language Preview

Learning Target

- Develop knowledge of a growing set of academic and social vocabulary to use in reading, speaking, and writing.

VOCABULARY PREVIEW

bore: (verb) to make a hole by using a twisting motion; to make someone tired or annoyed

bound: (adjective) sure or certain to happen; tied or held together tightly, either literally with string or something else or figuratively with promises or a close relationship

brute: (noun) a violent or rough person

inspiration: (noun) an idea about or willingness to do something

labored: (verb) to work hard

quiver: (noun) a case people carry arrows in

reeled: (verb) to fall or move very suddenly, usually from force

teeming: (adjective) to be filled with many of something

thrust: (verb) to throw or jab quickly

vengeance: (noun) the act of getting even or taking revenge

Vocabulary Practice

Use the definitions in the Vocabulary Preview or a dictionary to support your work.

Practice 1. Circle the word or phrase whose meaning is closest to the meaning of the vocabulary word.

Vocabulary Word	Words or Phrases to Choose From
brute	a sudden idea with kindness a cruel person
quiver	carrying case rattle weapon
labored	sleeping soundly working hard watching a play
thrust	throw quickly fall backward to make a hole
vengeance	permission revenge hard work

Practice 2. Using the context clues in the sentence, write the correct word in the blank. Some words may be used more than once.

1. Politicians want their speeches to be lively and interesting so they don't _____ the audience and make them fall asleep.
2. When the two countries started bombing each other, their citizens knew that war was _____ to happen.
3. Using her new electric drill, Keara _____ all the holes she needs to put up the curtain rods.
4. Jamal had a sudden _____ for the perfect hashtag for his tweet about the video.

Practice 3. Circle all the correct answers for the question.

1. Which of these pairs might be bound together?

   two distant relatives   a stack of papers and a rubberband   a dog and a cat

   a prisoner and handcuffs   a bride and groom at their wedding

2. Which of these things could be described as teeming?

   a lake with fish   a city with people

   an empty store   a blank wall

Learning Target
- Apply understanding of how epic poems are structured to comprehend the text.

Read and Annotate
Read the excerpt from the *Odyssey* and annotate the text as you read.
- ■ Use the My Notes area to write questions or ideas you have about the poem.
- ■ Underline any rich verbs that describe an action vividly.
- ■ Put a star next to trials the hero faces.
- ■ Put exclamation marks next to the times when the protagonist acts heroically.
- ■ Circle unknown words.

Epic Poem

From
the ODYSSEY

by Homer
Translation *by* Tony Kline

Book IX: 307–359
ODYSSEUS TELLS HIS TALE: OFFERING THE CYCLOPS WINE

1 As soon as rosy-fingered Dawn appeared, Cyclops relit the fire. Then he milked the ewes, and bleating goats in order, putting her young to each. When he had busied himself at his tasks, he again seized two of my men and began to eat them. When he had finished he drove his well-fed flocks from the cave, effortlessly lifting the huge door stone, and replacing it again like the cap on a quiver. Then whistling loudly he turned his flocks out on to the mountain slopes, leaving me with murder in my heart searching for a way to take vengeance on him, if Athene[1] would grant me inspiration. The best plan seemed to be this:

2 The Cyclops' huge club, a trunk of green olive wood he had cut to take with him as soon as it was seasoned, lay next to a sheep pen. It was so large and thick that it looked to us like the mast of a twenty-oared black ship, a broad-beamed merchant vessel that sails the deep ocean. Approaching it, I cut off a six-foot length, gave it to my men and told them to smooth the wood. Then standing by it I sharpened the end to a point, and hardened the point in the blazing fire, after which I hid it carefully in a one of the heaps of dung that lay around the cave. I ordered the men to **cast lots** as to which of them should dare to help me raise the stake and twist it into the Cyclops' eye when sweet sleep took him. The lot fell on the very ones I would have chosen, four of them, with myself making a fifth.

3 He returned at evening, shepherding his well-fed flocks. He herded them swiftly, every one, into the deep cave, leaving none in the broad yard, commanded

My Notes

cast lots: to throw a set of objects in order to impartially decide something

[1] **Athene:** goddess of wisdom, the arts, and war

Interpret the Text Using Close Reading

premonition: a vision of the future

draught: a liquid that one drinks

ambrosia and nectar: the food and drink that the gods ate

fuddled: made confused

subtle: not obvious

My Notes

treachery: a betrayal of trust

to do so by a god, or because of some **premonition**. Then he lifted the huge door stone and set it in place, and sat down to milk the ewes and bleating goats in order, putting her young to each. But when he had busied himself at his tasks, he again seized two of my men and began to eat them. That was when I went up to him, holding an ivy-wood bowl full of dark wine, and said: "Here, Cyclops, have some wine to follow your meal of human flesh, so you can taste the sort of drink we carried in our ship. I was bringing the drink to you as a gift, hoping you might pity me and help me on my homeward path: but your savagery is past bearing. Cruel man, why would anyone on earth ever visit you again, when you behave so badly?"

4 At this, he took the cup and drained it, and found the sweet drink so delightful he asked for another **draught**: "Give me more, freely, then quickly tell me your name so I may give you a guest gift, one that will please you. Among us Cyclopes the fertile earth produces rich grape clusters, and Zeus' rain swells them: but this is a taste from a stream of **ambrosia and nectar**."

Book IX: 360–412
ODYSSEUS TELLS HIS TALE: BLINDING THE CYCLOPS

5 As he finished speaking I handed him the bright wine. Three times I poured and gave it to him, and three times, foolishly, he drained it. When the wine had **fuddled** his wits I tried him with **subtle** words: "Cyclops, you asked my name, and I will tell it: give me afterwards a guest gift as you promised. My name is Nobody. Nobody, my father, mother, and friends call me."

6 Those were my words, and this his cruel answer: "Then, my gift is this. I will eat Nobody last of all his company, and all the others before him."

7 As he spoke, he reeled and toppled over on his back, his thick neck twisted to one side, and all-conquering sleep overpowered him. In his drunken slumber he vomited wine and pieces of human flesh. Then I thrust the stake into the depth of the ashes to heat it, and inspired my men with encouraging words, so none would hang back from fear. When the olivewood stake was glowing hot, and ready to catch fire despite its greenness, I drew it from the coals, then my men stood round me, and a god breathed courage into us. They held the sharpened olivewood stake, and thrust it into his eye, while I threw my weight on the end, and twisted it round and round, as a man bores the timbers of a ship with a drill that others twirl lower down with a strap held at both ends, and so keep the drill continuously moving. We took the red-hot stake and twisted it round and round like that in his eye, and the blood poured out despite the heat. His lids and brows were scorched by flame from the burning eyeball, and its roots crackled with fire. As a great axe or adze causes a vast hissing when the smith dips it in cool water to temper it, strengthening the iron, so his eye hissed against the olivewood stake. Then he screamed, terribly, and the rock echoed. Seized by terror we shrank back, as he wrenched the stake, wet with blood, from his eye. He flung it away in frenzy, and called to the Cyclops, his neighbors who lived in caves on the windy heights. They heard his cry, and crowding in from every side they stood by the cave mouth and asked what was wrong: "Polyphemus, what terrible pain is this that makes you call through deathless night, and wake us? Is a mortal stealing your flocks, or trying to kill you by violence or **treachery**?"

8 Out of the cave came mighty Polyphemus' voice: "Nobody, my friends, is trying to kill me by violence or treachery."

9 To this they replied with winged words: "If you are alone, and nobody does you violence, it's an inescapable sickness that comes from Zeus: pray to the Lord Poseidon, our father."

Interpret the Text Using Close Reading

Book IX: 413–479

ODYSSEUS TELLS HIS TALE: ESCAPE

My Notes

10 Off they went, while I laughed to myself at how the name and the clever scheme had deceived him. Meanwhile the Cyclops, groaning and in pain, groped around and labored to lift the stone from the door. Then he sat in the entrance, arms outstretched, to catch anyone stealing past among his sheep. That was how foolish he must have thought I was. I considered the best way of escaping, and saving myself, and my men from death. I dreamed up all sorts of tricks and schemes, as a man will in a life or death matter: it was an evil situation. This was the plan that seemed best. The rams were fat with thick **fleeces**, fine large beasts with deep black wool. These I silently tied together in threes, with twists of willow on which that lawless monster, Polyphemus, slept. The middle one was to carry one of my men, with the other two on either side to protect him. So there was a man to every three sheep. As for me I took the pick of the flock, and curled below his shaggy belly, gripped his back and lay there face upwards, patiently gripping his fine fleece tight in my hands. Then, sighing, we waited for the light.

fleece: the coat of wool on a ram

11 As soon as rosy-fingered Dawn appeared, the males rushed out to graze, while the un-milked females udders bursting bleated in the pens. Their master, tormented by agonies of pain, felt the backs of the sheep as they passed him, but foolishly failed to see my men tied under the rams' bellies. My ram went last, burdened by the weight of his fleece, and me and my teeming thoughts. And as he felt its back, mighty Polyphemus spoke to him:

12 "My fine ram, why leave the cave like this last of the flock? You have never lagged behind before, always the first to step out proudly and graze on the tender grass shoots, always first to reach the flowing river, and first to show your wish to return at evening to the fold. Today you are last of all. You must surely be grieving over your master's eye, blinded by an evil man and his wicked friends, when my wits were fuddled with wine: Nobody, I say, has not yet escaped death. If you only had senses like me, and the power of speech to tell me where he hides himself from my anger, then I'd strike him down, his brains would be sprinkled all over the floor of the cave, and my heart would be eased of the pain that nothing, Nobody, has brought me."

13 With this he drove the ram away from him out of doors, and I loosed myself when the ram was a little way from the cave, then untied my men. Swiftly, keeping an eye behind us, we shepherded those long-limbed sheep, rich and fat, down to the ship. And a welcome sight, indeed, to our dear friends were we, escapees from death, though they wept and sighed for the others we lost. I would not let them weep though, but stopped them all with a nod and a frown. I told them to haul the host of fine-fleeced sheep on board and put to sea. They boarded swiftly and took their place on the benches then sitting in their rows struck the grey water with their oars. When we were almost out of earshot, I shouted to the Cyclops, mocking him: "It seems he was not such a weakling, then, Cyclops, that man whose friends you meant to tear apart and eat in your echoing cave. Stubborn brute not shrinking from murdering your guests in your own house, your evil deeds were bound for sure to fall on your own head. Zeus and the other gods have had their revenge on you."

Interacting in Meaningful Ways: Academic Collaboration

Learning Targets

- Ask and answer questions about an epic poem in collaborative conversations, demonstrating active listening, and drawing upon an expanding pool of language resources for discussing literature.
- Express and support opinions of an epic poem in conversation.

Turn to your partner or small group to discuss each question about the *Odyssey*. After you have discussed a question, write notes about your answer before going on to the next question.

1. From which character's point of view does the author write the poem?

> The poem is told from the point of view of ____.

2. How does the author portray the two main characters?

> The author portrays Odysseus as ____ and Cyclops as ____.

3. What archetypal role does the narrator play in the epic? What stage of the Hero's Journey archetype do the plot events show?

> The narrator fits the archetypal role of ____.

4. What narrative techniques does the author use in paragraph 13?

> The author uses the narrative techniques of ____ and ____.

Asking Questions

Heroes often use trickery to defeat their enemies. With your partner or small group, read aloud paragraphs 13–14 from the *Odyssey*. Discuss what questions you have about what Odysseus is doing. Write one question to share with the whole class.

_____

_____

Interacting in Meaningful Ways: Evaluate Diction

Learning Targets

- Apply understanding of diction to comprehending and writing texts.
- Evaluate and explain in conversation how vivid verbs help readers to visualize the story's action.
- Write a short argument that analyzes the author's diction and explains its effect on the story.

Using Precise Diction

An epic poem that describes the Hero's Journey is full of action and adventure. Therefore, writers use diction that will emphasize the action and help readers see exactly what is happening. An important part of the diction in epics is vivid verbs, which are verbs that portray the action, danger, and drama that the hero faces. Notice how the vivid verbs below make the action more colorful, precise, and interesting.

Language Resources: Vivid Verbs

Verb	Definition	Vivid Verbs	Sentence
walk	to use your legs and feet to move	stride, stroll, stagger, march	The band left to _____ to the parking lot.
hit	using a hand or object to touch something with force	punch, smash, bash, whack, crash	A car might _____ the bicycle in the driveway.
jump	using your legs to move your body up or forward from the ground	leap, bounce, soar, fly	The coach wants players who can _____

Skim the *Odyssey* and look for the vivid verbs you underlined. If you are not sure of the meaning, use context clues and a dictionary to help you define the words. Use the chart below to list synonyms the author could have used instead and then revise the sentence with one of the synonyms. Use a thesaurus to help you find synonyms.

Vivid Verbs	Synonyms	Revised Sentence
drained	guzzled, gulped, inhaled	At this, he took the cup and guzzled it.

Quick Conversation

● Share your work with a partner. Read aloud the original and revised sentences. Discuss how they compare and which verbs you prefer. How did the new verbs change the story? Which verbs better help you visualize the action? Record notes from your discussion.

> The verb _____ helps me see _____.

> In my opinion, the verb _____ is the most vivid because _____.

> I think the verb _____ should be replaced with _____.

Write a Short Argument

After analyzing and evaluating diction in the *Odyssey*, you have enough information to write a short argument. Choose a vivid verb from your chart that comes from the story. Write a short argument in which you explain the author's diction, state your opinion of how effective it is, and give a reason why. Before writing, read the model short argument provided. Notice what information is in each of the sentences. Try structuring your argument in the same way.

_____

_____

_____

_____

_____

_____

_____

_____

_____

MODEL: SHORT ARGUMENT

The author uses the vivid verb "guzzled" to describe how Cyclops drinks the wine Odysseus gives him. This verb shows how quickly Cyclops drinks, and it also shows how greedy and selfish he is. He doesn't stop to offer anyone else a drink, and he doesn't use any manners at all in the way he drinks. The diction that Homer uses helps the reader see the action and understand how Cyclops is a true monster, even in the way he drinks a gift.

Interacting in Meaningful Ways: Analyze Imagery

Learning Targets

- Analyze and explain in conversation and writing how imagery supports the hero archetype.

- Evaluate and explain in conversation and writing how effectively the author uses imagery.

- Express and justify opinions in conversation and writing by providing text evidence.

Using Imagery to Support the Hero Archetype

Homer uses strong imagery in the *Odyssey* to draw the reader into the trials that the hero faces. The imagery also helps to emphasize the heroic qualities of Odysseus, the hero, and the evil qualities of Cyclops, the enemy. In this activity, you will identify, analyze, and evaluate the epic's imagery.

Language Resources

Imagery	Words that appeal to the five senses and help the reader create mental word pictures.

Language Resources

Imagery
Imagery appeals to the five senses. The following images are examples that appeal to each sense.

Sight	orange sun
Sound	crackling fire
Touch	cold wind
Taste	salty tears
Smell	sour milk

Read paragraph 17 of the *Odyssey*. Find four examples of imagery that directly support the Hero's Journey archetype. Look for imagery that emphasizes the heroic qualities of Odysseus, the dangers of the Road of Trials, or the evil enemy. Write the imagery in the chart. Then analyze each example to understand the effect the author is trying to create. Finally, evaluate how effective the imagery is in supporting the archetype.

Imagery	Analyze the Effect	Evaluate Effectiveness in Supporting Archetype
"vomited wine and pieces of human flesh"	This image helps the reader see, hear, and smell the vomiting of the violent and disgusting monster. The image shows what a difficult trial and enemy Odysseus is facing.	The image is highly effective in portraying the trials part of the archetype, which often includes monsters.

Quick Conversation

- Share your work with a partner. Take turns explaining your analysis and evaluation of the imagery. Discuss whether your partner agrees or disagrees with your evaluation. Record notes from your discussion.

In my opinion, this imagery is ____ effective because ____.

Do you agree with my evaluation?

I disagree with your analysis because ____.

I agree with your evaluation and ____.

Write a Short Argument

After analyzing and evaluating imagery in the *Odyssey*, you have enough information to write a short argument. Choose an image from your chart. Write a short argument in which you explain the image, state your opinion of how effective it is, and give a reason why. Before writing, read the model short argument provided. Notice what information is in each of the sentences. Try structuring your argument in the same way.

_____

_____

_____

_____

_____

_____

_____

_____

MODEL: SHORT ARGUMENT

The author uses the image of Cyclops vomiting "wine and pieces of human flesh" to portray Cyclops as a disgusting monster. This image reminds the reader how violent Cyclops is and what danger Odysseus is in. The image supports the Hero's Journey archetype by showing the terrible trials and the hero's bravery. In my opinion, this imagery is definitely effective because it makes the reader understand how brave the hero must be to face a man-eating monster.

Interacting in Meaningful Ways: Writing a Dialogue

Learning Targets

- Express and justify opinions about an epic in conversation and writing.

- Write a scene of dialogue that portrays characteristics of a hero and the Hero's Journey archetype.

- Use imagery and vivid verbs effectively to create precision and shades of meaning while writing.

Review your annotations and notes on the *Odyssey* and use them to complete the graphic organizer.

Road of Trials	Heroic Characteristics	Vivid Verbs and Imagery
What trials does Odysseus face? How does he overcome them?	What does Odysseus do, say, feel, or think that shows he is a hero?	What vivid verbs and imagery are used to support the hero archetype?

> **Language Resources**
>
> **heroic characteristics:** the actions, words, feelings, and thoughts that show how strong, fast, brave, or smart the hero is
>
> **Road of Trials:** the stage in the Hero's Journey archetype when the hero faces mental and physical challenges he must overcome
>
> **dialogue:** the words a character says, which are set off in quotation marks
>
> **dialogue tag:** the words that indicate which character is speaking and how the words are spoken, such as *he said, Cyclops shouted, they whispered.*

Quick Conversation

Share your work with your partner. Compare your ideas about the heroic characteristics of Odysseus.

Next, read aloud the last paragraph of the story:

> I would not let them weep though, but stopped them all with a nod and a frown.

Discuss the sentence. What does it tell you about the hero? Why doesn't he let his men grieve over the loss of their shipmates? What does the hero want to do first? Why is this important? Record notes from your discussion.

I think the hero doesn't let his men cry because ____.

I agree because ____

Based on ____, I think the hero first wants to ____.

Could you explain that please?

Planning a Dialogue

Use the graphic organizer to write a brief dialogue between Odysseus and his men after he mocks Cyclops. Think about how Odysseus will summarize what happened to him in Cyclops' cave. What details will he include in his story that prove that he is a hero? Make notes in the graphic organizer below by answering the questions.

Road of Trials	Heroic Characteristics	Vivid Verbs and Imagery
How does Odysseus overcome the trials? How will he describe the trials to his men?	What does Odysseus do, say, feel, or think that shows he is a hero?	What vivid verbs and imagery will support the hero archetype as Odysseus describes the adventure?

Dialogue Writing Prompt

Write a draft of your dialogue. Be sure to:

■ Describe what Odysseus says to the men about his adventure with Cyclops.

■ Include specific details of what Odysseus does, says, and thinks that show his heroic characteristics.

■ Use vivid verbs to describe what happens between Odysseus and Cyclops.

■ Include the men's reactions to Odysseus's story.

_____

_____

_____

_____

_____

_____

_____

_____

_____

_____

_____

_____

Part Three

Selecting Language Resources

Learning Targets

- Develop language resources to use while speaking and writing about poetry.

- Use an expanded set of words to speak and write precisely.

- Adjust language choices to suit the academic setting.

The chart presents words and phrases you will use in discussion and writing. Think about each word or phrase. Circle Q, H, or T to indicate how well you know it. Work with a partner, asking your partner to explain each word or phrase. Listen closely to the explanation, and then write your partner's name in the In Our Own Words column along with his or her condensed idea.

> **WORD CONNECTIONS**
>
> **Multiple Meaning Words**
>
> The word *tone* is a specific literary term, but it also has many other meanings. It can refer to specific sounds, such as the critical *tone* in a friend's voice or the high *tones* in a flute or musical instrument. *Tone* is also used to describe color, including the shade or amount of color. A painting might have bright red *tones* while a pale yellow dress might have a gold *tone*.

Rating	Q	H	T
	I have seen this word or phrase, but I have **questions** about its meaning.	I have **heard** this word or phrase, but do not know it well.	I know this word or phrase so well that I could **teach** it to someone else.

Word or Phrase	Definition	In Our Own Words
allegory Rating Q H T	A story or poem that uses an extended metaphor to create two levels of meaning. One meaning is the surface or literal story; the other meaning is what the characters, events, and objects symbolize outside the literal story.	
tone Rating Q H T	A writer's or speaker's attitude toward a subject	
represent Rating Q H T	to be a sign or example of something	
symbol Rating Q H T	something that represents something else	
stanza Rating Q H T	a set of lines in a poem	
connotation Rating Q H T	a feeling or idea associated with a word, but that is not its direct definition	

Academic and Social Language Preview

Learning Target
- Develop knowledge of a growing set of academic and social vocabulary to use in reading, speaking, and writing.

VOCABULARY PREVIEW

bouquets: (noun) a bunch of flowers that are tied or bundled together

mass: (noun) a large group of people; a large amount of something

nor: (conjunction) a negative form of the word *or*, meaning not; usually joins two things or clauses, joining the second part

object: (noun) a goal or purpose for an activity; a thing that is not alive and can be touched and seen

pale: (adjective) very light in color or lacking color

steady: (adverb) held firmly in one position without shaking

sought: (verb) looked for, searched for; past tense of seek

tread: (noun) step, in the sense of walking

will: (noun) a desire or choice

Vocabulary Practice
Use the definitions in the Vocabulary Preview or a dictionary to support your work.

Practice 1. Circle the word or phrase whose meaning is closest to the meaning of the vocabulary word.

Vocabulary Word	Words or Phrases to Choose From
steady	moving up and down not moving moving from side to side
pale	very light very heavy very dark
object	something alive an argument a goal
nor	not but and
mass	a small amount a noisy group a large amount
bouquets	flowers money a bad smell
sought	found pursued failed
will	desire fate future
tread	tire track footstep

Practice 2. Complete each sentence, paying attention to the **bold** vocabulary word.

1. The photographer tried to keep the camera steady **because** she wanted

_____

2. **Whenever** my sister looks pale, she will

_____

3. **Neither** my cousin nor my uncle could

_____

4. The store manager did not want the mass of shoppers to wait outside; **therefore**, she

_____

5. **Because** Mr. Gomez's object was to have all the students hear the movie, he

_____.

Practice 3. Choose the antonym, or the opposite word or phrase, for the vocabulary word.

Vocabulary Word	Words of Phrases to Choose From
steady	vibrating to move very slowly to trick
pale	heavy dark afraid
mass	one person a large group a choir
bouquet	a bunch of daisies a pile of acorns a single rose
will	wish obligation aim

Practice 4. Choose the correct vocabulary word to fill in the blanks. Some words may be used more than once.

1. A huge bouquet could be described as a _____ of flowers.
2. Since her _____ was to stay as pale as possible, Emma never went out into the sun.
3. A _____ of cold air caused the bitter cold temperatures in our area last week.
4. Even though he was scared, he tried to keep his hands _____.
5. Neither the doll nor the truck was the _____ the child wanted to play with today.
6. She never listened to anything she was told and always did everything according to her own

    _____.

7. Everyone in the house was asleep, so I walked down the hallway with a light _____.

My Notes

Learning Target
● Apply understanding of how an allegory is structured to comprehend a text.

Read and Annotate
Read "O Captain! My Captain!" and annotate the text as you read.
■ Use the My Notes area to write questions or ideas you have about the poem.
■ Underline words and phrases related to ships.
■ Put a star next to any repeated phrases.
■ Circle unknown words and phrases.

Poem

O Captain! My Captain!

by Walt Whitman

> O Captain! my Captain! our fearful trip is done;
> The ship has weather'd every **rack**, the prize we sought is won;
> The port is near, the bells I hear, the people all exulting,
> While follow eyes the steady keel, the **vessel** grim and daring:
> 5 But O heart! heart! heart!
> > O the bleeding drops of red,
> > > Where on the deck my Captain lies,
> > > > Fallen cold and dead.
>
> O Captain! my Captain! rise up and hear the bells;
> 10 Rise up—for you the flag is flung—for you the bugle trills;
> For you bouquets and ribbon'd wreaths—for you the shores a-crowding,
> For you they call, the swaying mass, their eager faces turning;
> Here Captain! dear father!
> > This arm beneath your head;

rack: a windy storm

vessel: a ship

15   It is some dream that on the deck,
            You've fallen cold and dead.

My Captain does not answer, his lips are pale and still;

My father does not feel my arm, he has no pulse nor will;

The ship is anchored safe and sound, its voyage closed and done;

20 From fearful trip the victor ship comes in with object won:

Exult O shores, and ring O bells!

    But I with **mournful** tread,

        Walk the deck my Captain lies,

            Fallen cold and dead.

My Notes

mournful: sad

Interacting in Meaningful Ways: Academic Collaboratio

Learning Targets

- Ask and answer questions about a poem in collaborative conversations, demonstrating active listening, and drawing upon an expanding pool of language resources for discussing literature.

- Express and support opinions of a poem in conversation.

Turn to your partner or small group to discuss each question about "O Captain! My Captain!" After you have discussed a question, write notes about your answer before going on to the next question.

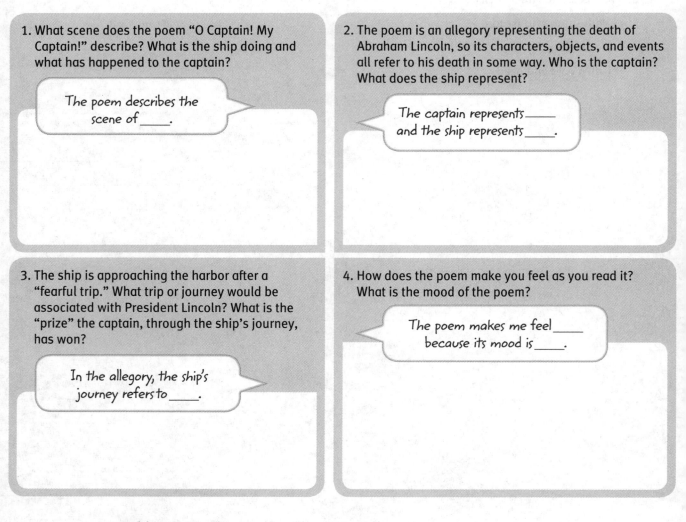

1. What scene does the poem "O Captain! My Captain!" describe? What is the ship doing and what has happened to the captain?

> The poem describes the scene of _____.

2. The poem is an allegory representing the death of Abraham Lincoln, so its characters, objects, and events all refer to his death in some way. Who is the captain? What does the ship represent?

> The captain represents _____ and the ship represents _____.

3. The ship is approaching the harbor after a "fearful trip." What trip or journey would be associated with President Lincoln? What is the "prize" the captain, through the ship's journey, has won?

> In the allegory, the ship's journey refers to _____.

4. How does the poem make you feel as you read it? What is the mood of the poem?

> The poem makes me feel _____ because its mood is _____.

Asking Questions

Allegories have two levels of meaning: the surface story and the symbolic meaning. The surface story "O Captain! My Captain!" is about a ship, whose captain has died, coming into harbor. With your part▪ or small group, read aloud the poem again. Discuss what questions you have about the symbolic meaning or the historical event it describes. Write one question to share with the whole class.

_____

_____

Interacting in Meaningful Ways: Differentiate Tone

Learning Targets

- Apply understanding of tone to comprehending and writing texts.
- Analyze and explain in conversation and writing how tone produces effects on the poem.
- Evaluate and explain in conversation and writing how effectively the author creates tone.
- Express and justify opinions in conversation and writing by providing text evidence.

Tone

A writer's tone is the attitude the writer expresses in a poem or other literary work. The writer's tone is determined by the words the writer chooses, called diction. Writers choose words that express the right tone because of their connotation, or feelings associated with the word. Notice the different connotations for the words *hot* and *ask* in the box below.

Language Resources: Connotation

	Denotation (a word's definition)	Positive Connotation	Neutral Connotation	Negative Connotation
hot	high in temperature	tropical, summery	heated, warm	blazing, scorching
ask	to put a question to or make a request	appeal, plea	request, inquire	challenge, nag, demand

Skim through "O Captain! My Captain!" and look for words that describe how the speaker feels about the captain. Then find words the speaker uses to describe the festivities on land. Decide whether the words and phrases are positive or negative and enter them into the correct box. Then describe how the narrator feels and choose a word that summarizes the tone.

The subject of the poem:	Positive tone words and phrases	Negative tone words and phrases	How the narrator feels about the subject	Words that summarize the tone
the captain Stanza 1 Stanza 2 Stanza 3	calls him "my" captain	cold and dead bleeding drops		
festivities on land Stanza 1 Stanza 2 Stanza 3	bells I hear			

Quick Conversation

- Share your work with a partner. Discuss whether the words and phrases describing the captain and the festivities are mostly positive or mostly negative. Based on the words you listed, how does the speaker feel about each one? What is the effect of the contrast of the words about death and the words about victory or joy? Record notes from your discussion.

> The speaker's attitude about the captain is mostly _____.

> I think the speaker's attitude about the festivities is mostly_____.

> In my opinion, the contrast in tone about the captain and the festivities emphasizes_____.

Write a Short Argument

After analyzing and evaluating tone in "O Captain! My Captain!" you have enough information to write a short argument. Choose examples from your chart from either stanza two or stanza three. Write a short argument in which you explain the speaker's tone about the captain and the festivities, using the words and phrases from the poem to explain your opinion. Before writing, read the model short argument provided. Notice what information is in each of the sentences. Try structuring your argument in the same way.

_____

_____

_____

_____

MODEL: SHORT ARGUMENT

The speaker's tone about the captain in stanza one is sorrowful. He refers to the captain as "my" captain, which shows how close he feels to the captain. He ends the stanza by describing the captain as "cold and dead." This image emphasizes the personal grief he feels over the captain's death, so the tone is one of deep sorrow. However, his tone about the festivities in stanza one is one of excitement. He hears "the bells," which are ringing because the ship has arrived safely. This image of the bells carries a joyful tone, which contrasts with his sorrowful tone about the captain.

Interacting in Meaningful Ways: Analyze Mood

Learning Targets

- Analyze and explain in conversation and writing how mood produces effects on the reader.

- Evaluate and explain in conversation and writing how effectively the author uses mood.

- Express and justify opinions in conversation and writing by providing text evidence.

Mood

Walt Whitman in his poem "O Captain! My Captain!" creates a mood of shocked mournfulness over the death of the ship's captain. Mixed in with this sorrowful mood is also a joyful mood of celebration as the excited crowds welcome the ship home. In this activity, you will analyze how Whitman creates these moods and evaluate how he does it.

Skim through poem looking for nouns, verbs, and adjectives that evoke an emotional reaction. Write five more examples in the chart. Then find synonyms for each word. Try to find synonyms that carry a different connotation. Consult a thesaurus to help you locate synonyms. Evaluate how the synonym changes the poem's mood.

 Language Resources

Synonym: a word that has the same or a very similar definition as another word
Connotation: the emotional association that a word carries
Thesaurus: a book or online tool that shows words that are related to each other; a book of synonyms

ACADEMIC VOCABULARY

Evoke is a verb that means to bring about or to cause to happen. Words, imagery, and pictures can **evoke** or cause feelings or memories. **Evocative** describes a work that **evokes** strong feelings or memories. A picture of a flag with an eagle flying over it might be described as evocative because it brings about feelings of patriotism in the United States.

Verbs from the Poem	Synonyms	Evaluation of Change in Mood
weather'd	endured or survived	*endured* or *survived* are less poetic, emotional terms and don't convey a sad, stately mood as well as *weather'd* does

Nouns from the Poem	Synonyms	Evaluation of Change in Mood

Adjectives from the Poem	Synonyms	Evaluation of Change in Mood

Quick Conversation

- Share your work with a partner. Take turns explaining the synonyms you chose and your evaluation of how they affected the poem's mood. Discuss whether your partner agrees or disagrees with your evaluation. Record notes from your discussion.

> In my opinion, this synonym changes the mood by ____.

> Do you agree with my evaluation?

> I disagree with your analysis because ____.

> I agree with your evaluation because ____.

Write a Short Argument

After analyzing and evaluating mood in "O Captain! My Captain!" you have enough information to write a short argument. Choose one word or phrase that evokes the poem's mood. Write a short argument in which you explain the connotation of the word, state your opinion of how effective it is in communicating the poem's mood, and give a reason why. Before writing, read the model short argument provided. Notice what information is in each of the sentences. Try structuring your argument in the same way.

_____

_____

_____

_____

MODEL: SHORT ARGUMENT

The speaker uses the verb "weather'd" to describe the ship's journey. This verb carries a negative connotation because it implies being battered by harsh weather and other forces. This verb helps to emphasize the difficult journey of the ship, which is appropriate for describing the long and difficult Civil War. If the speaker had used the verbs _endured_ or _survived_, the mood of the poem would be less solemn. The poem's mood is so mournful because the captain dies at the end of a difficult journey, and he cannot even enjoy the ship's coming home. The verb "weather'd" helps to create that mournful mood for the reader.

Definition Essay of a Hero
Informative/Explanatory Writing

Step 1: Introduction

You will be writing an explanatory essay about a hero. Think about each of the main characters in this unit. What qualities and actions help define them as heroes? Based on their qualities and actions, write an essay that defines the characteristics of a hero.

Expository Essay Writing Prompt:

You will write an explanatory essay that defines a hero based on one or two of the characters from this unit. Be sure to:

- State a strong thesis statement that defines three characteristics of a hero.
- Include supporting details and examples from the text.
- Use transitions to add details about the central idea.
- Use a variety of adjectives, adverbs, and vivid verbs to describe and explain the heroic qualities.
- Vary your sentence structure by using long, short, or combined clauses.
- End your expository paragraph by restating your thesis.

Step 2: Brainstorming

Now you are ready to start thinking about how to define a hero. Work in small groups or with a partner to brainstorm ideas using the graphic organizer below.

Ideas for Definition Essay		
	A hero is someone who is/acts ...	
Character	**Qualities**	**Actions**
Joby		
Odysseus		
President Lincoln		

Definition Essay of a Hero
Informative/Explanatory Writing

Discuss the ideas that you brainstormed with your partner or group. Use the sentence frames below to help you in your discussion. Remember to take turns sharing your ideas and ask each other questions.

> I think the most important quality of a hero is _____ because _____ .

> The character _____ shows this quality when he _____ .

> Another action a hero would take would be _____ .

> The character is heroic when he _____ .

After your discussion, do a quickwrite paragraph of at least 4–5 sentences, using the following sentence frame:

The character _____ is a hero because he _____

Get together with a partner and exchange quickwrites. Read aloud your quickwrites to each other, then exchange quickwrites and add more ideas in writing to each other's quickwrites.

Step 3: Prewriting

With your partner, read your revised quickwrites to each other. Then discuss how to summarize your ideas into one clear sentence about why the character is a hero. Your definition of a hero will be the thesis or central idea for your essay. If you were writing about Batman, for example, your thesis might be *Batman is a hero because he fights against crime, uses technology to beat the bad guys, and puts his life in danger for other people.*

Narrative/Explanatory Writing

Use these sentence frames to help you gather ideas about what defines a hero.

In my opinion, a hero has these three qualities: _____.

The reason I believe _____ is that _____.

The text evidence suggests that _____ .

I agree with your point that _____ , but I disagree that _____.

Record notes from your discussion.

_____

_____

_____

Based on your collaborative discussion with your partner, use the graphic organizer to begin to organize your ideas about why your character is a hero.

Introduction (Thesis/Central Idea)

Body Paragraphs	Supporting Details from Text	Supporting Details from Text
Quality/Action #1:		
Quality/Action #2:		
Quality/Action #3:		
Conclusion (Restatement of Thesis)		

Definition Essay of a Hero
Informative/Explanatory Writing

Language Resources
Heroic Characteristics

Adjectives	Adverbs
smart	courageously
brave	quickly
determined	firmly

Vivid Verbs	Figurative Language
concentrate	heard the rat-a-tat of his drum
heave	felt the heavy weight of his role
conquer	twisted it like a screw

Writing Checklist
- Review the Expository Writing Rubric
- Review the Student Expository Writing Exemplar
- Review your draft
- Participate in peer editing
- Revise
- Publish
- Present

Step 4: Drafting

Before you begin the draft of your essay, review the scoring guide with your partner so that you understand how your essay will be assessed. Ask your partner questions if you do not understand any of part of the scoring guide.

Use your completed graphic organizer and brainstorming document to help you as you begin to draft your definition essay. As you explain the three qualities and actions that define a hero, remember to use adjectives, adverbs, vivid verbs, and figurative language that will help show the heroic characteristics you are describing.

Be sure to include in your draft:

- specific qualities and actions that show the character is a hero
- supporting examples and details from the text
- transitions between and within paragraphs
- vivid verbs, adjectives, and adverbs and figurative language that emphasize the heroic characteristics
- a variety of long, short, and combined clauses in your sentences

Step 5: Editing and Revising

Exchange drafts with your partner. Then review the scoring guide again and look at the Student Expository Text Exemplar, which you will receive from your teacher. Read each other's drafts. Use this checklist as you read your partner's draft.

Peer Editing Checklist

☐ Did the writer follow the prompt and discuss one or two characters from the unit?

☐ Did the writer state a strong thesis statement that defines a hero?

☐ Did the writer include supporting details and examples from the text?

☐ Is the writing organized in a way that makes sense?

☐ Did the writer include adjectives, adverbs, and vivid verbs in describing the character?

☐ Did the writer include transitions to add details about the central idea and connect supporting paragraphs?

☐ Does the essay end with a restatement of the thesis?

☐ Are there any spelling or punctuation mistakes?

☐ Are there any grammar errors?

Look at the peer editing checklist that your partner completed and discuss it together, using these sentence frames. Takes notes on what you discuss.

- I really liked _____ about the essay.
- Another thing I liked about the essay is _____.
- One part of the essay that could have been clearer is _____.
- One part of the essay that needs stronger support is _____.
- One thing I think the writer could do to improve the essay is _____.

Definition Essay of a Hero
Informative/Explanatory Writing

Use your notes to help you revise your draft. Complete your revised draft on a computer, if possible. You may include graphics or photos from the Internet to include in your final draft, but make sure they are appropriate. Check your final essay against the scoring guide before you submit it to your teacher.

Step 6: Sharing

Present your expository essay orally. You may use visual aids to make your presentation more interesting. Use the following charts to help you present and listen actively when others present their essays.

Tips for Presenting
• Practice your presentation before you give it. You can practice in front of classmates, friends, or family members.
• Speak loudly and clearly.
• Maintain eye contact with your audience.
• Listen respectfully to any questions from your audience, and respond thoughtfully to their questions.

Active Listening	
What was the presenter's purpose?	The presenter's purpose was _____.
What was the presenter's main point?	The presenter's main point was _____.
Did the presenter make eye contact?	☐ Yes ☐ No
Did the presenter use a clear, loud voice?	☐ Yes ☐ No
What is one thing you liked about the presentation?	One thing I liked about the presentation was ____.
What is a question you still have about the presentation?	A question I still have about the presentation is ____.

My Notes

Definition Essay of a Hero
Informative/Explanatory Writing

My Notes

Step 7: Feedback

After presenting your essay orally, take the feedback you received from your classmates and make notes in the chart below. Use this feedback to plan and evaluate future presentations.

What Went Well	What Needs Improvement

Definition Essay of a Hero
Informative/Explanatory Writing

SCORING GUIDE

Scoring Criteria	4	3	2	1
Ideas	The essay • has a clearly focused thesis statement that defines a hero • shows three qualities/actions of the character that make him a hero • integrates strong supporting details from the text.	The essay • has a clear thesis statement • shows some qualities/actions that make the character a hero • integrates some evidence and supporting details.	The essay • has a thesis statement • includes vague or inadequate qualities/actions that make the character a hero • uses irrelevant or insufficient evidence and lacks supporting details.	The essay • has no real thesis statement • does not define a hero; response is vague or confusing • uses minimal evidence and supporting details.
Structure	The essay • introduces the main idea with an engaging hook • organizes ideas into three clear and logical support paragraphs • uses a variety of transitions to create coherence and integrate ideas • provides a clear restatement of the thesis in the conclusion.	The essay • introduces the topic with a thesis statement • organizes ideas into support paragraphs that progress logically • uses transitions to create coherence • provides a restatement of the thesis statement in the conclusion.	The essay • includes a partial or ineffective introduction • uses undeveloped or weak support paragraphs • uses transitions ineffectively or inconsistently • provides a weak, illogical, or repetitive restatement of the thesis in the conclusion.	The essay • does not include a thesis statement in the introduction • has little or no obvious support paragraphs • uses few or no transitions • lacks a conclusion.
Use of Language	The essay • uses precise and accurate diction to explain the topic • demonstrates command of the conventions of standard English capitalization, punctuation, spelling, grammar, and usage (including parallel structure, commas in a series, and semicolons).	The essay • uses diction that is appropriate to the topic and purpose • demonstrates adequate command of the conventions of standard English capitalization, punctuation, spelling, grammar, and usage (including parallel structure, commas in a series, and semicolons).	The essay • uses basic diction inappropriate to the topic or purpose • demonstrates partial or inconsistent command of the conventions of standard English capitalization, punctuation, spelling, grammar, and usage (including parallel structure, commas in a series, and semicolons).	The essay • uses diction that is vague or confusing • lacks command of the conventions of standard English capitalization, punctuation, spelling, grammar, and usage; frequent errors obscure meaning.

Definition Essay of a Hero
Informative/Explanatory Writing

Scoring Criteria	4	3	2	1
Collaboration	Student exceeds expectations in working collaboratively with others.	Student works collaboratively with others.	Student is weak in working collaboratively with others.	Student does not collaborate with others.
How English Works	The essay • uses adjectives, adverbs, and vivid verbs consistently to help the reader visualize details about the hero.	The essay • uses some adjectives, adverbs, and vivid verbs that help the reader visualize some details.	The essay • uses weak vivid verbs and adjectives or uses them inconsistently.	The essay • lacks the use of adjectives, adverbs, and vivid verbs to help the reader visualize details.
Interacting in Meaningful Ways	The essay • uses a variety of long, short, and combined clauses • uses imagery or figurative language to emphasize the hero's abilities.	The essay • uses accurate and consistent sentence construction and clauses • includes some imagery or figurative language to define the hero.	The essay • uses basic sentence construction and clauses • uses imagery or figurative language that is ineffective in adding details.	The essay • uses sentence construction that is inaccurate • lacks the use of imagery or figurative language.

THE CHALLENGE OF UTOPIA:
Analyzing and Evaluating Literary and Informational Texts

Visual Prompt: The perfect society may mean different things to different people. What type of society does each image represent? What does each say about what is important to the people who prefer one over the other?

Unit Overview

We probably all agree that we would like to live in an ideal society where everyone is happy, but what does that actually mean, and why do definitions of the ideal society differ so greatly? In this unit, you will read, write, and engage in various types of collaborative discussions to explore these universal questions.

ACTIVITY
1.1

Selecting Language Resources

Roots and Affixes

The word ***dystopia*** is created from the Latin prefix *dys-* ("bad, abnormal") and the word ***utopia***, which means "good place." The prefix *dys-* is used in other words to indicate the opposite, such as ***dysfunctional***, which means "not functioning" or "functioning in an abnormal way."

Learning Targets

- Develop language resources to use while speaking and writing about short stories.
- Use an expanded set of words to speak and write precisely.
- Adjust language choices to suit the academic setting.

The chart presents words and phrases you will use in discussion and writing. Think about each word or phrase. Circle Q, H, or T to indicate how well you know it. Work with a partner, asking your partner to explain each word or phrase. Listen closely to the explanation, and then write your partner's name in the In Our Own Words column along with his or her condensed idea.

Rating	Q	H	T
	I have seen this word or phrase, but I have **questions** about its meaning.	I have **heard** this word or phrase, but do not know it well.	I know this word or phrase so well that I could **teach** it to someone else.

Word or Phrase	Definition	In Our Own Words
science fiction Rating Q H T	a genre of fiction that tells stories usually set in the future, about the effects of new or possible scientific discoveries	
utopia Rating Q H T	an ideal or perfect community or society, whether real or imagined	
dystopia Rating Q H T	a community or society, usually fictional, that is undesirable or frightening	
setting Rating Q H T	the time and place that a story takes place	
theme Rating Q H T	the central message or insight about life that a piece of literature portrays through its characters, plot, imagery, and other details	
figurative language Rating Q H T	imaginative language that is not meant to be interpreted literally, but to create an effect on the reader	
connotations Rating Q H T	the feelings or associations that a word carries, separate from its literal definition	
evidence Rating Q H T	details used to support an argument or analysis	
dialogue Rating Q H T	the words characters say in a story	

Academic and Social Vocabulary Preview

Learning Target

● Develop knowledge of a growing set of academic and social vocabulary to create precise shades of meaning in reading, speaking, and writing.

VOCABULARY PREVIEW

advantage: (noun) a helpful effect or gain

average: (adjective) ordinary or typical

compete: (verb) to try to win or be the best at something against others

differ: (verb) to be different

genius: (noun) a very smart person

instance: (noun) an example

normal: (adjective) usual or typical; not strange

reckon: (verb) to think that something is true or possible

refer: (verb) to talk about or write about something; to mention

realization: (noun) the act of understanding something

since: (conjunction) in the period following the time when

vague: (adjective) not clear or specific

Vocabulary Practice

Use the definitions in the Vocabulary Preview or a dictionary to support your work.

Practice 1. Circle the word or phrase whose meaning is closest to the meaning of the vocabulary word.

Vocabulary Word	Words or Phrases to Choose From
advantage	a bad effect a helpful effect a silly effect
compete	to go against to work together to pretend
genius	a funny person a sensitive person a brilliant person
normal	usual boring similar
refer	to whisper to mention to understand
vague	helpful false not clear
realization	understanding confusion success

Practice 2. Complete each sentence, paying attention to the **bold** vocabulary word.

1. The sisters differ in the way they dress; **therefore,** _____

2. The puppy was very naughty. For **instance,** he _____

3. The players have not played well **since** _____

4. The instructions on the test were **vague,** so the class _____

5. His height was a great **advantage** for him when he _____

Practice 3. Circle the word that best fits the context of the sentence.

1. The nurse quickly reassured the worried mother that her baby's temperature was completely normal /average.

2. Jaden's average /ordinary grades did not bother her, but her mother wanted her to make the highest grades possible.

Interpret the Text Using Close Reading

Learning Targets

- Draw and support inferences from a close reading of the text.
- Learn the meanings of unfamiliar words from the text.
- Apply understanding of word connotations and the effects they have on the reader.
- Read closely and annotate the text to apply understanding of how short stories are structured.

Read and Annotate

Read "Harrison Bergeron" and annotate the text as you read.

- Use the My Notes area to write questions or ideas you have about the story.
- Underline words and phrases that have strong connotations and figurative language that help you visualize the characters, setting, and events.
- Put exclamation marks next to events that are humorous and horrifying at the same time.
- Circle unknown words and phrases.

Short Story

Harrison Bergeron

by Kurt Vonnegut, Jr.

1 THE YEAR WAS 2081, and everybody was finally equal. They weren't only equal before God and the law. They were equal every which way. Nobody was smarter than anybody else. Nobody was better looking than anybody else. Nobody was stronger or quicker than anybody else. All this equality was due to the 211th, 212th, and 213th Amendments to the Constitution, and to the **unceasing vigilance** of agents of the United States Handicapper General.

2 Some things about living still weren't quite right, though. April for instance, still drove people crazy by not being springtime. And it was in that clammy month that the H-G men took George and Hazel Bergeron's fourteen-year-old son, Harrison, away.

3 It was tragic, all right, but George and Hazel couldn't think about it very hard. Hazel had a perfectly average intelligence, which meant she couldn't think about anything except in short bursts. And George, while his intelligence was way above normal, had a little mental handicap radio in his ear. He was required by law to wear it at all times. It was tuned to a government transmitter. Every twenty seconds or so, the transmitter would send out some sharp noise to keep people like George from taking unfair advantage of their brains. /

4 George and Hazel were watching television. There were tears on Hazel's cheeks, but she'd forgotten for the moment what they were about, as the ballerinas came to the end of a dance.

5 A buzzer sounded in George's head. His thoughts fled in panic, like bandits from a burglar alarm.

My Notes

How can everyone be as smart and good-looking as everyone else?

unceasing: relentless; persistent; continuous
vigilance: watchfulness; alertness

Interpret the Text Using Close Reading

6 "That was a real pretty dance, that dance they just did," said Hazel.

7 "Huh," said George.

8 "That dance—it was nice," said Hazel.

9 "Yup," said George. He tried to think a little about the ballerinas. They weren't really very good—no better than anybody else would have been, anyway. They were burdened with sash weights and bags of birdshot, and their faces were masked, so that no one, seeing a free and graceful gesture or a pretty face, would feel like something the cat drug in. George was toying with the vague notion that maybe dancers shouldn't be handicapped. But he didn't get very far with it before another noise in his ear radio scattered his thoughts.

10 George winced. So did two out of the eight ballerinas.

11 Hazel saw him wince. Having no mental handicap herself, she had to ask George what the latest sound had been.

ball-peen hammer: a hammer used in metalworking, distinguished by a hemispherical head

12 "Sounded like somebody hitting a milk bottle with a **ball peen hammer**," said George.

13 "I'd think it would be real interesting, hearing all the different sounds," said Hazel a little envious. "All the things they think up."

14 "Um," said George.

15 "Only, if I was Handicapper General, you know what I would do?" said Hazel. Hazel, as a matter of fact, bore a strong resemblance to the Handicapper General, a woman named Diana Moon Glampers. "If I was Diana Moon Glampers," said Hazel, "I'd have chimes on Sunday—just chimes. Kind of in honor of religion."

16 "I could think, if it was just chimes," said George.

17 "Well—maybe make 'em real loud," said Hazel. "I think I'd make a good Handicapper General."

18 "Good as anybody else," said George.

19 "Who knows better than I do what normal is?" said Hazel.

20 "Right," said George. He began to think glimmeringly about his abnormal son who was now in jail, about Harrison, but a twenty-one-gun salute in his head stopped that.

21 "Boy!" said Hazel, "that was a **doozy**, wasn't it?"

doozy: something that is unusually good, bad, severe, etc.

22 It was such a doozy that George was white and trembling, and tears stood on the rims of his red eyes. Two of the eight ballerinas had collapsed to the studio floor, were holding their temples.

23 "All of a sudden you look so tired," said Hazel. "Why don't you stretch out on the sofa, so's you can rest your handicap bag on the pillows, honeybunch." She was referring to the forty-seven pounds of birdshot in a canvas bag, which was padlocked around George's neck. "Go on and rest the bag for a little while," she said. "I don't care if you're not equal to me for a while."

24 George weighed the bag with his hands. "I don't mind it," he said. "I don't notice it any more. It's just a part of me."

25 "You been so tired lately—kind of wore out," said Hazel. "If there was just some way we could make a little hole in the bottom of the bag, and just take out a few of them lead balls. Just a few."

Interpret the Text Using Close Reading

26 "Two years in prison and two thousand dollars fine for every ball I took out," said George. "I don't call that a bargain."

27 "If you could just take a few out when you came home from work," said Hazel. "I mean—you don't compete with anybody around here. You just sit around."

28 "If I tried to get away with it," said George, "then other people'd get away with it—and pretty soon we'd be right back to the dark ages again, with everybody competing against everybody else. You wouldn't like that, would you?"

29 "I'd hate it," said Hazel.

30 "There you are," said George. The minute people start cheating on laws, what do you think happens to *society*?"

31 If Hazel hadn't been able to come up with an answer to this question, George couldn't have supplied one. A siren was going off in his head.

32 "Reckon it'd fall all apart," said Hazel.

33 "What would?" said George blankly.

34 "Society," said Hazel uncertainly. "Wasn't that what you just said?

35 "Who knows?" said George.

36 The television program was suddenly interrupted for a news bulletin. It wasn't clear at first as to what the bulletin was about, since the announcer, like all announcers, had a serious speech **impediment**. For about half a minute, and in a state of high excitement, the announcer tried to say, "Ladies and Gentlemen."

37 He finally gave up, handed the bulletin to a ballerina to read.

38 "That's all right—" Hazel said of the announcer, "he tried. That's the big thing. He tried to do the best he could with what God gave him. He should get a nice raise for trying so hard."

39 "Ladies and Gentlemen," said the ballerina, reading the bulletin. She must have been extraordinarily beautiful, because the mask she wore was **hideous**. And it was easy to see that she was the strongest and most graceful of all the dancers, for her handicap bags were as big as those worn by two-hundred pound men.

40 And she had to apologize at once for her voice, which was a very unfair voice for a woman to use. Her voice was a warm, luminous, timeless melody. "Excuse me—" she said, and she began again, making her voice absolutely uncompetitive.

41 "Harrison Bergeron, age fourteen," she said in a **grackle** squawk, "has just escaped from jail, where he was held on suspicion of plotting to overthrow the government. He is a genius and an athlete, is under-handicapped, and should be regarded as extremely dangerous."

42 A police photograph of Harrison Bergeron was flashed on the screen—upside down, then sideways, upside down again, then right side up. The picture showed the full length of Harrison against a background calibrated in feet and inches. He was exactly seven feet tall.

43 The rest of Harrison's appearance was Halloween and hardware. Nobody had ever borne heavier handicaps. He had outgrown **hindrances** faster than the H-G men could think them up. Instead of a little ear radio for a mental handicap, he wore a tremendous pair of earphones, and spectacles with thick wavy lenses. The spectacles were intended to make him not only half blind, but to give him whanging headaches besides.

My Notes

impediment: a physical defect that prevents normal speech

grackle: any of several blackbirds smaller than a crow

hindrances: obstacles; deterrents

Interpret the Text Using Close Reading

My Notes

symmetry: balance; arrangement
consternation: alarm;
bewilderment

44 Scrap metal was hung all over him. Ordinarily, there was a certain **symmetry**, a military neatness to the handicaps issued to strong people, but Harrison looked like a walking junkyard. In the race of life, Harrison carried three hundred pounds.

45 And to offset his good looks, the H-G men required that he wear at all times a red rubber ball for a nose, keep his eyebrows shaved off, and cover his even white teeth with black caps at snaggle-tooth random. "If you see this boy," said the ballerina, "do not—I repeat, do not—try to reason with him."

46 There was the shriek of a door being torn from its hinges.

47 Screams and barking cries of **consternation** came from the television set. The photograph of Harrison Bergeron on the screen jumped again and again, as though dancing to the tune of an earthquake.

48 George Bergeron correctly identified the earthquake, and well he might have—for many was the time his own home had danced to the same crashing tune. "My God—" said George, "that must be Harrison!"

49 The realization was blasted from his mind instantly by the sound of an automobile collision in his head.

50 When George could open his eyes again, the photograph of Harrison was gone. A living, breathing Harrison filled the screen.

51 Clanking, clownish, and huge, Harrison stood—in the center of the studio. The knob of the uprooted studio door was still in his hand. Ballerinas, technicians, musicians, and announcers cowered on their knees before him, expecting to die.

52 "I am the Emperor!" cried Harrison. "Do you hear? I am the Emperor! Everybody must do what I say at once!" He stamped his foot and the studio shook.

53 "Even as I stand here," he bellowed, "crippled, hobbled, sickened—I am a greater ruler than any man who ever lived! Now watch me become what I can become!"

54 Harrison tore the straps of his handicap harness like wet tissue paper, tore straps guaranteed to support five thousand pounds.

55 Harrison's scrap-iron handicaps crashed to the floor.

56 Harrison thrust his thumbs under the bar of the padlock that secured his head harness. The bar snapped like celery. Harrison smashed his headphones and spectacles against the wall.

57 He flung away his rubber-ball nose, revealed a man that would have awed Thor, the god of thunder.

58 "I shall now select my Empress!" he said, looking down on the cowering people. "Let the first woman who dares rise to her feet claim her mate and her throne!"

59 A moment passed, and then a ballerina arose, swaying like a willow.

60 Harrison plucked the mental handicap from her ear, snapped off her physical handicaps with marvelous delicacy. Last of all he removed her mask.

61 She was blindingly beautiful.

62 "Now—" said Harrison, taking her hand, "shall we show the people the meaning of the word dance? Music!" he commanded.

63 The musicians scrambled back into their chairs, and Harrison stripped them of their handicaps, too. "Play your best," he told them, "and I'll make you barons and dukes and earls."

64 The music began. It was normal at first—cheap, silly, false. But Harrison snatched two musicians from their chairs, waved them like batons as he sang the music as he wanted it played. He slammed them back into their chairs.

65 The music began again and was much improved.

66 Harrison and his Empress merely listened to the music for a while—listened gravely, as though synchronizing their heartbeats with it.

67 They shifted their weights to their toes.

68 Harrison placed his big hands on the girl's tiny waist, letting her sense the weightlessness that would soon be hers.

69 And then, in an explosion of joy and grace, into the air they sprang!

70 Not only were the laws of the land abandoned, but the law of gravity and the laws of motion as well.

71 They reeled, whirled, swiveled, flounced, capered, **gamboled**, and spun.

72 They leaped like deer on the moon.

73 The studio ceiling was thirty feet high, but each leap brought the dancers nearer to it.

74 It became their obvious intention to kiss the ceiling. They kissed it.

75 And then, neutralizing gravity with love and pure will, they remained suspended in air inches below the ceiling, and they kissed each other for a long, long time.

76 It was then that Diana Moon Glampers, the Handicapper General, came into the studio with a double-barreled ten-gauge shotgun. She fired twice, and the Emperor and the Empress were dead before they hit the floor.

77 Diana Moon Glampers loaded the gun again. She aimed it at the musicians and told them they had ten seconds to get their handicaps back on.

78 It was then that the Bergerons' television tube burned out.

79 Hazel turned to comment about the blackout to George. But George had gone out into the kitchen for a can of beer.

80 George came back in with the beer, paused while a handicap signal shook him up. And then he sat down again. "You been crying" he said to Hazel.

81 "Yup," she said.

82 "What about?" he said.

83 "I forget," she said. "Something real sad on television."

84 "What was it?" he said.

85 "It's all kind of mixed up in my mind," said Hazel.

86 "Forget sad things," said George.

87 "I always do," said Hazel.

88 "That's my girl," said George. He winced. There was the sound of a riveting gun in his head.

89 "Gee—I could tell that one was a doozy," said Hazel.

90 "You can say that again," said George.

91 "Gee—" said Hazel, "I could tell that one was a doozy."

My Notes

gamboled: leapt; pranced

Interact in Meaningful Ways: Academic Collaboration

Learning Targets

● Ask and answer questions about a short story in collaborative conversations, demonstrating active listening, and drawing upon an expanding pool of language resources for discussing literature.

● Express and support opinions of a short story in conversation.

Turn to your partner or small group to discuss each question about "Harrison Bergeron." After you have discussed a question, write notes about your answer before going on to the next question.

1. What are handicaps in the story? What problem in society are the handicaps supposed to solve?

> The handicaps are ____. They are supposed to solve the problem of ____.

2. Why do the characters accept their handicaps? What are the consequences for not wearing them?

> The consequences for not wearing the handicaps are ____.

3. What words and phrases are used to show how and why Harrison is a threat to society? Which words are most effective to people in that society?

> Harrison is a threat to society because ____.

4. What is the central conflict in the story? How do the characters react to it and why?

> The central conflict of the story is ____, and the characters react by ____.

Asking Questions

Short stories often end by showing how characters respond to the resolution of the main conflict. With your partner or small group, read aloud the ending of "Harrison Bergeron" paragraphs 80–87. Discuss what questions you have about the ending. Write one question to share with the whole class.

_____

_____

How English Works: Vivid Verbs

Learning Targets

- Use different verbs to convey different meanings and effects.
- Discuss and explain how words and phrases convey shades of meaning and connotations.
- Analyze how specific verbs produce different effects on the reader.

> **Language Resources**
> **connotation:** the feelings or association that a word carries, separate from its literal definition

Vivid Verbs

In "Harrison Bergeron," Kurt Vonnegut, Jr., uses vivid verbs to help readers see the action of the story and to create a positive or negative image through a word's connotation. Notice in the chart below the shades of meaning and connotations associated with verbs that all mean "to cry." Some of the verbs are much more vivid because they carry a strong connotation.

Language Resources: Shades of Meaning

Verb:	cry	whimper	moan	sob	wail	howl
Definition/ Shade of Meaning	to shed tears, with or without sound	to cry with low, broken sounds	to make a long, low sound because of sadness or pain	to cry noisily with short, gasping breaths	to make a loud, long cry of pain or sadness	to cry out loudly in pain or anger
Connotation	neutral to negative	Slightly negative	more negative	more negative	strongly negative	strongly negative

Read paragraphs 52–60 of "Harrison Bergeron," looking for examples of vivid verbs. Write examples in the chart. Use the Language Resources: Shades of Meaning chart for support.

Technique	Example from "Harrison Bergeron"	Shade of Meaning	Connotation and Effect on the Reader
Vivid Verb	he bellowed	to bellow is to use a very loud, angry voice	strongly negative because only someone very angry bellows; helps the reader understand how angry and scary he is.
Vivid Verb			
Vivid Verb			

Quick Conversation

- Share your work with a partner. Read aloud the examples and discuss their connotations and effects. Record notes from your discussion.

> The word _____ has a shade of meaning of _____.

> The author made a good choice when he used the verb _____ because _____.

> Would you consider any of these verbs as figurative language? Why?

Determine Shades of Meaning

The words below are all vivid verbs that could be substituted for the verb *ring* in the following sentence: She awoke from a vivid dream in which she heard a bell *ring*.

buzz   peal   clang   chime   roar   jingle

Put the words in order of their connotations, from least intense sound to most intense sound. Use a dictionary to understand the word's shade of meaning. Then make an oral presentation in which you explain the ranking you made of the words and their connotations. Make notes for your presentation in the space below.

_____

_____

_____

_____

_____

_____

_____

_____

Interact in Meaningful Ways: Identify Theme

Learning Targets
- Express and justify opinions in conversation and writing by providing text evidence and using nuanced modal expressions and phrases.
- Analyze theme and how it is communicated through a close reading of dialogue, connotative language, and events.

Theme

Short stories portray characters who are struggling with a problem or conflict in a real or imagined world. Besides entertaining the reader, the writer also wants to communicate a deeper message or truth about life. This message is called the story's theme, and the writer conveys a story's theme through the details of the story. In this activity, you will identify, analyze, and evaluate theme.

One theme of "Harrison Bergeron" relates to the dangers of trying to make everyone equal. Skim through "Harrison Bergeron" looking for textual evidence that will support this thematic statement "A central theme of 'Harrison Bergeron' is that trying to create complete equality can rob people of personal choice and happiness." Look for dialogue, description, figurative language, and plot details that show characters who do not have personal choices or are not happy. Write two examples in the chart. Then analyze each example by explaining how the textual evidence supports the theme.

Theme of "Harrison Bergeron"		
Textual evidence	**Specific details from the textual evidence**	**Explain how the details support the theme**
"It was such a doozy that George was white and trembling and tears stood on the rims of his red eyes."	George is "white and trembling" "tears" on his "red eyes"	Shows that George is unhappy – he is "white and trembling" and has tears on his bloodshot eyes.

Language Resources
Literary Terms
theme: the central message or truth about life that a story communicates through its characters, plot, setting, imagery, and other details
dialogue: the words the characters say in the story or play
textual evidence: details from the text, including dialogue, plot events, descriptions of characters and setting, objects, imagery, and title

ACADEMIC VOCABULARY
Imply is a verb that means "suggests or expresses something without saying it directly." A friend might **imply** disapproval with a look or a frown.

Language Resources
Connotative Language
Connotative language includes words and images that imply theme. Below are words that suggest unhappiness or loss of choices.

Verbs
padlocked
cowered
winced

Adjectives
hideous
tired
abnormal

Images
buzzer
hammer
red rubber ball

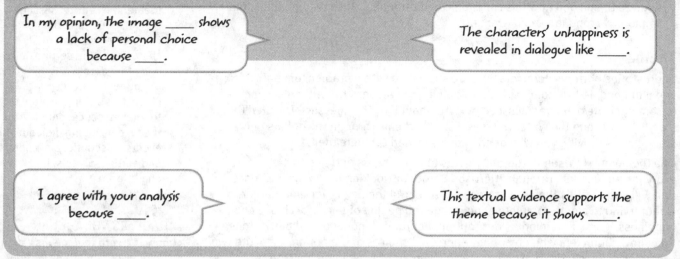

Quick Conversation

Share your work with a partner. Take turns explaining your textual evidence and analysis of how it supports the theme. Discuss whether your partner agrees or disagrees with your analysis. Record notes from your discussion.

In my opinion, the image ____ shows a lack of personal choice because ____.

The characters' unhappiness is revealed in dialogue like ____.

I agree with your analysis because ____.

This textual evidence supports the theme because it shows ____.

Write a Short Argument

After finding and analyzing textual evidence to support the theme of "Harrison Bergeron," you have enough information to write a short argument. Choose one piece of textual evidence from your chart. Write a short argument in which you explain the meaning of the textual evidence and how it supports the theme. Before writing, read the model short argument provided. Notice what information is in each of the five sentences. Try structuring your argument in the same way.

_____

_____

_____

_____

_____

_____

_____

MODEL: SHORT ARGUMENT

One theme of "Harrison Bergeron" is that trying to create complete equality can rob people of personal choices and happiness. George is a man of above average intelligence, but he must wear a transmitter to keep his thoughts scattered. The sounds are so loud and disruptive that he turns "white and trembling" and his "red eyes" have tears in them. A person who is pale and shaking with bloodshot eyes is not happy. Making George equal has made him less happy, not more happy.

Interact in Meaningful Ways: Writing a Comparison-Contrast Essay

Learning Targets
- Express and justify opinions about an expository essay in conversation and writing by providing text evidence or relevant background knowledge.

- Write an essay using the comparison-contrast text structure.

- Use transition words effectively to write cohesively.

Review your annotations and notes on "Harrison Bergeron" and use them to complete the graphic organizer.

Language Resources
Transitions
transitions: words or phrases that link ideas together
transitions to compare: likewise, similarly, in the same way, also
transitions to contrast: on the other hand, instead, in contrast, rather, however

Society's Attitudes	Text Evidence	Lesson or Theme
How much personal choice are characters allowed?	What is the role of handicapping? What details in the story show the society's attitude toward equality?	What is the story warning our society about?

Quick Conversation

Share your work with your partner. Compare your ideas about the society's attitudes, the textual evidence, and the theme of the story.

Next, read aloud paragraphs 85–91 of the story:

> "Forget sad things," said George.
> "I always do," said Hazel.

Discuss the dialogue. What sad thing are George and Hazel talking about? Would this advice be given in today's society? What does it tell you about their society? Record notes from your discussion.

To me, this advice is strange because ____.

But in our own society ____.

What evidence do you have that suggests ____?

What are some words we can use to compare and contrast?

Planning a Comparison-Contrast Essay

Use the graphic organizer to plan your essay that compares and contrasts the attitudes about personal choice in the story's society with the attitudes in our society. Are people in our society allowed to make their own choices? How much are they allowed to be individuals? How does this compare with the story's society? Make notes in response to the questions that follow.

Society's Attitudes	Evidence	Lesson or Theme
How much personal choice are people allowed in our society?	What examples, laws, and events show our society's attitude toward personal choice and equality? Does our society practice handicapping?	Would our society agree or disagree with the lesson of the story? Why or why not?

Comparison-Contrast Writing Prompt

Write a draft of your comparison-contrast essay. Be sure to:

■ Describe the attitude toward equality in the story.

■ Use dialogue, events, character details and other textual details to show the attitude.

■ Compare and contrast the story's attitude with our society's attitudes.

■ Explain how the attitudes are similar or different.

■ Use transitions to make the comparisons smooth and clear.

■ End your essay by reflecting on what lesson or warning the story has for our society.

_____

_____

_____

_____

_____

_____

Novel Excerpt

Selecting Language Resources

Learning Targets

- Develop language resources to use while speaking and writing about personal narratives.
- Use an expanded set of words to speak and write precisely.
- Adjust language choices to suit the academic setting.

The chart presents words and phrases you will use in discussion and writing. Think about each word or phrase. Circle Q, H, or T to indicate how well you know it. Work with a partner, asking your partner to explain each word or phrase. Listen closely to the explanation, and then write your partner's name in the In Our Own Words column along with his or her condensed idea.

> **WORD CONNECTIONS**
>
> Cognates
>
> The English word **perspective** and the Spanish word **perspectiva** are cognates. They both mean "a way of looking or thinking" and come from the Latin verb *perspicere*, meaning "to inspect carefully."

Rating	Q	H	T
	I have seen this word or phrase, but I have **questions** about its meaning.	I have **heard** this word or phrase, but do not know it well.	I know this word or phrase so well that I could **teach** it to someone else.

Word or Phrase	Definition	In Our Own Words
protagonist Rating Q H T	the main character in a story	
characterization Rating Q H T	the way an author develops a story's characters, by describing the character's appearance, actions, words, and thoughts	
setting Rating Q H T	the time and place of a story	
conflict Rating Q H T	the problems or struggles that the main character faces in a story	
dialogue Rating Q H T	the words characters say to each other	
perspective Rating Q H T	the attitude, beliefs, or point of view toward something	
Socratic Rating Q H T	an adjective referring to the ancient philosopher Socrates, who used questions to help followers discover truth	

Academic and Social Language Preview

Learning Target

- Develop knowledge of a growing set of academic and social vocabulary to create precise shades of meaning in reading, speaking, and writing.

VOCABULARY PREVIEW

absurdity: (noun) the state of being ridiculous, very foolish, silly, or unreasonable

concentrate: (verb) to focus attention on an activity

conversation: (noun) the casual talking between two people or a small group

curiously: (adverb) strangely; done out of interest or desire to know more about something or someone

definitely: (adverb) without doubt; certainly

extremely: (adverb) to a very large degree or extent

instant: (noun) a moment or very short period of time

instead: (adverb) in the place of something else; one thing chosen over another

still: (adverb) continuing on in time

though: (conjunction) although, in spite of the fact that

Vocabulary Practice

Use the definitions in the Vocabulary Preview or a dictionary to support your work.

Practice 1. Circle the word or phrase whose meaning is closest to the meaning of the academic vocabulary word.

Vocabulary Word	Words or Phrases to Choose From
instead	next to in place of continuing on
extremely	to a very large degree to a certain degree to a very small degree
definitely	with doubt with certainty with fear
still	stopping waiting continuing on
absurdity	foolishness hilarity anger
curiously	sadly equally interestingly

Practice 2. Complete each sentence, paying attention to the **bold** vocabulary word.

1. Because he saw the thief for just an **instant**, _____

2. **Though** she found it hard to concentrate on the math problems, _____

3. He was **still** hungry so he _____

4. She was **extremely** angry at her brother because he _____

Practice 3. Circle all the correct responses for the following questions.

1. Which of these things would be considered a conversation?
   a debate about climate change   a speech about politics
   a family meeting   a college lecture

2. Which items demonstrate the concept of "absurdity"?
   a ringing cell phone   a dog in a bikini   sunglasses at the beach
   a raincoat in the desert   chewing gum   hitting your thumb with a hammer on purpose

Interpret the Text Using Close Reading

Learning Targets

- Read closely and annotate the text to find a character's changing ideas.
- Apply understanding of how novels are structured to comprehending the text.

Read and Annotate

Read *The Giver* excerpt and annotate the text as you read.

- ■ Use the My Notes area to write questions or ideas you have about the story.
- ■ Underline the points Jonas makes in favor of choices.
- ■ Put stars next to the reasons Jonas gives against choices.
- ■ Circle unknown words and phrases.

Novel Excerpt

The Giver *from*

by Lois Lowry

Jonas lives in a utopian world controlled by the Elders. There is no war, hunger, violence, or suffering. However, there is also no music, art, color, or strong emotions—and no privacy or personal choice. Everyone accepts this way of life and does not question it, because it is all they have ever known. Now age 12, Jonas has been assigned a special career in his community: He will become the "Receiver of Memory," training for his role under the man who has held that position for years and is now "The Giver."

Through his mind, the Giver shares with Jonas the memories of what life was like in earlier times, before "Sameness." Jonas begins to feel emotions and see things he has never experienced. Through the Giver, Jonas has learned about and seen color for the first time, and he is starting to see bits of it in his daily life.

1   Days went by, and weeks. Jonas learned, through the memories, the names of colors; and now he began to see them all, in his ordinary life (though he knew it was ordinary no longer, and would never be again). But they didn't last. There would be a glimpse of green— the landscaped lawn around the Central Plaza; a bush on the riverbank. The bright orange of pumpkins being trucked in from the agricultural fields beyond the community boundary— seen in an instant, the flash of brilliant color, but gone again, returning to their flat and hueless shade.

2   The Giver told him that it would be a very long time before he had the colors to keep.

3   "But I want them!" Jonas said angrily. "It isn't fair that nothing has color!"

4   "Not fair?" The Giver looked at Jonas curiously. "Explain what you mean."

My Notes

5 "Well . . ." Jonas had to stop and think it through. "If everything's the same, then there aren't any choices! I want to wake up in the morning and *decide* things! A blue tunic, or a red one?"

6 He looked down at himself, at the colorless fabric of his clothing. "But it's all the same, always."

7 Then he laughed a little. "I know it's not important, what you wear. It doesn't matter. But—"

8 "It's the choosing that's important, isn't it?" The Giver asked him.

9 Jonas nodded. "My little brother—" he began, and then corrected himself. "No, that's inaccurate. He's not my brother, not really. But this newchild that my family takes care of— his name's Gabriel?"

10 "Yes, I know about Gabriel."

11 "Well, he's right at the age where he's learning so much. He grabs toys when we hold them in front of him— my father says he's learning small-muscle control. And he's really cute."

12 The Giver nodded.

13 "But now that I can see colors, at least sometimes, I was just thinking: what if we could hold up things that were bright red, or bright yellow, and he could *choose*? Instead of the Sameness."

14 "He might make wrong choices."

15 "Oh." Jonas was silent for a minute. "Oh, I see what you mean. It wouldn't matter for a newchild's toy. But later it does matter, doesn't it? We don't dare to let people make choices of their own."

16 "Not safe?" The Giver suggested.

17 "Definitely not safe," Jonas said with certainty. "What if they were allowed to choose their own mate? And chose *wrong*?

18 "Or what if," he went on, almost laughing at the absurdity, "they chose their own *jobs*?"

19 "Frightening, isn't it?" The Giver said.

20 Jonas chuckled . "Very frightening. I can't even imagine it. We really have to protect people from wrong choices."

21 "It's safer."

22 "Yes," Jonas agreed. "Much safer."

23 But when the conversation turned to other things, Jonas was left, still, with a feeling of frustration that he didn't understand.

24 He found that he was often angry, now: irrationally angry at his groupmates, that they were satisfied with their lives which had none of the vibrance his own was taking on. And he was angry at himself, that he could not change that for them.

25 He tried. Without asking permission from The Giver, because he feared— or knew— that it would be denied, he tried to give his new awareness to his friends.

Interpret the Text Using Close Reading

26 "Asher," Jonas said one morning, "look at those flowers very carefully." They were standing beside a bed of geraniums planted near the Hall of Open Records. He put his hands on Asher's shoulders, and concentrated on the red of the petals, trying to hold it as long as he could, and trying at the same time to transmit the awareness of red to his friend.

27 "What's the matter?" Asher asked uneasily. "Is something wrong?" He moved away from Jonas's hands. It was extremely rude for one citizen to touch another outside of family units.

28 "No, nothing. I thought for a minute that they were wilting, and we should let the Gardening Crew know they needed more watering." Jonas sighed, and turned away.

Interact in Meaningful Ways: Academic Collaboration

Learning Targets

- Ask and answer questions about a science fiction novel in collaborative conversations, demonstrating active listening, and drawing upon an expanding pool of language resources for discussing literature.

- Express and support opinions of a novel in conversation.

Turn to your partner or small group to discuss each question about the excerpt from *The Giver*. After you have discussed a question, write notes about your answer before going on to the next question.

1. Who is the protagonist of this novel? What does he want?

> The protagonist of the story is _____.
> He wants _____.

2. What can you infer about the setting of this novel from the conversation Jonas and the Giver have? How does the setting compare to the real world of the present?

> Based on this scene, I can infer that the setting is _____ because _____.

3. How does the Giver respond to Jonas's questions? Why do you think he does this?

> The Giver responds to Jonas's questions by _____.

4. Summarize what Jonas realizes about making choices. How does his perspective change?

> Jonas first believes that choices are _____. Then he believes choices are _____ because _____.

Asking Questions

Protagonists usually change in important ways during a story. With your partner or small group, read aloud paragraphs 24–28 of the excerpt. Discuss what questions you have about the changes in Jonas. Write one question to share with the whole class.

_____

_____

H EW How English Works: Verbal Moods

Learning Target
● Use a variety of verbal moods in writing and in conversation.

⚙ Language Resources

Verbal Moods		
Mood	**Definition**	**Example**
Indicative	verbs that indicate a fact or opinion	The author of the novel *The Giver* <u>is</u> Lois Lowry.
Imperative	verbs that express a command or request	<u>Read</u> Chapter 4 for homework. <u>Please sharpen</u> your pencil.
Interrogative	verbs that ask a question	<u>Did</u> you <u>like</u> the book?
Conditional	verbs that express something that hasn't happened or something that can happen if a certain condition is met	I <u>would have written</u> a different ending to the book.
Subjunctive	verbs that describe a state that is uncertain or contrary to fact (When using the verb "to be" in the subjunctive, always use *were* rather than *was*.)	If Lois Lowry <u>were</u> here, I <u>would ask</u> her about the ending.

⚙ Language Resources

Punctuation
The end punctuation of a sentence can provide clues about which verbal mood is used.

End Punctuation	Type of Verbal Mood
Period	indicative, imperative, conditional, subjunctive
Question Mark	interrogative, subjunctive
Exclamation Mark	indicative, imperative, conditional, subjunctive

> **ACADEMIC VOCABULARY**
>
> **Interrogative** is a grammar term describing something in the form of a question. The verb **interrogate** means "to ask questions, usually in forceful way." Detectives might **interrogate** a suspect. The person asking the questions is known as the **interrogator**.

Verbal Moods

Authors use all five of the verbal moods in their writing to describe different situations and create realistic dialogue. In this activity, you will identify and practice writing the five verbal moods.

Skim through *The Giver* excerpt looking for examples of each verbal mood. Don't forget to look carefully at the dialogue for examples. Use the Language Resources on Punctuation to help you identify and write the different types of verbal moods.

Mood	Sentence from excerpt	Your own sentence
Indicative	Yes, I know about Gabriel.	Yesterday at school ...
Imperative	Explain what you mean.	Please ...
Interrogative	It's the choosing that's important, isn't it?	Does Jonas ...
Conditional	The Giver told him it would be a very long time before he had the colors to keep.	I would have ...
Subjunctive	What if we could hold up things that were bright red, or bright yellow, and he could choose?	If I were Jonas ....

Quick Conversation

Share your work with a partner. Take turns reading your own sentences. Discuss your answers to the last sentence. What would each group member do if they were Jonas? Record notes from your discussion.

> In my opinion, Jonas should ____.

> Do you agree with my opinion?

> I agree with your opinion because ____.

> If I were Jonas, I would ____.

Write a Short Opinion Paragraph

After discussing what choices you would make if you were Jonas, you have enough ideas to write a short opinion paragraph. Write a paragraph in which you finish the sentence "If I were Jonas ..." as the topic sentence. Your paragraph should focus on doing something different than what happens in the book or excerpt. Give a reason for your choice. Before writing, read the model short opinion paragraph provided. Notice what information is in each of the four sentences. Try structuring your opinion in the same way.

_____
_____
_____
_____
_____
_____
_____
_____
_____
_____

MODEL: SHORT OPINION

If I were Jonas, I would ask the Giver more questions. The Giver asks Jonas questions about choices, but the Giver doesn't really say very much about what he thinks. I would keep the conversation going about choices and argue with the Giver a little more. Jonas lets the conversation change too quickly, so he feels unsettled.

Interact in Meaningful Ways: Analyze Characters' Perspectives

Language Resources

Socratic questioning: A question-and-answer technique named after the ancient philosopher Socrates, who used questions to help followers discover truth.

Learning Targets

- Discuss and write ideas about how a character changes.

- Express and justify personal opinions by giving relevant support and using basic modal expressions.

- Apply understanding of characters' perspectives to comprehending and writing texts.

Characters' Perspective

In *The Giver*, Jonas discovers new information about the society he lives in as he talks to the Giver. In the excerpt, Jonas feels unsettled as he wrestles with his own conflicting perspectives and feelings about his world. His perspective shifts as the Giver uses Socratic questioning to lead Jonas to think about the consequences of his beliefs.

Language Resources: Perspectives

Term	Definition	Example
Perspective	an attitude or belief about something	A child's perspective on taking a bath might be that it's a waste of time. A school's perspective on uniforms might be that they will make students more equal.
Conflicting perspectives	attitudes or beliefs that disagree or conflict with each other; can be between two people or groups, or between a person and society	A school wants to start using uniforms, but the students object because they see uniforms as being too restrictive and limiting personal freedom. These perspectives are conflicting.
Shifting perspective	attitudes or beliefs on something that change over time	Some parents who once supported school uniforms begin to change their opinions when they see the hassles the uniforms cause for students.

Skim through the excerpt of *The Giver*, looking for how Jonas's perspective changes as he talks to the Giver. Think about what Jonas wants at the beginning of the conversation. Write down his perspective and give textual evidence. Then think about how he changes his perspective. Summarize what he believes at the end of the conversation and give textual support for it.

Tracing Jonas's Shifting Perspective		
	Jonas's Perspective	Textual Evidence
At the beginning of the conversation		
At the end of the conversation		

Quick Conversation

Share your work with a partner. Read aloud how you described Jonas's shifting perspective. Discuss how and why his perspective changes. Then discuss your perspective. Do you agree that Jonas's shifting perspective is right? Record notes from your discussion.

Jonas's perspective shifts from _____ to _____.

My perspective is that choices _____.

I disagree with your perspective because _____.

In my opinion, Jonas was right to change his perspective because _____.

Present an Oral Argument

After analyzing Jonas's shifting perspective in *The Giver*, you have enough information to present a short oral argument on whether you agree or disagree with Jonas. First, use your chart to explain how Jonas's perspective shifts. Then state whether you agree with Jonas. Should Jonas have changed his perspective? Or is his first perspective right after all? Clearly state your opinion and give a reason for your opinion. Write your notes below.

_____

_____

_____

_____

_____

_____

_____

_____

_____

_____

_____

_____

_____

Interact in Meaningful Ways:
Writing a Dialogue

Punctuating Dialogue
Quotation marks go around
the words the character says:
"Don't come here," she said.

Use a **dialogue tag** to show
who is speaking the words.

Commas go inside the
quotation marks at the end of
the words the character says:
"I didn't hear you," she said.

A **period** goes after the
dialogue tag.

Put question marks and
exclamation points inside
the quotation marks: "Why
not?" she asked. "It's too
dangerous!" he replied.

Learning Targets

- Express ideas and opinions with some basic modal expressions.
- Apply understanding of how Socratic discussions and dialogue are structured to read closely and write dialogue.
- Write dialogue, using appropriate verbal moods.

Review your annotations and notes on the excerpt from *The Giver* and use them to complete the graphic organizer.

Topic	Conflicting Perspectives	Shifting Perspectives
What issue do Jonas and the Giver discuss? What is Jonas's perspective on the issue?	**What is the Giver's perspective on the issue? What questions does the Giver ask Jonas?**	**How does Jonas's perspective change during the conversation?**

Quick Conversation

Share your work with your partner. Compare your ideas about the conflicting perspectives and the way Jonas changes his perspective.

Next, read aloud paragraph 23 of the excerpt:

> But when the conversation turned to other things, Jonas was left, still, with a feeling of frustration that he didn't understand.

Discuss the sentence. What does it tell you about Jonas and how he feels about the issue of choices? Is he completely settled in his perspective? Does this passage indicate Jonas may change his perspective again? Why or why not? Record notes from your discussion.

I think Jonas feels _____ about the issue of choices because _____.

I disagree because _____.

Based on _____, I think Jonas's final perspective on choices will be _____.

Will you please explain that?

Planning a Dialogue

Use the graphic organizer to plan a scene of dialogue in which a young person and an older person engage in a Socratic discussion about an aspect of today's society. Choose an issue that the younger person feels should be changed. The dialogue should include questions that help the young person's perspective to shift in some way. Consider issues that you feel strongly about, and make notes in response to the questions that follow. Use the sentence frames to help you develop your ideas and the dialogue.

Issue	Conflicting Perspectives	Shifting Perspectives
What issue will your two characters discuss? What is the young person's perspective on the issue?	What is the older person's perspective on the issue? What questions does the older person ask?	How does the young person's perspective change during the conversation?
Issue: Young person's perspective:	Older person's perspective:	Change in perspective:
Dialogue starters:	**Dialogue starters:**	**Dialogue starters:**
It isn't fair that … I wish _____ was different because _____ If _____ changed, then _____ would happen.	Why isn't it fair? Have you thought about _____? What will happen when _____?	I never thought about _____ I agree with you that _____

Dialogue Writing Prompt

Write a draft of your dialogue. Be sure to:

- Establish the young person's perspective on the issue.
- Have the older person ask thoughtful questions that lead the young person to see the issue in a new way.
- Use three different verbal moods in the dialogue, and use language that reveals each character's perspective.
- Show a shift in the young person's perspective by the end of the dialogue.

_____

_____

_____

_____

_____

_____

_____

_____

_____

ACTIVITY 3.1

Selecting Language Resources

WORD CONNECTIONS

Cognates

The English word *argument* and the Spanish word *argumento* are cognates. They both mean "to make a case for" and come from the Latin verb *arguere*, meaning "to prove."

Learning Targets

- Develop language resources to use while speaking and writing about non-fiction articles.
- Use an expanded set of words to speak and write precisely.
- Adjust language choices to suit the academic setting.

The chart presents words and phrases you will use in discussion and writing. Think about each word or phrase. Circle Q, H, or T to indicate how well you know it. Work with a partner, asking your partner to explain each word or phrase. Listen closely to the explanation, and then write your partner's name in the In Our Own Words column along with his or her condensed idea.

Rating	Q	H	T
	I have seen this word or phrase, but I have **questions** about its meaning.	I have **heard** this word or phrase, but I do not know it well.	I know this word or phrase so well that I could **teach** it to someone else.

Word or Phrase	Definition	In Our Own Words
argument Rating Q H T	a logical appeal, supported by reasons and evidence, to persuade an audience to take an action or agree with a point of view	
claim Rating Q H T	an assertion of something as true, real, or factual	
evidence Rating Q H T	knowledge or data on which to base belief; used to prove truth or falsehood	
reasoning Rating Q H T	logical conclusions, judgments, or inferences based on evidence	
counterclaim/ counterargument Rating Q H T	a claim based on knowledge of the other side of a controversial issue; used to demonstrate understanding of the audience, expertise in the subject, and credibility	
purpose Rating Q H T	the specific reason for writing or speaking; the goal the writer or speaker wishes to achieve	
audience Rating Q H T	the specific person or group of people the writer is trying to convince (the opposition); one must consider the audience's values and beliefs before writing the argument	
debatable Rating Q H T	having two or more sides or opinions that can be argued	

Academic and Social Language Preview

Learning Target

- Develop knowledge of a growing set of academic and social vocabulary to create precise shades of meaning in reading, speaking, and writing.

VOCABULARY PREVIEW

ban: (verb) to outlaw or forbid

confirm: (verb) to show or say something is true or correct

data: (noun) facts, statistics, or pieces of information

effect: (noun) a change that happens as a result of something else

impact: (noun) a strong effect

issue: (noun) a topic or matter that people are concerned or talking about

nor: (conjunction) a negative form of the word *or*, meaning not; usually joins two things or clauses

similar: (adjective) to be alike or resemble something

theory: (noun) an explanation or idea to explain something

whether: (conjunction) indicating choices or possibilities

yield: (verb) to produce something as a result of work, effort or time

Vocabulary Practice

Use the definitions in the Vocabulary Preview or a dictionary to support your work.

Practice 1. Circle the word or phrase whose meaning is closest to the meaning of the vocabulary word.

Vocabulary Word	Words or Phrases to Choose From
data	opinions lies facts
theory	an explanation a question a set of proven facts
similar	identical alike same
ban	to forbid to allow to punish
nor	either not or
whether	indicating choices forbidden the result of work

Practice 2. Complete each sentence, paying attention to the **bold** vocabulary word.

1. **Because** the medicine had such a positive effect, the doctor

_____

2. The lawyer expected the witness to confirm her client's alibi; **however,**

_____

Practice 3. Use the context clues in the sentence to pick the correct vocabulary word.

1. The effect/issue of doing all those sit-ups was so small that he quit doing them.

2. Long after the debate, the students continued to discuss the issue/yield of racism.

3. He knew the tutoring would yield/impact better grades, but he was still surprised when he made the highest grade in the class.

4. The speaker made such a strong impact/issue on the audience that he received a standing ovation.

Learning Targets

- Explain ideas and identify evidence through a close reading of the text.
- Make inferences and draw conclusions based on a close reading of the text.

Read and Annotate

Read "Cellphones and driving: As dangerous as we think?" and annotate the text as you read.

- ▣ Use the My Notes area to write questions or ideas you have about the article.
- ▣ Underline specific evidence that supports the idea that cellphones cause accidents.
- ▣ Put a star next to the evidence you think is strongest.
- ▣ Put exclamation marks next to challenging passages or information.
- ▣ Circle unknown words and phrases.

Article

Cellphones and driving: As dangerous as we think?

Despite calls for cellphone bans, there's no conclusive data on handheld devices and safe driving

March 26, 2012 | By Matthew Walberg, *Chicago Tribune* reporter

1   A bill pending in Springfield would ban all drivers in Illinois from using handheld cellphones in Illinois. An **ordinance** being considered in Evanston would go further and prohibit motorists in that town from talking on cellphones of any kind—including hands-free.

2   It's a matter of safety, proponents of both measures say.

3   But two decades of research done in the U.S. and abroad have not yielded **conclusive** data about the impact cellphones have on driving safety, it appears. Nor is there a **consensus** that hands-free devices make for safer driving than handheld cellphones.

4   In theory, the effect of cellphones on driver performance should be relatively easy to determine: Compare crash data against phone records of drivers involved in accidents. But phone records are not easily obtained in the United States, forcing researchers in this country to find less direct ways to analyze the danger of cellphone distraction. The issue is further clouded because auto accidents overall have been decreasing, even as cellphones become more common.

My Notes

ordinance: statute; law

conclusive: definitive; clear
consensus: general agreement

Interpret the Text Using Close Reading

correlation: relation of two or more things or parts

5 "The expectation would be that as cellphone use has skyrocketed we would see a **correlation** in the number of accidents, but that hasn't happened," said Jonathan Adkins, spokesman for the Governors Highway Safety Association.

6 Adkins said the association believes that states should simply enforce their current cellphone laws, if any, and wait for further research to better understand exactly how much of a role cellphone use plays in automobile accidents.

7 "We know it's distracting, we know it increases the likelihood of a crash," Adkins said. "It just hasn't shown up in data in a lot of cases—in other words, it's hard to prove that a crash was caused because someone was on their cellphone."

prohibition: the action of forbidding something, especially by law

8 Proponents of cellphone restrictions—whether total bans or **prohibition** of handheld phones—can cite some studies to back up their positions.

9 A 2005 study published in the British Medical Journal looked at crash data for 456 cellphone subscribers in Perth, Australia, who had an auto accident that required medical attention. The study, which essentially confirmed a similar 1997 study conducted in Toronto, concluded that drivers talking on their phones were about four times more likely to be involved in an accident than those who were not on the phone.

intoxicated: inebriated; drunk

10 Another highly publicized 2006 study from the University of Utah concluded that drivers who talked on cellphones were as impaired as drivers who were **intoxicated** at the legal blood-alcohol limit of 0.08. The study, however, found that using hands-free devices did little to improve drivers' performances.

11 There is some evidence suggesting state and local bans have caused some drivers to talk less while on the road.

My Notes

_____

_____

_____

fatalities: deaths

_____

_____

_____

_____

_____

_____

_____

_____

_____

_____

_____

_____

_____

12 This month, California's Office of Traffic Safety released the results of a study showing a sharp decrease in the number of accidents caused by cellphone use that resulted in death or injury.

13 Researchers tracked the number of accident reports that listed cellphone use as a factor during the two-year periods before and after the 2008 passage of a statewide ban on handheld devices. The study concluded that while overall traffic **fatalities** of all kinds dropped by 22 percent, fatalities caused by drivers who were talking on a handheld phone at the time of the crash dropped nearly 50 percent. Similar declines were found for drivers using hands-free devices.

14 The study followed the agency's 2011 survey of more than 1,800 drivers that found that only about 10 percent of drivers reported that they regularly talked on the phone while driving—down from 14 percent from the previous year's survey. In addition, the survey saw increases in the number of people who said they rarely or never use their cellphone behind the wheel.

15 Those surveyed, however, overwhelmingly believed that hands-free devices made cellphone use safer, a perception that runs counter to research showing such tools do little to reduce the distraction.

16 "If there is an advantage, it's only because a person may have two hands on the wheel, but most people drive with one hand all the time anyway," said Chris Cochran, spokesman for the Office of Traffic Safety. "In reality, it's the conversation, not the phone itself."

Source: http://articles.chicagotribune.com/2012-03-26/news/ct-met-cell-phone-safety-studies-20120326_1_handheld-cellphones-cellphone-restrictions-cellphone-subscribers

Interact in Meaningful Ways:
Academic Collaboration

Learning Targets

- Ask and answer questions about an article in collaborative conversations, demonstrating active listening, and drawing upon an expanding pool of language resources for discussing literature.

- Express and support opinions of an article in conversation and by providing textual evidence.

- Express and support inferences and conclusions drawn from the text.

Turn to your partner or small group to discuss each question about "Cellphones and driving: As dangerous as we think?" After you have discussed a question, write notes about your answer before going on to the next question.

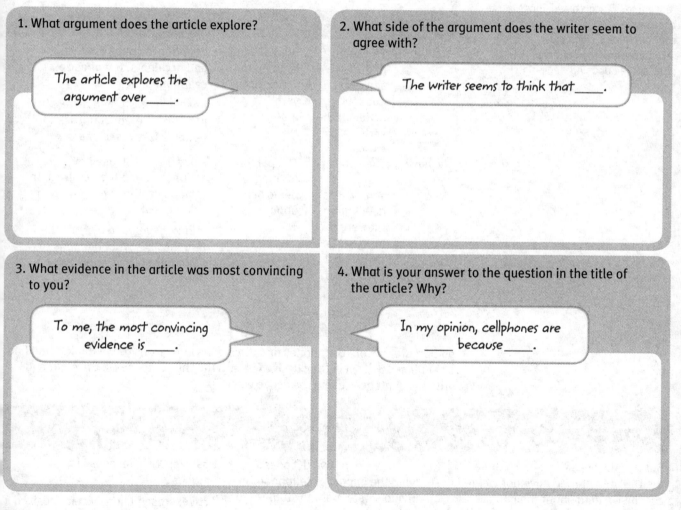

1. What argument does the article explore?

> The article explores the argument over _____.

2. What side of the argument does the writer seem to agree with?

> The writer seems to think that _____.

3. What evidence in the article was most convincing to you?

> To me, the most convincing evidence is _____.

4. What is your answer to the question in the title of the article? Why?

> In my opinion, cellphones are _____ because _____.

Asking Questions

Articles exploring arguments often include counterarguments. With your partner or small group, read aloud paragraphs 15–16. Discuss what questions you have about the counterarguments. Write one question to share with the whole class.

_____

_____

HEW How English Works: Active and Passive Voice

Learning Targets
- Analyze the use and effects of active and passive verbs.
- Apply understanding of how arguments are structured to comprehending and writing texts.

Active and Passive Voice

Arguments are written to persuade readers to believe a certain way, and writers use evidence and reasoning to convince them. They also select the active and passive voice of verbs carefully, depending what they want to emphasize.

Language Resources

Structure of an Argument

purpose: the goal the writer or speaker wishes to achieve

audience: the specific person or group of people the writer is trying to convince

claim: an assertion of something as true, real, or factual

evidence: knowledge or data used to prove truth or falsehood

reasoning: logical conclusions based on evidence

counterclaim: a claim that recognizes and then argues against the opposing viewpoints

Language Resources: Voice

Voice	Definition	Emphasizes	Example
Active	The subject of the sentence does the action of the verb.	Who or what is doing the action of the verb	Cellphones <u>cause</u> distractions and accidents. (emphasizes *cellphones*) Researchers <u>studied</u> drivers in three different countries. (emphasizes *researchers*)
Passive	The subject of the sentence is acted upon; the verb is a form of "be" with a past particple.	The person or thing being acted upon	Accidents <u>are caused</u> by cellphones and their distractions. (emphasizes *accidents* more than *cellphones*). Frida <u>was hugged</u> by Felipe! (Emphasizes what happens to *Frida* rather than what *Felipe* does.)

Read paragraph 4 of "Cellphones and driving: As dangerous as we think?" and find two sentences written in the passive voice. Write the sentences in the chart and rewrite the sentences using the active voice.

Sentences Using Passive Voice	Rewritten Sentence Using Active Voice	Emphasis of the Sentence
But two decades of research done in the U.S. and abroad have not yielded conclusive data about the impact cellphones have on driving safety, it appears.	Researchers spent two decades studying the impact of cellphones on driving safety, but the studies did not yield conclusive data.	**Passive:** "two decades" is emphasized **Active:** "researchers" is emphasized
		Passive: **Active:**
		Passive: **Active:**

💬 Quick Conversation

- Share your work with a partner. Read aloud the original and revised sentences. Discuss how they compare.

- What is emphasized in the passive voice compared to the active voice?
  Why might the writer have chosen the passive voice? Is the passive voice effective?
  Record notes from your discussion.

> I think the ____ -voice sentence emphasizes ____.

> In my opinion, the writer used the passive voice because ____.

> I disagree with your evaluation because ____.

> The passive voice is effective because ____.

Write a Short Argument

After analyzing the use of the active and passive voice, you have enough information to write a short argument. Choose one of the sentences from your chart and explain why the writer chose the passive voice. Then evaluate the effectiveness of the choice. Before writing, read the model short argument provided. Notice what information is in each of the four sentences. Try structuring your argument in the same way.

_____

_____

_____

_____

MODEL: SHORT ARGUMENT

In the article "Cellphones and driving: As dangerous as we think?" Matthew Walberg uses the passive voice when he describes research on the impact of cellphones. In my opinion, he chooses the passive voice to emphasize the "two decades" of research. He does this to show how much research and study has been done on the issue. The use of the passive voice is effective because it emphasizes that even a long period of study has not given enough data to answer the question about cellphones and driver safety.

Interact in Meaningful Ways: Embedding Quotations

Language Resources

Embedding Quotations

TLQC: a format to embed direct quotations
transition: words and phrases that link ideas
lead-in: introduces the context or background for the quote
quote: the exact words from the source, used with quotation marks
citation: Author's last name and page number in parentheses

ACADEMIC VOCABULARY

Cite is a verb that means to quote or mention something as an example. Writers might **cite** statistics; your mother might **cite** your messy room as an example of your laziness. A **citation** is the details about where the information came from, such as a book or a Web site.

Language Resources

Types of Evidence
expert testimony: statements or details from experts or authorities
facts and statistics: proven and reliable facts and numbers
analogies: comparisons to similar situations
references: details from history, religious texts, and classic literature

Learning Targets

- Analyze and explain how arguments are structured and evidence is presented.

- Evaluate and explain how convincing a writer's evidence is.

- Express and justify opinions by providing text evidence and using nuanced modal expressions and phrases.

Citing Evidence

When writing an argument, authors must weave evidence smoothly into their argument by introducing and citing it. In this activity, you will identify transitions, lead-ins, and quotes (TLQC), and then practice weaving evidence into your own writing.

Read paragraphs 8–10 in the article looking for the elements of TLQC that the writer uses. Write the examples in the chart. The example provided has analyzed paragraphs 11–13.

TLQC Elements	Examples from Text	Examples from Text
Type of Evidence	Facts and statistics	
Transition	"There is some evidence suggesting state and local bans have caused some drivers to talk less while on the road."	
Lead-in	"This month, California's Office of Traffic Safety released the results of a study…"	
Quote/Paraphrase	"…overall traffic fatalities of all kinds dropped by 22 percent…"	
Citation	California's Office of Traffic Safety –(part of the lead-in)	

Quick Conversation

Share your work with a partner. Read aloud your examples and take turns explaining your answers. Then discuss whether you think the evidence in your example is convincing and clear. Record notes from your discussion.

> In my example, the transition the writer used is _____.

> For the lead-in, the writer used the words _____.

> In my opinion, the evidence was not convincing because _____.

> Do you agree with my evaluation?

Write a Short Argument

After analyzing the transitions and the writer's evidence from the article, you can practice incorporating evidence into your own writing. First decide if you believe the evidence in your example was convincing. Then write a topic sentence that states your claim about the evidence. Use a transition and lead-in to introduce the evidence you have chosen. Instead of a paraphrase, use a direct quote. Then explain your reasoning for why the evidence is or is not convincing. Be sure your paragraph includes all four elements of the TLQC. Before writing, read the model short argument provided. Notice what information is in each of the sentences. Try structuring your argument in the same way.

_____

_____

_____

_____

MODEL: SHORT ARGUMENT

In the article "Cellphones and driving: As dangerous as we think?" Matthew Walberg presents convincing evidence. To show that state and local bans on cellphones have had an effect, he presents statistics from a study by the California Office of Traffic Safety. He says the study showed that "overall traffic fatalities of all kinds dropped by 22 percent" (Walberg). This evidence is convincing because 22 percent is a big change, and it shows that cellphone bans do save lives.

My Notes

Step 1: Introduction

You will be writing an argument essay that addresses the question: Should parents use devices or apps that disable the use of cell phones in cars by their teenage drivers? Think about the article in this unit on cell phone use and distracted driving. What does the evidence say about this issue? Also consider "Harrison Bergeron" and the excerpt from *The Giver*. What do these stories say about personal choices? Should societies limit choices and personal freedom? Should parents limit the choices their teenage drivers can make for the sake of safety?

Argumentative Essay Writing Prompt:

Write an argumentative essay that states a claim on one side or the other of the following question: Should parents use devices or apps that disable the use of cell phone in cars by their teenage drivers? Decide which side of the debate you stand on, and write an essay in which you convince parents to agree with you. Be sure to:

● Make a strong claim that clearly states your position on the issue.

● Consider your audience and the reasons and evidence that will best convince them.

● Gather information from credible sources.

● Introduce and respond to one counterclaim by your audience.

● Use a vivid verbs and connotative language that supports your claim and reasons.

● Weave evidence and quotations smoothly into your argument.

Step 2: Brainstorming

If you have an instant reaction to the question, pause and think about it. Try to develop responses to both sides of the issue. This will help you make an informed decision about where you stand. It will also help you to understand your audience and to address counterclaims, no matter which side you support. Work in small groups or with a partner to brainstorm ideas using the graphic organizer below.

Should parents use devices/apps to disable cellphones by teenage drivers?	
Yes	**No**
Because ...	Because ...
Because ...	Because ...
Because ...	Because ...

Argumentative Essay About Cell Phone Use
Argument Writing

Discuss the reasons that you brainstormed with your partner or group. Use the sentence frames below to help you in your discussion. Remember to take turns sharing your ideas and ask each other questions.

> I think the strongest reason for YES is _____ because _____ .

> Parents would probably respond to that reason by saying _____ .

> I think the strongest reason for NO is _____ because _____ .

> You make a good point about _____, but have you considered _____?

After your discussion, choose what you believe is the strongest reason to support your claim. Then do a quickwrite paragraph of at least 4–5 sentences, using the following sentence frames:

Parents should/should not use devices to disable cellphones while their teenagers are driving because …

_____

_____

The evidence shows that …

_____

_____

My audience is likely to argue that _____, so I will counter by arguing or pointing out that …

_____

_____

Step 3: Prewriting

Work with a partner and read your quickwrites to each other. Then discuss what questions research can help you answer about your claim. For example, if you are answering *Yes* to the prompt, you might want to do research that helps you answer this question: *How do devices that disable cell phones affect accident rates?* After you develop a research question, then discuss where you might find sources to answer the question. Is there evidence in any of the articles in your textbook?

Argumentative Essay About Cell Phone U Argument Writing

My Notes

_____
_____
_____
_____
_____
_____
_____

Language Resources

Embedding Quotations

TLQC: a format to embed direct quotations

transition: words and phrases that link ideas

lead-in: introduces the context or background for the quote

quote: the exact words from the source, used with quotation marks

citation: Author's last name and page number in parentheses

Will you do an Internet search? What search terms and sources will be most helpful? Record notes from your discussion.

_____

_____

_____

Now use the graphic organizer below to gather the research for your argument.

Claim:

Research Question:

Source	Evidence

Step 4: Drafting

Before you begin the draft of your essay, review the scoring guide with your partner so that you understand how your essay will be assessed. Then use the graphic organizer below to develop the reason, evidence, and counterclaim for your argument.

Introduction:		
Claim		
Reason #1	Evidence and Source	Evidence and Source
Counterclaim	Reasoning/Evidence Against	Reasoning/Evidence Against
Conclusion: Restatement of Claim		

Argumentative Essay About Cell Phone Use
Argument Writing

Use your completed graphic organizer and brainstorming document to help you as you begin to draft your argument essay. Review the elements of TLQC to help you weave in quotations from your research.

Be sure to include in your draft:

- Present your claim clearly.
- Use evidence from your research to support your claim.
- Use the TLQC format to weave quotations smoothly into your writing.
- Use the active voice, but use one sentence in the passive voice for effect.
- Present a counterclaim and point out why the counterclaim is weak or wrong.

Step 5: Editing and Revising

Exchange drafts with your partner. Then review the scoring guide again and look at the Student Argument Text Exemplar, which you will receive from your teacher. Read each other's drafts. Use this checklist as you read your partner's draft.

Peer Editing Checklist

☐ Did the writer follow the prompt and state a clear claim that answers the prompt?

☐ Did the writer include one reason and supporting evidence for the claim?

☐ Did the writer present and argue against a counterclaim?

☐ Did the writer use the TLQC format to embed quotations smoothly into the essay?

☐ Did the writer use the active voice effectively and include one use of the passive voice for effect?

☐ Does the essay end with a restatement of the claim?

☐ Are there any spelling or punctuation mistakes?

☐ Are there any grammar errors?

> The most convincing evidence in the writer's argument is _____.

> One thing I liked about the writer's essay is _____.

> I think the writer could do _____ to improve the essay.

> Could you explain that?

Look at the peer editing checklist that your partner completed. Use it to help you revise your draft. Use a classroom computer to revise and complete your draft. You may include graphics or photos from the Internet to include in your final draft, but make sure they are appropriate. Check your final essay against the scoring guide before you submit it to your teacher.

Writing Checklist
☐ Review the Argument Writing Rubric.
☐ Review the Student Argument Writing Exemplar.
☐ Review your draft.
☐ Participate in peer editing.
☐ Revise
☐ Publish
☐ Present

My Notes

Step 6: Sharing

Present your argument essay orally. You may use visual aids to help you. Use the following charts to help you present and listen actively when others present their essays.

Presentation Tips
• Practice your presentation before you give it.
• Speak loudly and clearly.
• Maintain eye contact with your audience.
• Listen respectfully to any questions from your audience, and respond to any questions from your audience.

Active Listening	
What was the presenter's claim?	The presenter's claim was _____.
What main evidence did the presenter use to support the claim? Was the evidence effective?	The presenter used _____ . The evidence was/was not effective because _____.
Did the presenter make eye contact?	☐ Yes ☐ No
Did the presenter use a clear, loud voice?	☐ Yes ☐ No
What is one thing you liked about the presentation?	One thing I liked about the presentation was ____.
What is a question you still have about the presentation?	I still have a question about _____.

Step 7: Feedback

After presenting your essay orally, take the feedback you received from your classmates and make notes in the chart below. Use this feedback to plan and evaluate future presentations.

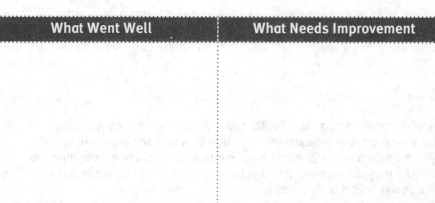

What Went Well	What Needs Improvement

Argumentative Essay About Cell Phone Use
Argument Writing

SCORING GUIDE

Scoring Criteria	4	3	2	1
Ideas	The essay • supports a claim with strong reasoning and evidence. • shows strong use of sources and the research process. • addresses the counterclaim effectively.	The essay • supports a claim with adequate reasoning and evidence. • shows use of sources and the research process. • addresses the counterclaim.	The essay • has an unclear or unfocused claim and/or inadequate support. • shows insufficient use of sources and the research process. • addresses the counterclaim ineffectively.	The essay • has no claim or claim lacks support. • shows little or no use of sources and the research process. • does not addresses the counterclaim.
Structure	The essay • has an engaging introduction that gives context for the issue. • follows a logical organizational structure. • contains an insightful conclusion.	The essay • has an introduction that gives some background about the issue. • follows an adequate organizational structure. • contains a conclusion.	The essay • has a weak introduction. • uses an ineffective or inconsistent organizational structure. • has an illogical, or unrelated conclusion.	The essay • lacks an introduction. • has little or no obvious organizational structure. • lacks a conclusion.
Use of Language	The essay • uses precise and accurate language to persuade the audience. • demonstrates command of the conventions of standard English capitalization, punctuation, spelling, grammar, and usage.	The essay • uses acceptable language to persuade the audience. • demonstrates adequate command of the conventions of standard English capitalization, punctuation, spelling, grammar, and usage.	The essay • uses basic or weak language to persuade the audience. • demonstrates partial command of the conventions of standard English capitalization, punctuation, spelling, grammar, and usage.	The essay • uses language that is vague or confusing • lacks command of the conventions of standard English capitalization, punctuation, spelling, grammar, and usage; frequent errors obscure meaning.
Collaboration	Student exceeds expectations in working collaboratively with others.	Student works collaboratively with others.	Student is weak in working collaboratively with others.	Student does not work collaboratively with others.

Argumentative Essay About Cell Phone U
Argument Writing

Scoring Criteria	4	3	2	1
How English Works	The essay • uses vivid verbs and connotative language consistently to help persuade the reader. • uses both the active and passive voice effectively.	The essay • uses some vivid verbs and connotative language to help persuade the reader. • uses both the active and passive voice.	The essay • uses weak vivid verbs and connotative language or uses them inconsistently. • shows weak use of the active and passive voice.	The essay • lacks the use of vivid verbs and connotative language. • does not use active and passive voice appropriately.
Interact in Meaningful Ways	The essay • uses an accurate TLQC format to embed quotations smoothly.	The essay • uses some elements of the TLQC format to embed quotations.	The essay • uses an incorrect TLQC format to embed quotations smoothly.	The essay • lacks the TLQC format to embed quotations.

UNIT

3

THE CHALLENGE TO MAKE A DIFFERENCE:
Evaluating and Presenting Arguments

Visual Prompt: What do you notice about this art? How does the artist use visual techniques for effect? How do you think the arts (artwork, music, literature, etc.) can help change the world?

Unit Overview

The world has dark pages in its history, and at times the challenge of righting such immeasurable wrongs seems impossible. In this unit, you will apply the lessons of the past to start making a difference today by raising awareness and encouraging people to take action about a significant national or global issue.

Novel Excerpt

Selecting Language Resources

WORD CONNECTIONS

Cognates

The English word *character* and the Spanish word *carácter* are cognates. They both mean "personality; how a person behaves" and come from the Latin word *kharaktēr*.

Learning Targets

- Develop language resources to use while speaking and writing about a short story.

- Use an expanded set of words to speak and write.

- Adjust language choices to suit the purpose, task, and audience.

The chart presents words and phrases you will use in discussion and writing. Think about each word or phrase. Circle Q, H, or T to indicate how well you know it. Work with a partner, asking your partner to explain each word or phrase. Listen closely to the explanation, and then write your partner's name in the In Our Own Words column along with his or her condensed idea.

Rating	Q	H	T
	I have seen this word or phrase, but I have **questions** about its meaning.	I have **heard** this word or phrase, but I do not know it well.	I know this word or phrase so well that I could **teach** it to someone else.

Word or Phrase	Definition	In Our Own Words
characterization Rating Q H T	the way a writer makes a person in a story, book, play, or movie seem like a real person	
description Rating Q H T	how a person, thing, or event looks, sounds, smells, feels, tastes	
inference Rating Q H T	a conclusion or opinion formed based on facts or evidence	
dialogue Rating Q H T	things that are said by two or more characters in a story, book, movie, play, etc.	
setting Rating Q H T	the time, place, and conditions in which the action in a book or movie takes place	
theme Rating Q H T	the main subject that is discussed or described in a piece of writing, a movie, etc.	
symbol Rating Q H T	an object that represents or expresses an idea	

Academic and Social Language Preview

Learning Target

- Use an expanded set of words to create precision and meaning while speaking and writing.
- Develop knowledge of how phrasing or different words with similar meanings produce shades of meaning.

VOCABULARY PREVIEW

anymore: (adverb) in the recent or present period of time; any longer

criticized: (verb) to be disapproved of

departing: (verb) leaving going away

different: (adjective) to be unlike

exploration: (noun) the act of studying or investigating a new area to learn about it

hesitated: (verb) stopped briefly before doing or saying something

nervously: (adverb) in a way that shows worry and fear of what might happen

noisy: (adjective) making a lot of noise; loud

opposite: (adjective) located across from something; completely different

obvious: (adjective) easy to see or notice; easy for the mind to understand

section: (noun) a particular area or part of a whole

served: (verb) gave food or drink to someone at a meal, in a restaurant, etc.

special: (adjective) for a specific purpose

won't know what's hit her: (idiom) to feel shocked because something, usually unpleasant, happens suddenly and unexpectedly

Vocabulary Practice

Use the definitions in the Vocabulary Preview or a dictionary to support your work.

Practice 1. Circle the word or phrase whose meaning is opposite to the meaning of the vocabulary word.

Vocabulary Word	Words or Phrases to Choose From
criticized	complimented rejected ridiculed
noisy	talkative loud silent
opposite	different same across
hesitated	hurried paused waited
different	unusual unlike similar

Practice 2. Complete each sentence, paying attention to the **bold** vocabulary word.

1. She **won't know what's hit her** when

_____

2. After grading the test, it was **obvious** to the teacher that the student

_____

3. My mother was mad at me because I wore my **special** shoes

_____

4. During the **exploration** of the cave, the divers

_____

5. She doesn't play volleyball **anymore** because

_____

Practice 3. Choose the right word in the pair that fits the sentence.

1. My vacation is over, so I am arriving/departing from the hotel tomorrow.
2. The young boy moved to the section/session of the stadium nearest the field to try and get his ball signed.
3. The famous chef served/ate us a delicious meal complete with dessert.
4. When it was his turn to sing, the newcomer hesitated boldly/nervously.

Interpret the Text Using Close Reading

Learning Targets

- Apply understanding of how novels are structured to comprehend the text.
- Explain how phrasing or different common words with similar meaning produce different effects on the audience.
- Draw and support inferences from a close reading of the text.
- Analyze theme and how it is communicated through a close reading of dialogue, connotative language, and events.
- Use knowledge of word structure, context, reference materials, and visual cues to determine the meaning of unknown and multiple-meaning words on familiar topics.

Read and Annotate

Read the excerpt from *The Boy in the Striped Pajamas* and annotate the text as you read.

- Use the My Notes area to write questions or ideas you have about the story.
- Underline descriptions that help you visualize the characters, setting, and events.
- Put a star next to dialogue that suggests the theme of the story.
- Put an exclamation mark next to dialogue that shows Bruno does not understand Shmuel's situation.
- Circle unknown words.

Novel Excerpt

from
The Boy in the Striped Pajamas

by John Boyne

1 Two boys were sitting on opposite sides of a fence.

2 "All I know is this," began Shmuel. "Before we came here I lived with my mother and father and my brother Josef in a small flat above the store where Papa makes his watches. Every morning we ate our breakfast together at seven o'clock and while we went to school, Papa mended the watches that people brought to him and made new ones too. I had a beautiful watch that he gave me but I don't have it anymore. It had a golden face and I wound it up every night before I went to sleep and it always told the right time."

3 "What happened to it?" asked Bruno.

4 "They took it from me," said Shmuel.

5 "Who?"

6 "The soldiers of course," said Shmuel as if it was the most obvious thing in the world.

My Notes

Who are the soldiers Shmuel mentions? Why did they take his watch?

My Notes

7 "And then one day things started to change," he continued. "I came home from school and my mother was making armbands for us from a special cloth and drawing a star on each one. Like this." Using his finger he drew a design in the dusty ground beneath him.

The star of David.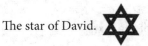

8 "And every time we left the house, she told us we had to wear one of these armbands."

9 "My father wears one too," said Bruno. "On his uniform. It's very nice. It's bright red with a black-and-white design on it." Using his finger he drew another design in the dusty ground on his side of the fence.

A swastika.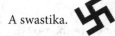

10 "Yes, but they're different, aren't they?" said Shmuel.

11 "No one's ever given me an armband," said Bruno. /

12 "But I never asked to wear one," said Shmuel.

13 "All the same," said Bruno, "I think I'd quite like one. I don't know which one I'd prefer though, your one or father's."

14 Shmuel shook his head and continued with his story. He didn't often think about these things anymore because remembering his old life above the watch shop made him very sad.

15 "We wore the armbands for a few months," he said. "And then things changed again. I came home one day and Mama said we couldn't live in our home any more."

16 "That happened to me too!" said Bruno, delighted that he wasn't the only boy who'd been forced to move. "The Fury came for dinner, you see, and the next thing I knew we moved here. And I *hate* it here," he added. "Did he come to your house and do the same thing?"

17 "No, but when we were told we couldn't live in our house we had to move to a different part of Cracow, where the soldiers built a big wall and my mother and father and my brother and I all had to live in one room."

18 "All of you?" asked Bruno. "In one room?"

"And not just us," said Shmuel. "There was another family there and the mother and father were always fighting with each other and one of the sons was bigger than me and hit me even when I did nothing wrong."

19 "You can't have all lived in the one room," said Bruno. "That doesn't make any sense."

20 "All of us," said Shmuel. "Eleven in total."

contradict: to express an opposite thought

Bruno opened to his mouth to **contradict** him again—he didn't really believe that eleven people could live in the same room together—but changed his mind.

21 "We lived there for some more months," continued Shmuel, "all of us in that one room. There was one small window in it but I didn't like to look out of it because then I would see the wall and I hated the wall because our real home was on the other side of it. And this part of town was a bad part because it was always noisy and it was impossible to sleep. And I hated Luka, who was the boy who kept hitting me even when I did nothing wrong."

22 "Gretel hits me sometimes," said Bruno. "She's my sister," he added. "And a Hopeless Case. But soon I'll be bigger and stronger than she is and she won't know what's hit her then."

23 "Then one day the soldiers all came with huge trucks," continued Shmuel, who didn't seem all that interested in Gretel. "And everyone was told to leave the houses. Lots of people didn't want to and they hid wherever they could find a place but in the end I think they caught everyone. And the trucks took us to a train and the train …" He hesitated for a moment and bit his lip. Bruno thought he was going to start crying and couldn't understand why.

24 "The train was horrible," said Shmuel. "There were too many of us in the carriages for one thing. And there was no air to breathe. And it smelled awful."

25 "That's because you all crowded onto one train," said Bruno, remembering the two trains he had seen at the station when he left Berlin. "When we came here, there was another one on the other side of the platform but no one seemed to see it. That was the one we got. You should have got on it too."

26 "I don't think we would have been allowed," said Shmuel, shaking his head. "We weren't able to get out of our carriage."

27 "The door's at the end," explained Bruno.

28 "There weren't any doors," said Shmuel.

29 "Of course there were doors," said Bruno with a sigh. "They're at the end," he repeated. "Just past the **buffet** section."

30 "There weren't any doors," insisted Shmuel. "If there had been, we would have gotten off."

31 Bruno mumbled something under his breath along the lines of "Of course there were," but he didn't say it very loud so Shmuel didn't hear.

32 "When the train finally stopped," continued Shmuel, "we were in a very cold place and we all had to walk here."

33 "We had a car," said Bruno, out loud now.

34 "And Mama was taken away from us, and Papa and Josef and I were put into the huts over there and that's where we've been since."

35 Shmuel looked very sad when he told this story and Bruno didn't know why; it didn't seem like such a terrible thing to him, and after all much the same thing happened to him.

36 "Are there many other boys over there?" asked Bruno.

My Notes

_____

buffet: a counter or table where food is served

_____

37 "Hundreds," said Shmuel.

38 Bruno's eyes opened wide. "Hundreds?" he said, amazed. "That's not fair at all. There's no one to play with on this side of the fence. Not a single person."

39 "We don't play," said Shmuel.

40 "Don't play? Why ever not?"

41 "What would we play?" he asked, his face looking confused at the idea of it.

42 "Well, I don't know," said Bruno. "All sorts of things. Football, for example. Or exploration. What's the exploration like over there anyway? Any good?"

43 Shmuel shook his head and didn't answer. He looked back towards the huts and turned back to Bruno then. He didn't want to ask the next question but the pains in his stomach made him.

44 "You don't have any food on you, do you?" he asked.

45 "Afraid not," said Bruno. "I meant to bring some chocolate but I forgot."

46 "Chocolate," said Shmuel very slowly, his tongue moving out from behind his teeth. "I've only ever had chocolate once."

47 "Only once? I love chocolate. I can't get enough of it although Mother says it'll rot my teeth."

48 "You don't have any bread, do you?"

49 Bruno shook his head. "Nothing at all," he said. "Dinner isn't served until half past six. What time do you have yours?"

50 Shmuel shrugged his shoulders and pulled himself to his feet. "I think I'd better get back," he said.

51 "Perhaps you can come to dinner with us one evening," said Bruno, although he wasn't sure it was a very good idea.

52 "Perhaps," said Shmuel, although he didn't sound convinced.

53 "Or I could come to you," said Bruno. "Perhaps I could come and meet your friends," he added hopefully. He had hoped that Shmuel would suggest this himself but there didn't seem to be any sign of that.

54 "You're on the wrong side of the fence though," said Shmuel.

55 "I could crawl under," said Bruno, reaching down and lifting the wire off the ground. In the centre, between two wooden telegraph poles, it lifted quite easily and a boy as small as Bruno could easily fit through.

56 Shmuel watched him do this and backed away nervously. "I have to get back," he said.

57 "Some other afternoon then," said Bruno.

58 "I'm not supposed to be here. If they catch me I'll be in trouble."

59 He turned and walked away and Bruno noticed again how small and skinny this new friend was. He didn't say anything about this because he knew only too well how unpleasant it was being criticized for something as silly as your height, and the last thing he wanted to do was be unkind to Shmuel.

60 "I'll come back tomorrow," shouted Bruno to the departing boy and Shmuel said nothing in reply; in fact he started to run off back to the camp, leaving Bruno all on his own.

Interact in Meaningful Ways: Academic Collaboration

Learning Targets

- Ask and answer questions about an excerpt from a novel in collaborative conversations.
- Demonstrate active listening and draw upon an expanding pool of language resources for discussing literature.
- Draw and support inferences from a close reading of the text.
- Analyze and evaluate how writers use language to explain characters and support ideas.

Turn to your partner or small group to discuss each question about *The Boy in the Striped Pajamas*. After you have discussed a question, write notes about your answer before going on to the next question.

1. Where does the story take place? How do you know?

> The text evidence in paragraph(s) _____ shows that the story takes place _____.

2. How do you characterize Bruno? What do you learn about him?

> I think I would characterize Bruno as _____ because _____.

3. What does Bruno not understand about Shmuel? How can you tell?

> The text evidence in paragraph (s) _____ indicates that Bruno does not understand _____.

4. What do you infer about why Shmuel runs off at the end? Does Bruno understand why?

> I believe Shmuel runs off because _____. In my opinion, Bruno _____.

Asking Questions

The author of *The Boy in the Striped Pajamas* has chosen a difficult and complex topic to write about. Do you think you understand why Bruno and Shmuel have very different lives even though they live near each other? With your partner or small group, look back at the excerpt. Discuss what questions you have about the text. Write one question you would like to ask the author about the ending of the excerpt. Share your question with the whole class.

_____

_____

HEW How English Works: Pronoun Antecedents

Language Resources
Contractions

A **contraction** is two words (usually one is a verb) combined to make one word. An apostrophe takes the place of the missing letters. You can combine a pronoun and a verb to create a contraction.

Contraction	Meaning
we've	we have
I'll	I will
she's	she is
I'd	I had, I would
they're	they are
what's	what has, what is

Learning Targets

- Apply understanding of how pronouns refer back to nouns in text and how pronoun antecedents make the text more cohesive.
- Analyze and evaluate how writers use language to explain characters and support ideas.

Pronoun Antecedents

In this excerpt from *The Boy in the Striped Pajamas*, the dialogue is between two boys. The author uses pronouns, such as *he*, to take the place of a noun so the character's name isn't used over and over. Because both characters in the excerpt are boys, it is important to understand who is speaking and who is being spoken about.

Language Resources: Pronoun Antecedents

pronoun: takes the place of a noun. Examples include *I, he, she, it, we, us, they*

antecedent: the object or person to which the pronoun refers. The antecedent tells you who is speaking or who is being spoken about. The author uses dialogue or context to help you identify the correct antecedent.

Skim through the excerpt from *The Boy in the Striped Pajamas*. Look for pronouns, including those used to form contractions, and try to determine their antecedents. At times, you may need to read further than the cited paragraph to know the antecedent. The location of the text is noted for you. Refer back to the text as needed. Answer the questions by recording your responses in the chart below. Use the Language Resources charts for support.

Excerpt from *The Boy in the Striped Pajamas*	Question	Answer
"Before we came here I lived with my mother and father and my brother Josef in a small flat above the store where Papa makes his watches." (paragraph 2)	Who is Shmuel talking about when he says, "we"?	
"They took it from me," said Shmuel. (paragraph 4)	Who is "they"?	
"Yes, but they're different aren't they," said Shmuel. (paragraph 10)	What is "they're" and "they" referring to?	
"That happened to me too!" said Bruno, delighted that he wasn't the only boy who'd been forced to move." (paragraph 16)	Who is "he" in this sentence?	
"And there was no air to breathe. And it smelled awful." (paragraph 24)	What is "it" referring to?	

• Share your work with a partner. Discuss your responses. How does knowing the correct antecedent help you understand the story and the characters? Did you find it easy or difficult to identify the correct antecedent? Were there any contractions in the excerpt that were new to you? What were they? Record notes from your discussion.

> I think knowing the correct antecedents when I'm reading is important because _____.

> In my opinion, the most difficult thing about identifying the correct antecedent is _____.

> I had never seen the contraction _____ before _____.

Write a Short Argument

After analyzing the author's use of pronoun antecedents in the excerpt from *The Boy in the Striped Pajamas*, you have enough information to write a short argument explaining why it's important to be able to identify the correct antecedent while reading. Cite one example from the text, and explain how misunderstanding the antecedent could impact your ability to fully understand the story. Before writing, read the model short argument provided. Try structuring your argument in the same way.

_____

_____

_____

_____

_____

_____

_____

_____

_____

_____

_____

MODEL: SHORT ARGUMENT

Shmuel often talks about "us" and "we," as in this sentence: "There were too many of us in the carriages for one thing." It is important to understand that he is referring to the Jewish people who were rounded up by the Nazis. Bruno's ignorance about who "us" and "we" are shows his complete misunderstanding of Shmuel and his situation.

Interact in Meaningful Ways:
Analyze Dialogue

⚙ **Language Resources**

A *symbol* is an object, a person, or a place that stands for something else. **Symbolism** is the use of symbols in a literary work. The excerpt opens with two boys on opposite sides of a fence. As we read, we learn that the two boys are on opposite sides in a much bigger sense, with Shmuel being Jewish and Bruno being the son of a Nazi.

ACADEMIC VOCABULARY

Effective is an adjective that can provide detail about, or modify, a noun or pronoun. Something that is described as effective produces an **effect** or result. Something that is not effective can be described as **ineffective**.

Learning Targets

- Express and justify opinions in conversation and writing by providing text evidence.

- Express attitude or opinions using familiar and nuanced expressions.

- Engage in conversation and express ideas about the author's use of dialogue.

- Draw and support inferences based on a close reading of the text.

- Plan and deliver a brief informative oral presentation.

Analyzing Dialogue to Understand Character and Theme

John Boyne uses dialogue in *The Boy in the Striped Pajamas* to tell us about the main characters, Bruno and Shmuel. He also uses dialogue to reveal theme in the story. In this exercise, you will identify, analyze, and evaluate the author's use of dialogue for characterization and to reveal theme.

⚙ **Language Resources**

Dialogue: words spoken between two or more characters in a literary work

Characters: people, animals, or imaginary creatures that take part in a story

Characterization: how a writer develops characters; for example, through description, actions, and dialogue

Theme: a writer's central idea or main message about life

Review the annotations you made identifying important dialogue in the excerpt from *The Boy in the Striped Pajamas*. Choose lines of dialogue that develop the characters and reveal the story's theme, and fill out the chart below. An example has been provided for you.

Character's Line of Dialogue	What is the Effect of the Dialogue?	What does the Dialogue Reveal About the Character?	What Theme Does the Dialogue Suggest?
Bruno: "You can't have all lived in the one room," said Bruno. "That doesn't make any sense."	The dialogue shows the difference between reality and Bruno's perspective.	Bruno assumes Shmuel is just like him, and he doesn't understand Shmuel's situation.	Bruno and Shmuel are living in completely different realities.
Bruno:			
Shmuel:			
Shmuel:			

Quick Conversation

- Share your work with a partner. Take turns explaining your analysis of how the author uses dialogue for characterization and to build theme. Discuss whether your partner agrees or disagrees with your analysis. Record notes from your discussion.

> In my opinion, Bruno's dialogue reveals _____.

> Do you agree with my analysis?

> Shmuel's dialogue has the effect of _____.

> I agree with your analysis because _____.

Write an Oral Presentation

After analyzing the use of dialogue in *The Boy in the Striped Pajamas*, you have enough information to prepare a brief oral presentation. Choose one line of dialogue from your chart. In your presentation, explain what the dialogue reveals about the character and the theme. State your opinion of how effective the dialogue is, and give a reason why. Before writing, read the model oral presentation provided. Notice what information is in each of the four sentences. Try structuring your presentation in the same way.

_____

_____

_____

_____

MODEL: ORAL PRESENTATION

When Shmuel says, "You're on the wrong side of the fence though," he seems to understand how different his world is from Bruno's. This line of dialogue also emphasizes the theme that the boys are not just on opposite sides of the fence but are on opposite sides of life. The dialogue is effective because it shows us something about Shmuel's character while at the same time revealing theme.

Interacting in Meaningful Ways: Presenting a Holocaust Narrative

Language Resources

Transitional words keep the reader or listener from getting lost and are most often found at the beginning of a sentence. Writers and speakers use transition words to help move the reader or listener from one idea to another.
Showing a time sequence: *first, next, finally, at the end, in summary*
Adding information: *and, not only, in addition*
Stating an example: *for example, for instance*
Showing a result: *so, as a result*

Learning Targets

- Plan and deliver a brief informative oral presentation.
- Apply understanding of how writers develop theme throughout a story using descriptions, dialogue, characterization, and other features. Demonstrate an understanding of the text and communicate informatively about it.
- Apply growing understanding of how ideas, events, or reasons are linked throughout a text using transitional words or phrases.
- Contribute to group discussions by asking relevant questions, adding evidence, and summarizing key ideas.
- Adjust language choices according to task, purpose, and audience.

Review your annotations and notes on *The Boy in the Striped Pajamas* and use them to complete the graphic organizer.

Holocaust Theme: the Excerpt	Holocaust Theme: Dialogue & Description	The Holocaust: What Do We Learn?
How does this excerpt relate to and develop the Holocaust theme, "finding the light in the darkness"?	How does the dialogue between Bruno and Shmuel illustrate the Holocaust theme? Explain how the descriptions from the excerpt also develop the theme.	What does this excerpt from Boyne's novel teach us about the Holocaust?

Quick Conversation

Share your work with your partner or group. Compare your ideas about the setting, character, and events.

Next, read aloud paragraph 59:

> He turned and walked away and Bruno noticed again how small and skinny this new friend was. He didn't say anything about this because he knew only too well how unpleasant it was being criticized for something as silly as your height, and the last thing he wanted to do was be unkind to Shmuel.

Discuss the paragraph. How does this paragraph illustrate the Holocaust theme of "finding light in the darkness"? What is ironic about Bruno not wanting to criticize Shmuel "for something as silly as your height"? From whose point of view is *The Boy in the Striped Pajamas* told? Why is this important? Record notes from your discussion.

> I think this paragraph illustrates the theme by ____.

> I agree/disagree because ____.

> In my opinion, Bruno's thoughts show that he ____.

_____
_____
_____
_____

Presenting a Holocaust Narrative

Use the graphic organizer below and all of your previous work to plan your presentation with your small group. First, your group must work together to choose a passage. Then, you must agree on which dialogue you will use and how to describe the scene for the audience. Lastly, you will work together to write your theme statement.

Small Group Roles

- Each person will play one role in the presentation:
- One person introduces the reading by setting the scene and reading any narration.
- Two people play the roles of the boys and read the group's chosen dialogue.
- One person reads the theme statement.

Work with your group and use the chart to prepare for writing your draft.

Holocaust Theme	Setting the Scene	Dialogue & Descriptions
What specific passage demonstrates the Holocaust theme of "finding light in the darkness"? What is your theme statement?	What descriptions can you use to set the scene in the passage you've chosen?	What dialogue in the passage you've chosen best illustrates the theme?

Presentation Prompt

Write a draft of your presentation. Be sure to:

- Describe how *The Boy in the Striped Pajamas* develops the Holocaust theme.
- Include a theme statement.
- Describe the scene in the passage you've selected.
- Use the dialogue from your passage that best illustrates the theme.
- Use pronouns and transitional words whenever appropriate.

_____

_____

_____

_____

_____

_____

_____

_____

_____

_____

ACTIVITY 2.1

Selecting Language Resources

WORD CONNECTIONS

Roots and Affixes

The word *logos* comes from the Greek *logos*, meaning "word" or "reason." This root gives us the word *logical*, meaning "sensible" or "reasonable." The word *pathos* comes also comes from the Greek *pathos*, meaning "suffering" or "feeling." This root gives us the word *empathy*, which means you can understand another person's feelings.

Learning Targets

- Develop language resources to use while speaking and writing about a speech.
- Use an expanded set of words to speak and write precisely.
- Adjust language choices to suit the setting and audience.

The chart presents words and phrases you will use in discussion and writing. Think about each word or phrase. Circle Q, H, or T to indicate how well you know it. Work with a partner, asking your partner to explain each word or phrase. Listen closely to the explanation, and then write your partner's name in the In Our Own Words column along with his or her condensed idea.

Rating	Q	H	T
	I have seen this word or phrase, but I have **questions** about its meaning.	I have **heard** this word or phrase, but I do not know it well.	I know this word or phrase so well that I could **teach** it to someone else.

Word or Phrase	Definition	In Our Own Words
argumentation Rating Q H T	the act of giving reasons for or against something	
audience Rating Q H T	a group of people who gather together to listen to something or watch something	
occasion Rating Q H T	a special event or time	
purpose Rating Q H T	the reason something is done	
tone Rating Q H T	a feeling or attitude expressed by the words someone is speaking or writing	
claim Rating Q H T	to say something is true	
appeals to logos Rating Q H T	appeals to reason	
appeals to pathos Rating Q H T	appeals to emotions	
call to action Rating Q H T	words that urge a reader or listener to take immediate action	
allusion Rating Q H T	a statement that calls attention to something by mentioning it indirectly	

Academic and Social Language Preview

Learning Targets

- Develop knowledge of a growing set of academic and social vocabulary to use in reading, speaking, and writing.
- Develop knowledge of how phrasing or different words with similar meanings produce shades of different meaning.

VOCABULARY PREVIEW

as long as: (phrase) provided that; since

committed: (verb) did something illegal or harmful

interpret: (verb) explain the meaning of

multitudes: (noun) a great number of people or things

national: (adjective) belonging to a nation as a whole

neutrality: (noun) the state of not supporting either side of an argument, fight, or war

oppressor: (noun) a person who treats a another person or a group of people in a cruel or unfair way

presence: (noun) existence; a person or thing that is present but not seen

quality: (noun) how good or bad something is

represent: (verb) to speak or act on behalf of someone or something

Vocabulary Practice

Use the definitions in the Vocabulary Preview or a dictionary to support your work.

Practice 1. Circle the word or phrase whose meaning is closest to the meaning of the vocabulary word.

Vocabulary Word	Words or Phrases to Choose From
presence	being kindness absence
interpret	confuse translate misunderstand
multitudes	many few minority
represent	pass over fight back speak for
oppressor	person who ignores others person who helps others person who mistreats others

Practice 2. Using the context clues in the sentence, write the correct word in the blank.

1. _____ is not good if one side is clearly right, and the other side is clearly wrong.
2. We cheered for our _____ soccer team at the World Cup.
3. Young people who abuse drugs and alcohol are much more likely to have _____ a crime.

Practice 3. Complete each sentence, paying attention to the **bold** vocabulary word or phrase.

1. **As long as** you are sixteen or older, you can

_____

2. The **quality** of the shirt was poor because when I put it on

_____

Interpret the Text Using Close Reading

Learning Target

- Apply understanding of how speeches are structured to comprehending the text.
- Explain how word choice produces effects on the audience.
- Draw and support inferences.
- Analyze theme and how it is communicated.
- Use word structure and context clues to understand unfamiliar words.

Read and Annotate

Read the excerpt from the speech and annotate the text as you read.

- ■ Use the My Notes area to write questions or ideas you have about the speech.
- ■ Underline the sentences that reveal the author's main idea.
- ■ Put stars next to events that the author uses to illustrate his ideas.
- ■ Place an exclamation mark by the call to action.
- ■ Circle unknown words.

My Notes

_____

_____

_____

_____

_____

_____

_____

_____

_____

_____

_____

Speech

from **The Nobel Acceptance Speech Delivered by Elie Wiesel**
in Oslo on December 10, 1986

1 I am moved, deeply moved by your words, Chairman Aarvik. And it is with a profound sense of **humility** that I accept the honor—the highest there is—that you have chosen to bestow upon me. I know your choice transcends my person.

humility: modesty

2 Do I have the right to represent the multitudes who have perished? Do I have the right to accept this great honor on their behalf? I do not. No one may speak for the dead, no one may interpret their **mutilated** dreams and visions. And yet, I sense their presence. I always do—and at this moment more than ever. The presence of my parents, that of my little sister. The presence of my teachers, my friends, my companions ...

mutilated: damaged beyond repair

3 This honor belongs to all the survivors and their children and, through us, to the Jewish people with whose destiny I have always identified.

4 I remember: it happened yesterday, or eternities ago. A young Jewish boy discovered the Kingdom of Night.   I remember his bewilderment, I remember his **anguish**. It all happened so fast. The ghetto. The **deportation**. The sealed cattle car. The fiery altar upon which the history of our people and the future of mankind were meant to be sacrificed.

anguish: agonizing pain
deportation: removal to another country

5 I remember he asked his father: "Can this be true? This is the twentieth century, not the Middle Ages. Who would allow such crimes to be committed? How could the world remain silent?"

6 And now the boy is turning to me. "Tell me," he asks, "what have you done with my future, what have you done with your life?" And I tell him that I have tried. That I have tried to keep memory alive, that I have tried to fight those who would forget. Because if we forget, we are guilty, we are accomplices.

naïve: simple; unsophisticated

jeopardy: peril; danger

My Notes

_____

_____

_____

_____

integrity: adherence to an ethical code
dissident: one who disagrees

7 And then I explain to him how **naïve** we were, that the world did know and remained silent. And that is why I swore never to be silent whenever wherever human beings endure suffering and humiliation. We must take sides. Neutrality helps the oppressor, never the victim. Silence encourages the tormentor, never the tormented. Sometimes we must interfere. When human lives are endangered, when human dignity is in **jeopardy**, national borders and sensitivities become irrelevant. Wherever men and women are persecuted because of their race, religion, or political views, that place must—at that moment—become the center of the universe.

8 There is so much injustice and suffering crying out for our attention: victims of hunger, of racism and political persecution—in Chile, for instance, or in Ethiopia—writers and poets, prisoners in so many lands governed by the Left and by the Right.

9 Human rights are being violated on every continent. More people are oppressed than free. How can one not be sensitive to their plight? Human suffering anywhere concerns men and women everywhere.

10 There is so much to be done, there is so much that can be done. One person—a Raoul Wallenberg, an Albert Schweitzer, Martin Luther King, Jr.—one person of **integrity**, can make a difference, a difference of life and death. As long as one **dissident** is in prison, our freedom will not be true. As long as one child is hungry, our life will be filled with anguish and shame. What all these victims need above all is to know that they are not alone; that we are not forgetting them, that when their voices are stifled we shall lend them ours, that while their freedom depends on ours, the quality of our freedom depends on theirs.

11 This is what I say to the young Jewish boy wondering what I have done with his years. It is in his name that I speak to you and that I express to you my deepest gratitude as one who has emerged from the Kingdom of Night. We know that every moment is a moment of grace, every hour an offering; not to share them would mean to betray them.

12 Our lives no longer belong to us alone; they belong to all those who need us desperately.

Interact in Meaningful Ways:
Academic Collaboration

Learning Targets

- Ask and answer questions and exchange ideas about a speech in collaborative conversations.
- Demonstrate active listening.
- Read a text closely to make meaning of and explain it.
- Use knowledge of word structure, context, reference materials, and visual cues to determine the meaning of unknown and multiple-meaning words on familiar topics.
- Analyze the parts of a speech.

Turn to your partner or small group to discuss each question about Elie Wiesel's speech. After you have discussed a question, write notes about your answer before going on to the next question.

1. What is the occasion of this speech? What is the speaker's purpose?

> The speaker's purpose is _____.

2. What central event does the speaker reference or allude to? How does this event serve as the basis for his speech?

> The speaker alludes to the _____. This serves as the basis of his speech by _____.

3. What is the speaker's tone, or attitude toward, his subject?

> The speaker's attitude toward his subject is _____.

4. What is the speaker's call to action? In other words, what does he want his audience to do?

> The speaker's call to action is _____.

Asking Questions

Elie Wiesel gave his speech with a specific purpose in mind. With your partner or small group, read aloud paragraphs 5 and 6 of the speech. Discuss how Wiesel issues a call to action in these paragraphs and throughout his speech. If you could ask Wiesel one question about his call to action, what would it be? Write the question to share with the class.

_____

_____

How English Works:
Adverbial and Adjectival Clauses

Language Resources
Subordinating Conjunctions

although	because
as long as	that
when	wherever
whenever	while

Language Resources

An **adjectival clause** tells *who, what, which one, what kind* and begins with a relative pronoun.

An **adverbial clause** tells *why, where, under what conditions, or to what degree* and begins with a subordinating conjunction.

Learning Targets

● Analyze and evaluate the use of adverbial and adjectival clauses in Wiesel's speech.

● Write a short argument citing an effective sentence with an adverbial or adjectival clause and explaining why it is effective.

Adverbial and Adjectival Clauses

A clause is a group of words with a subject and a verb, and a clause may or may not form a complete sentence. A subordinate clause cannot stand alone as a sentence and will begin with either a **subordinating conjunction** or a **relative pronoun**. An **adjectival clause** is a type of subordinate clause. It modifies a noun or pronoun and almost always appears right after the noun or pronoun. An **adverbial clause** is also a subordinate clause and usually modifies a verb. It can appear anywhere in a sentence and begins with a subordinating conjunction.

Language Resources: Relative Pronouns

Relative Pronoun	Sample Sentence with Adjectival Clause Underlined	What word does the clause modify?
which	Noodles, <u>which many of us enjoy,</u> can be messy to eat.	noodles
who	People <u>who are clever</u> can always find a way.	people

Skim the excerpt from the Nobel Acceptance Speech, and look for relative pronouns and subordinating conjunctions. Use the Language Resources charts as a reference. Place an RP by the relative pronouns and an SC by the subordinating conjunctions as you find them in the text. In the chart on the next page, write the sentences you found with **adjectival** or **adverbial** clauses in the first column, and underline the clause. In the second column, explain how the speaker's placement and use of the clause impacts the listener or reader. Examples have been provided for you.

Sentence with Adjectival/Adverbial Clause Underlined	Impact of the Clause: Use and Placement
Do I have the right to represent the multitudes <u>who have perished?</u>	The clause clarifies that Wiesel is questioning his right to speak on behalf of a great number of people, all of whom have died.
<u>As long as one child is hungry,</u> our life will be filled with anguish and shame.	Wiesel said, "As long as one dissident is in prison, our freedom will not be true," immediately prior. The parallel structure and repeated use of the adverbial clauses emphasizes Wiesel's condemnation of those who would allow even "one" to suffer.

Sentence with Adjectival/Adverbial Clause Underlined	Impact of the Clause: Use and Placement

Quick Conversation

- Share your work with a partner. Read aloud the sentences you chose and discuss your comments on the effectiveness of the speaker's use of adjectival and adverbial clauses. If you chose some of the same sentences, discuss any differences between your explanation and your partner's. Record notes from your discussion in the box below.

> In my opinion, the adjectival clauses are helpful because ____.

> I think the speaker's most effective adjectival or adverbial clause is ____.

Write a Short Argument

After analyzing and evaluating Elie Wiesel's use of adverbial and adjectival clauses in the excerpt from his Nobel Acceptance Speech, you have enough information to write a short argument. Choose one sentence with either an adjectival or adverbial clause from your chart. Write a short argument in which you explain the speaker's use of the clause, state your opinion of how effective it is, and give a reason why. Before writing, read the model short argument provided. Notice what information is in each of the sentences. Try structuring your argument in the same way.

_____

_____

_____

_____

MODEL: SHORT ARGUMENT
The speaker says, "As long as one child is hungry, our life will be filled with anguish and shame." The adverbial clause in the sentence captures Wiesel's sentiment that it is unacceptable for even one individual to suffer, and to allow this suffering is shameful. In my opinion, Wiesel's placement and use of this adverbial clause is effective in stirring the listener or reader. "As long as one child is hungry," is a clause that calls us to take responsibility because it's clear that one child and many more go hungry every day.

Interact in Meaningful Ways: Analyze an Argument

Language Resources

Connotative Diction

Notice how each set of words has a similar meaning but the emotion or feelings connected to each word is different. For example, describing someone as "nosy" carries a negative connotation. Saying someone is "confident" could be considered a compliment, while "smug" is an insult.

skinny	thin	slender
miserly	cheap	frugal
smug	confident	proud
nosy	curious	inquisitive

Language Resources

Imagery

Imagery appeals to the senses. The following words and phrases are examples of imagery used in Wiesel's speech.

Sight	sealed cattle car, Kingdom of Night
Sound	crying out, silent, stifled voices, speak
Touch	fiery altar
Taste	hungry

Learning Targets

- Analyze how writers and speakers use vocabulary and other language resources to persuade while considering the purpose, audience, and topic.
- Express and justify opinions in conversation and writing by providing text evidence.
- Apply understanding of why the structure of Wiesel's speech is effective as a call to action.
- Write a short argument.
- Draw inferences and conclusions based on a close reading of the text.

Using the SOAPSTone Strategy to Analyze the Wiesel Speech

Elie Wiesel uses strong imagery and connotative diction in his speech to draw the reader into the tragedy and loss that occurred during the Holocaust. He has a clear purpose or call to action, and he creates a specific appeal to his audience.

Language Resources

Imagery: Words that appeal to the five senses and help the reader create mental word pictures.

Tone: The attitude the writer expresses in a poem or other literary work.

Diction: The words the writer chooses.

Connotative Diction: The emotions and feelings connected to a word.

Read the excerpt from Elie Wiesel's speech and use the text to complete the questions for analysis in the SOAPSTone chart below. Refer to the Language Resources charts for help, and cite the text with your answers whenever possible.

Element	Question for Analysis	Answer & Textual Evidence
Speaker	Who is the speaker?	
Occasion	What event prompted the speaker to create this text?	
Audience	Who is the speaker's intended audience?	
Purpose	What is the speaker's call to action? What does he want people to do?	
Subject	How does the speaker appeal to emotions? How does he use logical reasoning?	
Tone	What is the speaker's attitude toward this subject? How does he use connotative diction and imagery to convey tone?	

Quick Conversation

Share your work with a partner. Take turns reviewing each of the elements and your corresponding answers in the SOAPSTone chart. Ask each other, "Which part of the speech made the biggest impression on you and made you want to take action?" Record notes from your discussion.

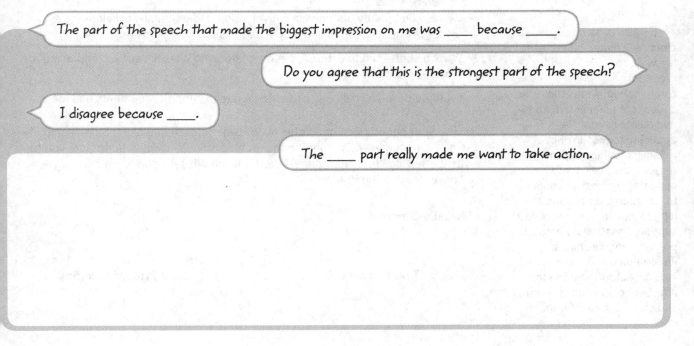

The part of the speech that made the biggest impression on me was ____ because ____.

Do you agree that this is the strongest part of the speech?

I disagree because ____.

The ____ part really made me want to take action.

Write a Short Argument

After completing and evaluating the questions for analysis in Wiesel's speech, you have enough information to write a short argument. Reference your chart and write a short argument in which you list and explain the elements of the speech that best support Wiesel's call to action. State your opinion of how effective it is, and give a reason why. Before writing, read the model short argument provided. Notice what information is in each of the sentences. Try structuring your argument in the same way.

_____

_____

_____

_____

MODEL: SHORT ARGUMENT

Wiesel's use of connotative diction and imagery create a powerful picture of how the horrors of the Holocaust live on in each person who suffers today. He says, "I remember: it happened yesterday or eternities ago." The connotation is that the memory and pain of the Holocaust never ends. Wiesel speaks of the "fiery furnace" and how the boy discovers the "Kingdom of Night." These images remind the listener of the consequences of "silence." In my opinion, the connotative diction and imagery are effective because they urgently compel the listener to do something. The listener is convinced that doing nothing is equivalent to inflicting the same suffering that happened in the Holocaust.

Interact in Meaningful Ways: Writing and Presenting a Speech

Language Resources

claim: the main point the writer or speaker will argue for

call to action: words that urge a reader or listener to take immediate action

appeal to logos: an appeal to logic; provides logical reasoning and evidence

appeal to pathos: an appeal to emotion; uses connotative language, imagery, and tone

supporting visuals: photos, posters, slogans, maps, illustrations, and other visual media strengthen the effectiveness of your speech and create interest for the audience

Learning Targets

- Express and justify opinions in conversation and writing by providing text evidence and using nuanced modal expressions and phrases.

- Write a short "call to action" speech referencing Wiesel's speech and using the features of an effective speech.

- Evaluate how well a speaker uses language to support arguments and ideas.

Review your annotations and notes on Wiesel's speech and use them to complete the graphic organizer. Completing the graphic organizer will help prepare you to write a brief "call to action" speech, referencing Wiesel's speech and urging listeners to "never forget" the Holocaust.

Wiesel's Claim:	
Text Evidence: Logos	**Text Evidence: Pathos**
Call to Action:	

Quick Conversation

Share your work with your partner. Compare your ideas about Wiesel's call to action.

Next, read aloud the following excerpt from the speech:

> We must take sides. Neutrality helps the oppressor, never the victim. Silence encourages the tormentor, never the tormented.

Discuss the excerpt. How does the excerpt support Wiesel's claim? What action does Wiesel urge the reader to take? Why is this important? Record notes from your discussion.

> I think this excerpt supports Wiesel's claim because ____.

> I agree, and ____.

> In my opinion, the call to action is ____ because ____.

> Will you please explain that?

Planning a Speech

Use the graphic organizer to prepare to write your own speech. Write your own claim and use evidence from Wiesel's speech to support your claim. Include a call to action, and use at least one effective visual.

What is your claim?

Text Evidence: Logos	Text Evidence: Pathos

What is your call to action?

Speech Writing Prompt

Write a draft of your speech. Be sure to:

- Clearly state your claim.
- Cite text evidence from Wiesel's speech to support the claim.
- State your call to action.
- Include effective visual support.

_____

_____

_____

_____

_____

_____

_____

_____

_____

_____

_____

_____

ACTIVITY 3.1

Selecting Language Resources

WORD CONNECTIONS

Roots and Affixes

The word **ethos** comes from the Greek *ethos*, meaning habitual and moral character; a person's disposition. The Greeks also used this word to refer to the power of music to influence listeners' emotions and behavior.

Learning Targets

- Develop language resources to use while speaking and writing about a speech.
- Use an expanded set of words to create precision and meaning while speaking and writing.
- Adjust language choices to suit the purpose, task, and audience.

The chart presents words and phrases you will use in discussion and writing. Think about each word or phrase. Circle Q, H, or T to indicate how well you know it. Work with a partner, asking your partner to explain each word or phrase. Listen closely to the explanation, and then write your partner's name in the In Our Own Words column along with his or her condensed idea.

Rating	Q	H	T
	I have seen this word or phrase, but I have **questions** about its meaning.	I have **heard** this word or phrase, but I do not know it well.	I know this word or phrase so well that I could **teach** it to someone else.

Word or Phrase	Definition	In Our Own Words
target audience Rating Q H T	a group at which a book, speech, or movie is aimed	
multimedia campaign Rating Q H T	using multiple forms of media (text, graphics, video, etc.) to reach an audience	
persuasive appeals Rating Q H T	convincing arguments an author or speaker uses to appeal to a reader or listener's logic, ethics, and emotion.	
pathos Rating Q H T	persuading by appealing to the reader or listener's emotion	
ethos Rating Q H T	persuading by using the author's or speaker's credibility, character, or position of authority	
logos Rating Q H T	persuading by appealing to the reader or listener's sense of logic and reason	

Academic and Social Language Preview

Learning Targets

- Develop knowledge of a growing set of academic and social vocabulary to use in reading, speaking, and writing.
- Develop awareness of shades of meaning.

VOCABULARY PREVIEW

according to: (preposition) as stated by

acute: (adjective) serious or dangerous

applied: (verb) put or spread something on a surface or the body

chronic: (adjective) occurring over and over for a long time

cycle: (noun) a set of events or actions that happen again and again in the same order

diagnosed: (verb) recognized a disease or condition

drift: (noun) a mass of particles piled up by the wind or moving water

exposed: (verb) left open to risk

irrigation: (noun) supplying something such, as land, with water by artificial means

labor force: (noun) those who work in a society

support: (verb) to provide what is needed

Vocabulary Practice

Use the definitions in the Vocabulary Preview or a dictionary to support your work.

Practice 1. Circle the word or phrase whose meaning is closest to the meaning of the vocabulary word or phrase.

Vocabulary Word	Words or Phrases to Choose From
chronic	minor repetitive rare
support	to help to ignore to rest
drift	pile tower hole
exposed	defended vulnerable careless
labor force	retirees workers children

Practice 2. Complete each sentence, paying attention to the **bold** vocabulary word or phrase.

1. The cause of the fire was unknown, **according to**

_____

2. The patient was devastated when **diagnosed**

_____

3. She got up, went to school, went home, went to bed, in an endless **cycle** until

_____

4. Because he had fair skin, he **applied**

_____

5. We had a seven foot snow **drift** because

_____

6. The farmer set up an **irrigation** system, so

_____

Practice 3. Choose the antonym, or word with an opposite meaning, for the vocabulary word.

Vocabulary Word	Words of Phrases to Choose From
acute	mild ugly sharp
applied	rubbed submitted removed
support	abandon enlist tighten
diagnosed	determined overlooked announced

Practice 4. Choose the correct vocabulary word or phrase to fill in the blanks.

1. The detective was _____ to danger when his cover was blown.

2. Pneumonia and _____ bronchitis share many of the same symptoms.

3. _____ the American Cancer Society, secondhand smoke is deadly.

Interpret the Text Using Close Reading

Learning Targets

- Draw and support inferences from a close reading of the text.
- Analyze theme and how it is communicated through a close reading of dialogue, connotative language, and events.
- Apply understanding of how a speech is structured.
- Apply understanding of how writers and speakers use language to support ideas and arguments.

Read and Annotate

Read the Address by Cesar Chavez, President United Farm Workers of America, AFL-CIO and annotate the text as you read.

- Use the My Notes area to write questions or ideas you have about the speech.
- Underline specific evidence that uses appeals to logos (reason).
- Put a star next to evidence that appeals to pathos (emotion).
- Put an exclamation mark next to the call to action.
- Circle unknown words and phrases.

Address by Cesar Chavez, President United Farm Workers of America, AFL-CIO

Pacific Lutheran University
March 1989, Tacoma, Washington

1 What is the worth of a man or a woman? What is the worth of a farm worker? How do you measure the value of a life?

2 Ask the parents of Johnnie Rodriguez.

3 Johnnie Rodriguez was not even a man; Johnnie was a five year old boy when he died after a painful two year battle against cancer.

4 His parents, Juan and Elia, are farm workers. Like all grape workers, they are exposed to pesticides and other agricultural chemicals. Elia worked in the table grapes around Delano, California until she was eight months pregnant with Johnnie.

5 Juan and Elia cannot say for certain if pesticides caused their son's cancer. But neuroblastoma is one of the cancers found in McFarland, a small farm town only a few miles from Delano, where the Rodriguezes live.

6 "Pesticides are always in the fields and around the towns," Johnnie's father told us. "The children get the chemicals when they play outside, drink the water or when they hug you after you come home from working in fields that are sprayed.

7 "Once your son has cancer, it's pretty hard to take," Juan Rodriguez says. "You hope it's a mistake, you pray. He was a real nice boy. He took it strong and lived as long as he could."

8 I keep a picture of Johnnie Rodriguez. He is sitting on his bed, hugging his Teddy bears. His sad eyes and cherubic face stare out at you. The photo was taken four days before he died.

Interpret the Text Using Close Reading

9 Johnnie Rodriguez was one of 13 McFarland children diagnosed with cancer in recent years; and one of six who have died from the disease. With only 6,000 residents, the rate of cancer in McFarland is 400 percent above normal.

10 In McFarland and in Fowler childhood cancer cases are being reported in excess of expected rates. In Delano and other farming towns, questions are also being raised.

carcinogen: a substance that causes cancer

pesticides: chemicals used to kill insects

leaching: draining

11 The chief source of **carcinogens** in these communities are **pesticides** from the vineyards and fields that encircle them. Health experts believe the high rate of cancer in McFarland is from pesticides and nitrate-containing fertilizers **leaching** into the water system from surrounding fields.

****

12 Farm workers and their families are exposed to pesticides from the crops they work. The soil the crops are grown in. Drift from sprays applied to adjoining fields-and often to the very field where they are working.

13 The fields that surround their homes are heavily and repeatedly sprayed. Pesticides pollute irrigation water and groundwater.

14 Children are still a big part of the labor force. Or they are taken to the fields by their parents because there is no child care.

toxic: poisonous

15 Pregnant women labor in the fields to help support their families. **Toxic** exposure begins at a very young age-often in the womb.

16 What does acute pesticide poisoning produce?

17 Eye and respiratory irritations. Skin rashes. Systemic poisoning.

18 Death.

19 What are the chronic effects of pesticide poisoning on people, including farm workers and their children, according to scientific studies?

20 Birth defects. Sterility. Still births. Miscarriages. Neurological and neuropsychological effects. Effects on child growth and development.

21 Cancer.

My Notes

_____

_____

_____

_____

_____

_____

_____

22 Do we feel deeply enough the pain of those who must work in the fields every day with these poisons? Or the anguish of the families that have lost loved ones to cancer? Or the heartache of the parents who fear for the lives of their children? Who are raising children with deformities? Who agonize the outcome of their pregnancies?

plague: a highly fatal epidemic affliction

23 Who ask in fear, 'where will this deadly **plague** strike next?'

24 Do we feel their pain deeply enough?

25 I didn't. And I was ashamed.

wanton: immoral and excessive

26 I studied this **wanton** abuse of nature. I read the literature, heard from the experts about what pesticides do to our land and our food.

27 I talked with farm workers, listened to their families, and shared their anguish and their fears. I spoke out against the cycle of death.

28 But sometimes words come too cheaply. And their meaning is lost in the clutter that so often fills our lives.

fast: stop eating for a period of time

29 That is why, in July and August of last year, I embarked on a 36-day unconditional, water-only **fast**.

30 The fast was first and foremost directed at myself. It was something I felt compelled to do to purify my own body, mind and soul.

31 The fast was an act of penance for our own members who, out of ignorance or need, cooperate with those who grow and sell food treated with toxics.

32 The fast was also for those who know what is right and just. It pains me that we continue to shop without protest at stores that offer grapes; that we eat in restaurants that display them; that we are too patient and understanding with those who serve them to us.

33 The fast, then, was for those who know that they could or should do more-for those who, by not acting, become bystanders in the poisoning of our food and the people who produce it.

34 The fast was, finally, a declaration of noncooperation with supermarkets that promote, sell, and profit from California table grapes. They are as culpable as those who manufacture the poisons and those who use them.

35 It is my hope that our friends everywhere will resist in many nonviolent ways the presence of grapes in the stores where they shop.

My Notes

Interact in Meaningful Ways:
Academic Collaboration

Learning Targets

- Ask and answer questions about a speech in collaborative conversations, demonstrating active listening, and drawing upon an expanding pool of language resources for discussing literature.

- Draw and support inferences from a close reading of the text.

- Express and justify opinions in conversation and writing by providing text evidence and using nuanced modal expressions and phrases.

Turn to your partner or small group to discuss each question about the address given by Cesar Chavez. After you have discussed a question, write notes about your answer before going on to the next question.

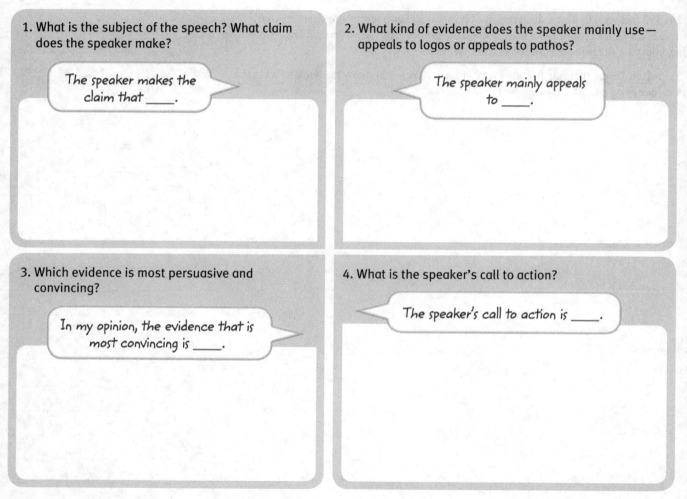

1. What is the subject of the speech? What claim does the speaker make?

The speaker makes the claim that _____.

2. What kind of evidence does the speaker mainly use—appeals to logos or appeals to pathos?

The speaker mainly appeals to _____.

3. Which evidence is most persuasive and convincing?

In my opinion, the evidence that is most convincing is _____.

4. What is the speaker's call to action?

The speaker's call to action is _____.

Asking Questions

Cesar Chavez opens his speech using an appeal to pathos in talking about the family whose son died from cancer. He then goes on to appeal to logos by creating a link between pesticides and various sicknesses. At the end of his speech, he delivers a very clear call to action. With your partner or small group, discuss the different examples of logos and pathos used throughout the speech. Consider why Chavez chose these examples. Write one question you would like to ask the author.

_____

_____

Learning Targets

- Apply understanding of how writers and speakers use verb tenses for effect.
- Use a variety of verbs in different tenses.
- Apply understanding of how writers and speakers use specific language to present ideas and support arguments.
- Write a short argument.
- Justify opinions or persuade others by providing textual evidence or relevant information.

Present Progressive Verb Tenses

The present progressive verb tense describes an ongoing action that is happening at the same time the statement is written. This tense is formed by using *am*, *is*, or *are* with the verb form ending in *-ing*. For example, look at the first sentence in paragraph 10 of the Chavez speech, "In McFarland... are being reported ..." The words "are being reported" show that the action was happening when the speaker gave this speech.

⚙ Language Resources: Verb Tenses

	Present Tense	Present Progressive
play	He plays.	He is playing.
work	They work.	They are working.
study	You study.	You are studying.
cry	I cry.	I am crying.

Skim through the address by Cesar Chavez and look for examples of the present progressive tense. Annotate these examples with "PPT." Then rewrite each of the present-tense sentences below in the present progressive tense.

Present-Tense Sentence	Rewritten Sentence: Present Progressive
The children get the chemicals when they play outside.	
You hope it's a mistake.	
You pray.	
I keep a picture of Johnny Rodriquez.	

💬 **Quick Conversation**

• Share your work with a partner. Discuss how the speaker's use of the present progressive tense impacts his listeners. Why do you think Chavez chose the present progressive tense in the sentences you annotated with PPT? What is the difference in tone when the present tense is used instead of the present progressive? Record notes from your discussion.

> The speaker chose to use present progressive tense mainly because ____.

> The speaker uses present tense when ____.

> The present progressive tense makes the tone ____.

Write a Short Argument

After analyzing and evaluating verb tenses in the address by Cesar Chavez, you have enough information to write a short argument. Review the annotations you made in the text identifying the present progressive tense, as well as the sentences you rewrote and your Quick Conversation notes. Write a short argument in which you explain why the speaker's choice to use the present progressive tense is effective. Cite words and phrases from the speech to explain your opinion. Before writing, read the model short argument provided. Notice what information is in each of the sentences. Try structuring your argument in the same way.

_____

_____

_____

_____

MODEL: SHORT ARGUMENT

The speaker's use of present progressive tense creates a sense of urgency. The situations he is concerned about are happening as he speaks. In paragraph 10, Chavez says, "In McFarland and in Fowler childhood cancer cases are being reported in excess of expected rates." The present progressive tense reminds the listener that people are being poisoned now, even as he delivers his speech. This tense prompts the listener to respond quickly to the call to action.

Interact in Meaningful Ways:
Identify Syntax—Sentences and Fragments

Learning Targets

- Evaluate and explain in conversation and writing how effectively the author uses syntax.

- Express and justify opinions in conversation and writing by providing text evidence and using nuanced modal expressions and phrases.

- Use language resources, including conjunctions, to make texts more cohesive.

Language Resources
Sentences and Fragments

Complete Sentence	Fragment
He would never feel the breeze again or the warmth of the sun.	Or the warmth of the sun.
The pizza was cold, but I ate it anyway.	But I ate it anyway.
He will take the bus, or he will walk to school.	Or he will walk to school.

Language Resources

Conjunctions

A conjunction is a word or phrase that connects other words or groups of words. Conjunctions create cohesion. Conjunctions can begin sentences but in everyday writing, they are most often used within compound and complex sentences. Common conjunctions: *and*, *but*, *or* Everyday writing example: We are training daily *and* getting stronger.

WORD CONNECTIONS

Roots and Affixes

Syntax is the arrangement of words and phrases to create well-formed sentences. **Syntax** comes from the Greek *syn* meaning "together," and *taxis*, meaning "an ordering."

Syntax—Sentences and Fragments

A sentence fragment is an incomplete sentence that lacks a subject or a predicate, and is normally incorrect. We normally avoid sentence fragments when writing, but they can be effective when giving a speech. Sentence fragments can have a powerful effect on a listening audience. Cesar Chavez successfully uses many fragments in his speech. Skim through the speech looking for fragments and evaluate their effect. Write three examples of fragments in the chart. Then make the fragments into complete sentences. Evaluate how rewriting the fragments changes the effect of the words within the speech.

Fragment from the Speech	Fragment Rewritten as Complete Sentence	Evaluation of How the Rewrite Changes the Effect

Quick Conversation

- Share your work with a partner. Take turns explaining the sentence fragments you chose from the speech, your rewrites, and your evaluation of how the rewrites change the effect. Discuss why you think the speaker's use of fragments is effective, and whether your partner agrees or disagrees with your evaluation. Record notes from your discussion.

_____

_____

> In my opinion, converting the fragments into sentences changes the effect by ____.

> Do you agree with my evaluation?

> I think the use of fragments is effective because ____.

> I disagree with your evaluation because ____.

Write a Short Argument

After analyzing and evaluating the use of fragments in the speech by Cesar Chavez, you have enough information to write a short argument. Choose two fragments that the speaker uses effectively. Write a short argument in which you cite the fragments, state your opinion of how they are effective in the speech, and give a reason why. Before writing, read the model short argument provided. Notice what information is in each of the sentences. Try structuring your argument in the same way.

_____

_____

_____

_____

MODEL: SHORT ARGUMENT

Chavez uses sentence fragments effectively in his speech. In paragraph 28, Chavez says, "But sometimes words come too cheaply. And their meaning is lost in the clutter that so often fills our lives." Before these fragments, Chavez tells us how he talked to the farmworkers about the issue and how he spoke out against it. I think the use of the first fragment creates an abrupt stop that emphasizes that talking and speaking are not enough. The second fragment creates pause and reflection. The effect of these fragments would be lost if they were rewritten as complete sentences.

Presenting a Multimedia Campaign
Informative/Explanatory Writing

Step 1: Introduction

You will be identifying an important social issue you are interested in and feel strongly about. Next, you will write a brief informational introduction to use when you present a multimedia campaign with your group.

Informative Introduction Writing Prompt

Be sure to:

- Engage and inform the audience in the introduction.

- State your topic and claim clearly.

- Cite text evidence (logos and pathos) from your research to support the claim.

- State the call to action and reinforce it in the conclusion.

Step 2: Brainstorming

Now you are ready to start thinking about what you will present. Use the graphic organizer to brainstorm about your essay and presentation. Record your responses.

1. What social issue do you feel the most passionate about? What is your claim specific to the social issue?	2. What resources could provide more information about your issue? How will you use evidence to appeal to your audience?
3. What type of logo would best represent your claim? What slogan could you write to promote your claim and raise awareness?	4. What presentation tools could you use for your presentation? What types of media could you use to help you create a convincing presentation?

Collaborative Dialogue

Discuss the ideas that you brainstormed with your partner or group. Use the sentence frames below to help you in your discussion. Remember to take turns sharing your ideas and to ask each other questions.

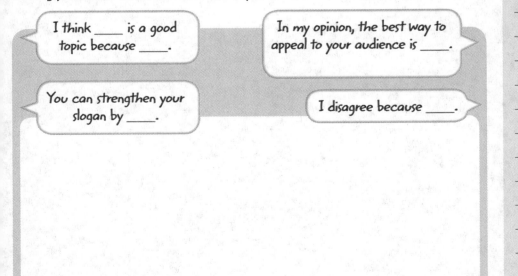

I think _____ is a good topic because _____.

In my opinion, the best way to appeal to your audience is _____.

You can strengthen your slogan by _____.

I disagree because _____.

Presenting a Multimedia Campaign
Informative/Explanatory Writing

Quickwrite

Write your claim, call to action, and two ideas for appealing to your audience. Next, take turns reading aloud what you've written, and asking each other the following questions: Is your claim well stated? Is your call to action clear? Are your ideas to appeal to the audience effective? Make notes from your conversation.

Step 3: Planning

Collaborative Dialogue

Work with your partner and use the sentence frames below to prepare for creating an outline of your introduction and presentation. Speaker 1 will ask the question, and Speaker 2 will answer the question and record it. Speaker 1 can give feedback on the answer or ask for clarification. Make sure you take turns asking and answering questions. Refer back to previous exercises and notes to help you. Remember to record your responses and to write down any new ideas or notes that will help you create your outline.

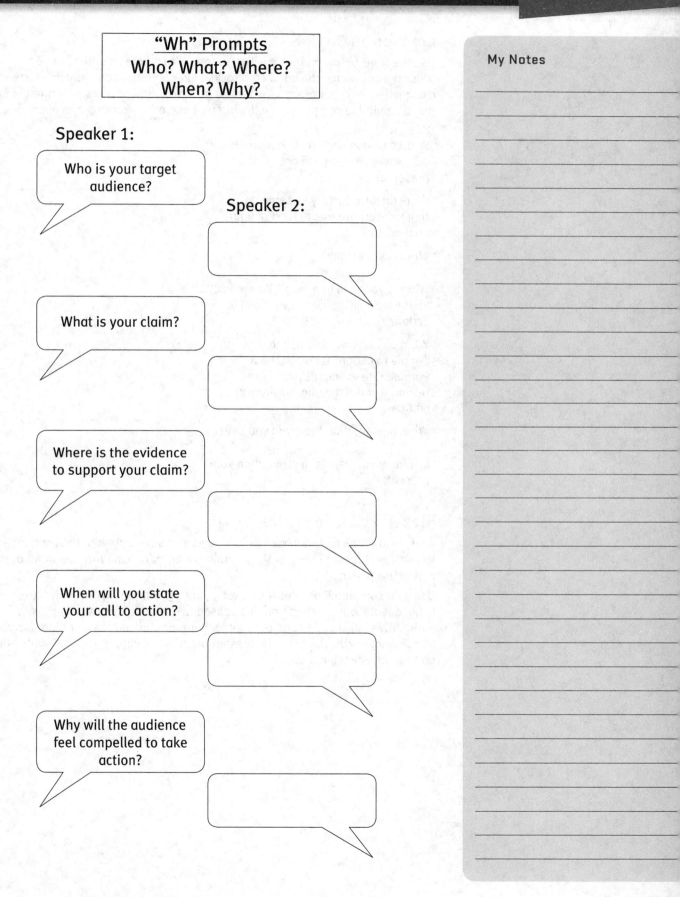

"Wh" Prompts
Who? What? Where?
When? Why?

My Notes

Speaker 1:

Who is your target audience?

Speaker 2:

What is your claim?

Where is the evidence to support your claim?

When will you state your call to action?

Why will the audience feel compelled to take action?

Presenting a Multimedia Campaign
Informative/Explanatory Writing

Creating an Outline

Use the chart below and work with your group to create an outline of your presentation. Match the numbered tasks below with the number you've been assigned within your group. The task or question that matches your number is your responsibility to complete. Use the Internet and other resources as needed.

Write a slogan and create a logo. How and where will you use both in your presentation?	1
Write an introductory statement that will capture the interest of your audience.	1
What is your claim?	2
What is your call to action? Where in your essay will you write your call to action?	2
What appeals will you use to urge people to action? (Logos/Ethos/Pathos) Cite examples from your research and remember to cite your sources.	3/4
What presentation tools will you use?	3/4
List ideas for visuals to strengthen your presentation.	ALL

Step 4: Practicing

Review all of the material from Unit 3, paying close attention to the Language Resources charts. Skim over the Informative Introduction Writing Prompt at the end of this activity.

Use your completed graphic organizers, your brainstorming document, the Language Resources charts on this page, and all of your notes to draft your informative introduction and prepare for your multimedia presentation. Include transitional words, imagery, the present progressive verb tense, and syntax that strengthen your claim.

Language Resources

Transitional words keep the reader or listener from getting lost and are most often found at the beginning of a sentence. Writers and speakers use transition words to help move the reader or listener from one idea to another.

Showing a time sequence: *first, next, finally, at the end, in summary*

Adding information: *and, not only, in addition*

Stating an example: *for example, for instance*

Showing a result: *so, as a result*

Presentation Prompt

Be sure your plans and preparation includes:

- A slogan and logo that support your cause
- Multimedia
- Notes regarding which presentation tool you will use
- Pronoun antecedents (page 9)
- Transitional words to guide the reader or listener (page 13)
- Imagery to convey your tone (page 22)
- The present progressive verb tense (page 33)
- Syntax that strengthens your claim (page 35)

Step 5: Editing and Revising

Use the Scoring Guide and work with your group to rate one Public Service Announcement from the website listed on the Multimedia Campaign Student Exemplar. Next, work with your partner to complete your assigned job within your group. Finally, reference the peer editing checklist and graphic organizer and collaborate with your group to review each other's work.

Peer Editing Checklist

☐ Did the presentation engage and inform the audience in the introduction?

☐ Did the presentation state the subject and claim clearly?

☐ Did the presentation cite text evidence and details to support the claim?

☐ Did the presentation state the call to action and reinforce it in the conclusion?

☐ Did the presentation include visual aids and multimedia?

☐ Did the presentation use pronoun antecedents?

☐ Did the presentation use transitional words?

☐ Did the presentation use imagery to convey tone?

☐ Is the presentation organized in a way that makes sense?

☐ Did the presentation use the present progressive verb tense?

☐ Did the presentation use syntax to strengthen the claim?

☐ Did the presentation use correct spelling and punctuation?

☐ Did the presentation use correct grammar?

Language Resources

multimedia campaign: The use of more than one form of communication at a time to promote interest and information specific to a cause. Examples: Internet, Facebook, YouTube, magazines, radio

logo: a symbol created or adopted by an individual or organization to aid and promote public recognition

slogan: a memorable phrase or motto used to identify or promote a product or group.

presentation tools: tools such as Prezi or PowerPoint that help you organize and present your campaign.

Writing and Presenting Checklist:

■ Review the Scoring Guide
■ Review the Exemplar
■ Review your draft
■ Participate in peer editing
■ Revise
■ Publish
■ Present

Presenting a Multimedia Campaign Informative/Explanatory Writing

Peer Editing: Quick Conversation

Share your notes and responses from the checklist with the other group. Discuss your responses, making sure that you take turns listening and providing feedback. Record notes from your discussion.

> I think your strongest use of imagery is _____ because _____.

> In my opinion, the one change you could make to strengthen your call to action is _____.

> I think the text evidence does/does not support your claim because _____.

> I like your introduction because _____.

Look at the peer editing checklist that the other group completed. Use the checklist and any other feedback and work with your group to revise your draft and presentation. Use a classroom computer to complete your draft and create your presentation in PowerPoint or Prezi. Because your presentation is multimedia, include graphics or photos from the Internet, but make sure they are appropriate and cited. Check your final essay against the Scoring Guide before you submit it to your teacher. Practice your presentation at home with a family member.

Step 6: Sharing

Your group will now share your presentation orally in the form of your multimedia campaign, created on PowerPoint or Prezi. You may use other visual aids to help you.

Presenting a Multimedia Campaign
Informative/Explanatory Writing

Keep these points in mind as you are presenting:

Tips for Presenting	Tips for Listening
Keep these points in mind as you are presenting: • Speak loudly and clearly. • Maintain eye contact with your audience. • Listen respectfully to any questions from your audience. • Respond thoughtfully to any questions from your audience.	As your classmates present, be an active listener: • Take notes. • Listen for the speaker's purpose and main point. • Listen for the *who? what? where? when? how? why?* • Jot down any questions you may have for the presenter.

When it is your turn to listen to other presentations, complete the following chart:

Active Listening

Presenter's name:

Content

The presenter's purpose was to _____.

The presenter's main point was _____.

I do / do not feel compelled to act after listening to the presenter because
_____.

Form

The presenter did/did not use a clear, loud voice.

The presenter did/did not make eye contact.

One thing the presenter could improve is _____.

Feedback

One thing I really liked about the presentation was _____.

A question I still have is _____.

Step 7: Feedback

Now that you have received feedback on your work, note what your group did well and what still needs improvement.

What Went Well	What Needs Improvement

My Notes

SCORING GUIDE

Scoring Criteria	4	3	2	1
Ideas	The presentation • supports a clear claim and addresses counterclaim(s) with relevant reasons and evidence from a variety of accurate sources • uses persuasive appeals effectively • integrates engaging multimedia and campaign features to clarify ideas.	The presentation • supports a claim and addresses counterclaim(s) with sufficient reasons and evidence from reliable sources • uses persuasive appeals (*logos, pathos,* and *ethos*) • includes adequate multimedia and campaign features to clarify ideas.	The presentation • has an unclear or unsupported claim, addresses counterclaim(s) ineffectively, and/or uses research from insufficient or unreliable sources • uses persuasive appeals unevenly • includes inadequate multimedia and campaign features.	The presentation • has no claim or counterclaim, and/or shows little or no evidence of research • does not use persuasive appeals • lacks multimedia or campaign features.
Structure	The presentation • demonstrates extensive evidence of collaboration and preparation • has an introduction that engages and informs the audience • sequences ideas and quotations smoothly with transitions • concludes with a clear call to action.	The presentation • demonstrates adequate evidence of collaboration and preparation • has an introduction that informs and orients the audience • sequences ideas and embeds quotations with transitions • includes a conclusion with a call to action.	The presentation • demonstrates insufficient or uneven collaboration and/or preparation • has a weak introduction • uses flawed or illogical sequencing; quotations seem disconnected • includes a weak or partial conclusion.	The presentation • demonstrates a failure to collaborate or prepare • lacks an introduction • has little or no evidence of sequencing or transitions • lacks a conclusion.

Presenting a Multimedia Campaign
Informative/Explanatory Writing

Scoring Criteria	4	3	2	1
Use of Language	The speaker • communicates to a target audience with a persuasive tone and precise diction • demonstrates command of the conventions of standard English grammar, usage, and language (including correct mood/voice) • cites and evaluates sources thoroughly in an annotated bibliography.	The speaker • communicates to a target audience with appropriate tone and some precise diction • demonstrates adequate command of the conventions of standard English grammar, usage, and language (including correct mood/voice) • cites and evaluates sources in an annotated bibliography.	The speaker • communicates to a target audience inappropriately; may use basic diction • demonstrates partial command of the conventions of standard English grammar, usage, and language • begins to cite and/or evaluate sources in an annotated bibliography; may use improper format.	The speaker • does not communicate clearly; uses vague or confusing diction • has frequent errors in standard English grammar, usage, and language • lacks an annotated bibliography.
Collaboration	Student exceeds expectations in working collaboratively with others.	Student works collaboratively with others.	Student is weak in working collaboratively with others.	Student does not collaboratively with others.
How English Works	Language • uses present progressive verb tense to effectively impact and persuade the listener • uses pronouns to refer back to nouns in text and strongly demonstrates how pronoun antecedents make the text more cohesive • uses strong transitions to add details that support the central idea	Language • uses present progressive verb tense with some impact to the listener • uses pronouns to refer back to nouns in text and demonstrates a limited understanding of how pronoun antecedents make the text more cohesive	Language • uses present progressive verb tense incorrectly or without effective placement • uses pronouns incorrectly	Language • lacks the use of present progressive verb tense • lacks the use of pronouns

Presenting a Multimedia Campaign
Informative/Explanatory Writing

Scoring Criteria	4	3	2	1
Interact in Meaningful Ways	Language • uses syntax thoughtfully and effectively to express and justify opinions • demonstrates strong understanding of how to use shades of meaning	Language • uses syntax to express and justify opinions • uses transitions to add details that support the central idea • demonstrates understanding of how to use imagery to convey tone	Language • uses basic syntax without variation • uses transitions that are ineffective in adding details that support the central idea • demonstrates partial understanding of how to use imagery to convey tone	Language • uses syntax that is inaccurate • lacks the use of transitions or clauses • lacks understanding of how to use imagery to convey tone

THE CHALLENGE OF COMEDY:
Critiquing and Creating Comedy

Visual Prompt: What makes people laugh?

Unit Overview

If laughter is truly the best medicine, then a study of challenges would not be complete without a close examination of the unique elements of comedy. Overcoming challenges is often easier when we are able to look at the humorous side of life. However, finding humor is not always easy; it can be a challenge in itself. In this unit, you will learn how authors create humor and how they use humor to reveal a universal truth (theme).

Selecting Language Resources

Cognates

The English word *diction*, the Spanish word *dicción*, and the Haitian Creole word *diction* are cognates. They all mean "a way of speaking" and come from the same Latin root *dict-*, meaning "to speak."

Learning Targets

- Develop language resources for speaking and writing about essays.
- Use an expanded set of words to speak and write precisely.
- Adjust language choices to suit the academic setting.

The chart presents words and phrases you will use in discussion and writing. Think about each word or phrase. Circle Q, H, or T to indicate how well you know it. Work with a partner, asking your partner to explain each word or phrase. Listen closely to the explanation. Then write your partner's name in the "In Our Own Words" column, along with his or her condensed idea.

Rating	Q	H	T
	I have seen this word or phrase, but I have **questions** about its meaning.	I have **heard** this word or phrase but do not know it well.	I know this word or phrase so well that I could **teach** it to someone else.

Word or Phrase	Definition	In Our Own Words
diction Rating Q H T	word choice; the way something is put into words	
expository Rating Q H T	meant to explain something; explanatory	
humor Rating Q H T	the quality of being funny or amusing	
technique Rating Q H T	a special way of using tools or materials to do something	
device Rating Q H T	something designed to bring about a certain result	
theory Rating Q H T	an explanation of how or why something happens	
pun Rating Q H T	a simple joke that plays off the sound, rather than the meaning, of a word	
satire Rating Q H T	a form of comedy that uses humor, irony, or exaggeration to expose and criticize issues in society or people's weaknesses	

Academic and Social Language Preview

Learning Targets

- Develop a growing set of academic and social vocabulary to create precise shades of meaning in reading, speaking, and writing.
- Adjust language choices to suit the academic setting.

VOCABULARY PREVIEW

arbitrary: (adjective) based only on what one wants or thinks; ignoring rules or others' opinions

cultures: (noun) societies

features: (verb) includes; presents

instance: (noun) an example; something that shows or proves

keen: (adjective) sharp and quick in seeing, hearing, or thinking

livelihood: (noun) means of supporting oneself

operator: (noun) a worker who answers a telephone

repetitive: (adjective) happening again and again

sequence: (noun) the order in which things follow one another

significant: (adjective) meaningful

typical: (adjective) usual; normal

Vocabulary Practice

Use the definitions in the Vocabulary Preview or a dictionary to support your work.

Practice 1. Circle the word or phrase whose meaning is **opposite** to the meaning of the vocabulary word.

Vocabulary Word	Words or Phrases to Choose From
keen	stupid careful interesting
significant	important major worthless
typical	average uncommon modern
arbitrary	comical unacceptable reasonable
repetitive	once secure frequent

Practice 2. Complete each sentence, paying attention to the **bold** vocabulary word.

1. Unexpected events can happen; for **instance,**

_____

2. I enjoy films and TV shows that **feature**

_____

3. When people from different **cultures** meet, they might

_____

4. If you do not perform the steps in **sequence,** then the experiment

_____

Practice 3. Use each vocabulary word to complete an analogy.

livelihood   operator   repetitive

1. Singer is to microphone as _____ is to telephone.
2. Employment is to _____ as exercise is to fitness.
3. Random is to disorder as _____ is to pattern.

Interpret the Text Using Close Reading

Learning Targets

- Apply understanding of how essays are structured to comprehending the text.

- Explain how phrasing or different common words with similar meanings produce different effects on the audience.

- Use general academic words and domain-specific words to create some precision while speaking and writing.

Read and Annotate

Read "Made You Laugh" independently or as a group. Annotate the text as you read.

■ Use the My Notes area to write questions or ideas you have about the text.

■ Underline words and phrases that are synonyms for "laugh" and "laughter."

■ Put a star next to the topic sentence in each section.

■ Circle unknown words and phrases.

Essay

Made You Laugh

by Marc Tyler Nobleman

1 Would you like to know a language everyone in the world understands? You already do—because you laugh. Any two people from vastly different cultures who don't speak a word of the other's language still know exactly what is meant when the other person laughs.

2 Think of laughter as the unofficial language of Earth. Yet how much do any of us really understand about humor?

On the Laugh Track

3 What makes things funny? READ asked John Ficarra, the editor of MAD magazine. After all, he should know. Here's what he said: "Monkeys. They're unbeatable. For example, show a photo of a dentist— not funny. Show a photo of a dentist with a monkey in his chair, and it's comedy gold. Try this theory out on a few of your family photos, and you'll see." OK, so monkeys are funny. What else? How about this?

4 Two hunters were in the woods, when one collapsed. He didn't seem to be breathing. The other called the emergency number and said, "My friend is dead! What can I do?" The operator said, "Calm down, I can help. First, let's make sure he's dead." After a second of silence on

My Notes

My Notes

I wonder how many people were tested for the project. Was it hundreds or thousands of people?

the hunter's end, the operator heard a gunshot. The hunter came back on the phone and said, "OK, now what?"

5 If you laughed, you're not alone. In the year 2001, that joke was voted the funniest in the world as part of a project called LaughLab. Psychologist Richard Wiseman's goal was to determine what makes people laugh and what is found to be funny among men and women, older and younger people, and people from different countries. His research team tested people in person and asked others to submit opinions online using a "Giggleometer," which ranked jokes on a scale of 1–5. More than 40,000 jokes were tested.

6 You may be saying to yourself, "Studying jokes? Is that science?" But plenty of smart people say yes. Laughter is a biological function.* It has a certain rhythm; laughter syllables build, then trail off, and they come out in a repetitive, not random, sequence. For example, "ha-ha-ho-ho-he" is typical, but "ha-ho-ha-ho-ha" or "he-ho-he" just doesn't happen.

7 Babies begin to laugh instinctively when they're about four months old, perhaps to form a connection with parents. Those born blind and deaf also laugh, so laughter is not dependent on sight and hearing. Other animals, notably chimps, exhibit laugh-like behavior when playing with one another. Even rats, when tickled, make high-pitched squeals that can be interpreted as laughter. (As you might guess, only a dedicated few know this firsthand.)

Comedy Is Serious Stuff

8 Comics know that the same jokes are not funny to everyone everywhere. Ed Hiestand, a writer for comedy great Johnny Carson, told READ, "Everyone who writes comedy needs to know the audience. On the Carson show, everybody would laugh on a Friday night. Nobody would laugh on a Monday." Even within one state or town or family, senses of humor are as varied as the people are. Professional comics do not assume a 10 p.m. audience will like a joke because a 7 p.m. audience did.

9 Comedians who test jokes for a living say it's hit or miss. "It's a tough gig, and you have to have a large threshold for pain," said stand-up Jay Nog. Performers whose jokes get a two-second laugh consider that a significant accomplishment.

10 Timing is critical. Starting stand-up Zubair Simonson said he's learning the hard way that "good timing can cause a weak joke to soar, while poor timing can cause a strong joke to falter." Authors and film actors do not often get immediate public feedback. But comics do.

11 What keeps the funny guys going? The laughs and after-effects. "The best humor has some sort of layer to it; it makes a statement of some kind or comment," said Margy Yuspa, a director at Comedy Central. "An example is [Dave] Chappelle. His comedy is funny on the surface and also often comments on race or social issues."

Funny You Said That

12 Comedians have their own theories about humor. "What makes us laugh is a surprise change in perspective that connects an unknown with a known idea in a unique manner," said Ronald P. Culberson, a humorist at FUNsulting.com. "For instance, a three-legged dog walks into an Old West saloon and says, 'I'm looking for the man who shot my paw.'"

13 Ask an average person why humans laugh, and he or she would probably say, "Because something was funny." But comics need to know what gives the giggles; their livelihood depends on it.

14 Comedian Anthony DeVito told READ that "people tend to laugh at things that reinforce what they already believe. Comedy tells them they're right."

Interpret the Text Using Close Reading

15 Gary Gulman, a finalist in Last Comic Standing, a reality TV show and comedy competition, gave specifics. "Sometimes it's a keen observation about something you thought you lived through. Sometimes it's a juxtaposition of words. Sometimes it's a gesture or a sound. An encyclopedia couldn't do this question justice."

What Are You Laughing At?

16 Yet laughter is not always a planned response to a joke. One study found that 80 percent of the time, we laugh at something that just happens. People often laugh just because someone else does. Like a yawn, a laugh is contagious. That's why some sit-coms use laugh tracks.

17 Laughter is also social, a way to bond with others. After all, how often do you laugh alone? When two or more people laugh at the same thing, it is as if nature reminds them of what they have in common.

18 Behavioral neuroscientist Robert R. Provine conducted a 10-year experiment in which he eavesdropped on 2,000 conversations in malls, at parties, and on city sidewalks. He found that the greatest guffaws did not follow intentionally funny statements; people laughed hardest at everyday comments that seemed funny only in a certain social context.

19 "Do you have a rubber band?" is not in and of itself humorous, but it is if it's said in response to "I like Amelia so much. I wish I could get her attention."

Theories of Funniness

20 There are three main theories about humor.

21 **Release theory**—Humor gives a break from tension. In a horror movie, as a character creeps through a dark house (often idiotically) to follow an eerie noise, he might open a door to find a cat playing with a squeeze toy. The audience laughs in relief. Humor also lets us deal with unpleasant or forbidden issues, such as death and violence. People are often more comfortable laughing at something shocking said by someone else, though they would never say it themselves. Comedian Keenen Ivory Wayans once said, "Comedy is the flip side of pain. The worst things that happen to you are hysterical—in retrospect. But a comedian doesn't need retrospect; he realizes it's funny while he's in the eye of the storm."

22 **Superiority theory**—Audience members laugh at those who appear to be more stupid than they judge themselves to be. Slapstick humor, such as seeing a guy slip on a banana peel, often falls into this category. This theory dates back to Plato in ancient Greece and was prominent in the Middle Ages, when people with deformities were often employed as court jesters.

23 Some comedians exploited this theory by building a routine—or even a **persona**—around the idea that they were losers who couldn't catch a break. Larry David, David Letterman, and Woody Allen are comedians who have done this, each in his own way.

24 **Incongruity theory**—People laugh when things that are not normally associated with each other are put together. Many comedy duos, from Laurel and Hardy to David Spade and Chris Farley, feature a thin man and a fat man, a visual contrast.

25 People also laugh when there is a difference between what they expect to happen and what actually occurs. They are being led in a certain direction, and then that direction abruptly changes, and the unpredictability makes them laugh. Children see birds all the time without reaction, but if one flies into their classroom through an open window, they will probably explode in giggles.

My Notes

Interpret the Text Using Close Reading

Got Laughs?

26 What we laugh at changes as we age. Here are some examples.

Audience	Often Likes
Young children	Slapstick, or silly **physical humor**
Elementary-school Children	**Puns,** simple jokes that play off the sound rather than the meaning of a word, such as "Lettuce all go to the salad bar"
Teens	**Jokes** about topics that authority figures would consider rebellious, a way to use humor to deal with nerve-racking subjects
Adults, particularly well-educated ones	**Satire,** which makes fun of the weaknesses of people and society

27 Generally, children laugh more than adults. One study found that adults laugh 20 times a day, while children laugh 200 times!

The Secrets of Humor

28 Certain comedic devices turn up again and again in jokes, comic strips, and filmed entertainment—because they succeed.

29 "There were tricks," said Hiestand of his days writing for *The Tonight Show* hosted by Johnny Carson, "things you would see, certain things always got laughs." One of the most popular is often called the rule of threes. That is a pattern in which two nonfunny elements are followed by a third that is funny (yet still makes sense within the context). Many jokes start off with a list of three, such as "A rabbi, a lawyer, and a duck walk into a bar." As the joke unfolds, the rabbi says something straightforward, then the lawyer does as well, but the duck finishes with something witty or absurd.

30 Three guys were stranded on an island. An antique lamp washed ashore. When the guys touched it, a genie came out. "I'll grant each of you one wish," the genie said. The first guy said, "I want to go home," then disappeared. The second guy said, "I also want to go home," and he too disappeared. The third man suddenly looked sad. He said, "I want my two friends back to keep me company."

31 Certain concepts seem to be more amusing than others. If you tell any joke involving an animal, and it doesn't matter which one you use, think Donald and Daffy. In the LaughLab experiment, scientists determined that the funniest animal is the duck. (It's not arbitrary that a duck was used in the rule-of-threes joke.)

Do Tell—But Do It Right

32 There are also known techniques for telling jokes well.

- **Keep it short**—Don't include any details that are not necessary to bring you to the punch line. In the genie joke, there was no need to specify it was a tropical island or to name the castaways. The quicker you tell a joke, the funnier it will be.
- **Be specific**—Some comedians swear that a joke is funnier if you say "Aquafresh" instead of "toothpaste." The attention to detail makes the story seem more real.

Interpret the Text Using Close Reading

- **Keep a straight face**—Deliver the joke deadpan, or without emotion. That way, any strangeness in the joke will seem even stranger because the person telling it doesn't seem to notice.

- **Don't laugh at your own joke**—Let your audience decide whether it is funny or foolish—or both.

33 Theories and techniques aside, much about humor remains a mystery. According to Hiestand, Carson many times said, "I don't understand what makes comedy a sure thing. There's no 100-percent surefire formula." Meanwhile, for most of us, laughter is never a problem. It does not need to be solved, just enjoyed.

My Notes

Interact in Meaningful Ways:
Academic Collaboration

Learning Targets

- Ask and answer questions about an informational text in collaborative conversations, demonstrating active listening, and drawing upon an expanding pool of language resources for discussing literature.

- Express and support opinions of a personal narrative in conversation.

Turn to your partner or small group to discuss each question about "Made You Laugh." After you have discussed a question, write notes about your answer before going on to the next question.

1. What is the key idea of the section "Comedy Is Serious Stuff," paragraphs 8–11? What details in the section support this idea?

> The key idea of the section is ____.

2. Find one of the jokes included in the text of the essay. What key idea does this joke illustrate or support?

> I think the joke about ____ illustrates the key idea that ____.

3. Why do you think there are so many "theories of funniness"? What can you conclude about humor from all these theories?

> I think the number of theories suggests ____.

4. Look at the chart in the section "Got Laughs?" In general, as people age, how does the humor they enjoy change?

> As people age, their tastes becomes more ____.

Asking Questions

The author of "Made You Laugh" has chosen a broad and complex topic to write about. Do you think you understand all the points he made? With your partner or small group, look back at the whole essay. Discuss what questions you have about the text. Write one question you would like to ask the author to clarify a point he made. Share your question with the whole class.

_____

_____

How English Works: Compound Sentences

Learning Target
- Apply understanding of independent clauses and compound sentences to comprehending and writing texts.

Connecting ideas
Combine clauses in an increasing variety of ways (e.g., creating compound and complex sentences) to make connections between and join ideas, for example, to express a reason (e.g., He stayed at home on Sunday to study for Monday's exam.) or to make a concession (e.g., She studied all night even though she wasn't feeling well.).

Compound Sentences
"Made You Laugh" is an expository essay that explores many aspects of a broad and complicated topic—humor. To do this, the author has used long sentences—compound and complex sentences. By combining two or more related clauses into one sentence, the author clarifies the connection between ideas and events.

Simple sentences: Those born blind and deaf also laugh.

Laughter is not dependent on sight and hearing.

Compound sentence: Those born blind and deaf also laugh, so laughter is not dependent on sight and hearing.

By linking the two independent clauses with the conjunction *so*, the author makes the relationship between the two ideas clearer.

Read the short, simple sentences on the left side of the chart. Combine the simple sentences into one compound sentence with two or three independent clauses. Your rewritten sentence should make the relationships between ideas clear. You can check your work against the author's sentences in "Made You Laugh."

> **Language Resources**
>
> **compound sentence:** a sentence formed from two or more independent clauses
> **coordinating conjunction:** a word that joins two simple sentences or independent clauses to form a compound sentence; the words *but*, *or*, and *so* are coordinating conjunctions
> **independent clause:** a group of words that expresses a complete thought and can stand by itself as a simple sentence
> **simple sentence:** a sentence with one independent clause

Short, Simple Sentences	Rewrite as Compound Sentences
They are being led in a certain direction. Then that direction abruptly changes. The unpredictability makes them laugh.	They are being led in a certain direction, and then that direction abruptly changes, and the unpredictability makes them laugh.
It [Laughter] has a certain rhythm. Laughter syllables build, then trail off. They come out in a repetitive, not random, sequence.	
"The best humor has some sort of layer to it. It makes a statement of some kind or comment."	
"Do you have a rubber band?" is not in and of itself humorous. It is if it's said in response to "I like Amelia so much. I wish I could get her attention."	

💬 Quick Conversation

- Share your work with a partner. Read aloud the original and revised sentences. Discuss how they compare and why the compound sentences show related ideas more clearly. Record notes from your discussion.

> In my opinion, the compound sentences _____.

> Short simple sentences tend to sound _____.

> I think the _____ sentences are effective because _____.

Create Compound Sentences

Work with a partner to create original compound sentences.

- On your own, first write an independent clause or simple sentence about something you find funny. Then, exchange your sentence with a partner.

- After reading your partner's sentence, think of a way you can add a conjunction and another independent clause to make it a compound sentence. The clause you add should state an idea that is clearly related to the first clause.

- Write your compound sentence on the lines below. Then, read it aloud and discuss it with the whole group.

_____

_____

_____

_____

_____

_____

_____

Interact in Meaningful Ways:
Analyze Precise Diction

Learning Targets

- Adjust language choices according to social setting and audience.
- Evaluate and explain in conversation and writing how effectively the author uses precise diction.

Precise Diction

Mark Tyler Nobleman, the author of "Made You Laugh," has written an expository essay about humor. Although he includes a number of jokes as examples, his main purpose is to inform readers about the scientific study of humor. To do this, he uses a thoughtful tone. One way he achieves this tone is by using precise diction—verbs, adjectives, and nouns. In the following paragraph, for example, notice how precise nouns, such as *function, rhythm, syllables,* and *sequence,* help create the serious tone. Similarly, the adjectives *biological, repetitive,* and *random* are what we'd expect in a piece about a scientific study.

> You may be saying to yourself, "Studying jokes? Is that science?" But plenty of smart people say yes. Laughter is a biological function. It has a certain rhythm; laughter syllables build, then trail off, and they come out in a repetitive, not random, sequence. For example, "ha-ha-ho-ho-he" is typical, but "ha-ho-ha-ho-ha" or "he-ho-he" just doesn't happen.

Read these sentences from "Made You Laugh." Underline one precise word in each sentence that shows the tone the author uses to write about a scientific study. Then write an original sentence using the underlined word.

Sentence from "Made You Laugh"	Original Sentence
Babies begin to laugh instinctively when they're about four months old.	
Even rats, when tickled, make squeals that can be interpreted as laughter.	
Those born blind and deaf also laugh, so laughter is not dependent on sight and hearing.	
Authors and film actors do not often get immediate public feedback. But comics do.	
Yet laughter is not always a planned response to a joke.	

Language Resources

Literary Terms

Diction: word choice; the way something is put into words

Tone: an author's attitude toward his or her subject

Precise: exact; specific

ACADEMIC VOCABULARY

Precise diction is the choice of clear and exact words that suit the style and tone of a piece of writing. The opposite of precise diction is vague and confusing word choice.

💬 Quick Conversation

- Share your work with a partner. Take turns explaining which word you chose in each sentence and what your understanding is of the word's meaning. Discuss whether your partner agrees or disagrees with your choices and how you used the words in sentences. Record notes from your discussion.

> In my opinion, the word _____ is precise because _____.

> Do you agree with my annotations?

> Can you tell me what the word _____ means?

> I disagree with how you used the word _____ because _____.

Write a Short Summary

Sum up one section of "I Made You Laugh" in five or six sentences. Use precise diction and a thoughtful tone to sum up the key ideas of the section. (Your summary should not include minor details.) Before writing, read the model short summary provided. Notice what information is in each of the sentences. Try structuring your summary in the same way.

_____

_____

_____

_____

MODEL: SHORT SUMMARY

The "Got Laughs?" section of the essay examines how age affects the enjoyment of humor. Very young children prefer broad physical humor, while older children typically find puns and word play more entertaining. The average teen enjoys jokes that might make adults uncomfortable, perhaps as a way to lessen anxiety on difficult topics. Finally, research indicates that satire—humor that focuses on people's weaknesses—is most popular among adults.

Interact in Meaningful Ways: Writing to Sources

Learning Targets

- Express and justify opinions about a text in conversation and writing by providing text evidence.

- Write a short expository text collaboratively and independently.

The essay "Made You Laugh" includes a number of jokes. Which joke did you think was funniest? In the chart below, summarize the joke. Then tell why you think it is funny. Finally, cite any information in the essay, such as one of the theories in paragraphs 20–25, that suggests why the joke is funny.

Joke	Why I Think It's Funny	Information in Essay That Explains Why It Is Funny

---

Quick Conversation

Share your work with your partner. Compare your ideas about the joke and why it was funny.

Next, read aloud this sentence from the last paragraph of the essay:

> Theories and techniques aside, much about humor remains a mystery.

Discuss the sentence. What does it tell you about attempts to understand humor scientifically? Record notes from your discussion.

> It's important to try to understand the sources of humor because _____.

> I agree with this statement because _____.

> Based on the theories the author describes, I think _____.

> Could you please explain to me why _____?

Planning an Expository Essay

Use the graphic organizer to plan your own expository essay about a time you had a good laugh. You can write about a joke you heard, a real-life event, or a person you met. Make notes about what you will include in your essay in the chart below.

Details About Joke/ Event/Person	Why I Thought It Was Funny	Information in Essay That Explains Why It Was Funny

Expository Essay Writing Prompt

Write a draft of your expository essay. Be sure to:

■ Describe the humorous joke, event, or person.

■ Explain why you thought it was humorous.

■ Cite evidence from the essay that explains why it was humorous.

■ Take a serious tone toward your subject.

■ Use precise diction to describe and explain.

_____

_____

_____

_____

_____

_____

_____

_____

_____

_____

_____

Selecting Language Resources

Learning Targets

- Develop language resources to use while speaking and writing about essays.
- Use an expanded set of words to speak and write precisely.
- Adjust language choices to suit the academic setting.

The chart presents words and phrases you will use in discussion and writing. Think about each word or phrase. Circle Q, H, or T to indicate how well you know it. Work with a partner, asking your partner to explain each word or phrase. Listen closely to the explanation, and then write your partner's name in the In Our Own Words column along with his or her condensed idea.

> **WORD CONNECTIONS**
>
> **Prefixes**
> The prefix *ir-* means "not," so *irreverent* means "not reverent." Similarly, the prefixes *il-*, *im-*, and *in-* also mean "not," as in *illogical*, *impossible*, and *insecure*.

Rating	Q	H	T
	I have seen this word or phrase, but I have **questions** about its meaning.	I have **heard** this word or phrase but do not know it well.	I know this word or phrase so well that I could **teach** it to someone else.

Word or Phrase	Definition	In Our Own Words
juxtaposition Rating Q H T	a writing technique that places words, phrases, and ideas that normally wouldn't be used together next to each other for effect	
description Rating Q H T	the type of writing that creates a colorful, exact picture of a person, place, object, or event	
syntax Rating Q H T	the relationships among the words, phrases, and clauses in sentences; sentence structure	
simile Rating Q H T	a comparison between two unlike things using the word *like* or *as*	
repetition Rating Q H T	the repeated use of the same words or phrases for effect	
audience Rating Q H T	the type of reader or readers for whom a piece of writing is intended	
irreverent Rating Q H T	unconventional; lacking respect for that which is usually respected	

Academic and Social Language Preview

WORD CONNECTIONS

Multiple Meaning Words

The word *expiring* is a multiple-meaning word. It has three commonly used meanings.
1. running out of time
2. dying
3. breathing out air from the lung

When reading, use the context of the surrounding sentences to figure out which meaning is intended.

Learning Target

- Develop knowledge of a growing set of academic and social vocabulary to comprehend when reading and to create precision shades of meaning in one's own speaking, and writing.

VOCABULARY PREVIEW

expiring: (verb) running out of time; dying

kicks the bucket: (verb) dies

mope: (verb) to act sad and dull

pacifist: (noun) someone who refuses to take part in war

pet peeves: (noun) things that a person finds very annoying

stand-ins: (noun) replacements

tedious: (adjective) boring

torso: (noun) the body without head, arms, or legs

unbeknownst: (adverb) without one's knowledge; unknown

vital signs: (noun) pulse, temperature, and other signals of a body's health

Vocabulary Practice

Use the definitions in the Vocabulary Preview or a dictionary to support your work.

Practice 1. Write the vocabulary word that matches the three words or phrases in the second column.

pet peeves   stand-ins   torso   vital signs

Vocabulary Word	Words or Phrases It Matches
	blood pressure heart rate oxygen level of blood
	squeaky doors flickering lights dripping faucets
	shoulders stomach chest
	substitute teachers actors' understudies pinch hitters

Practice 2. Complete each sentence, paying attention to the **bold** vocabulary word.

1. Outside the weather seemed lovely, but **unbeknownst** to us,

_____

2. Our time on the parking meter was **expiring**, so

_____

3. My summer job at the factory was **tedious** because

_____

Practice 3. Circle the word that does not belong.

1. pacifist   peace lover   warrior   dove
2. mope   dance   lie around   frown
3. kicks the bucket   passes away   survives   dies

Interpret the Text Using Close Reading

My Notes

Learning Targets
● Apply understanding of how essays are structured to comprehend the text.

● Use general academic words and domain-specific words to create some precision while speaking and writing.

● Explain how phrasing or different common words with similar meanings produce different effects on the audience.

Read and Annotate
Read the comedic essay independently or as a group. Annotate the text as you read.

■ Use the My Notes area to write any questions or ideas you have about the story.
■ Underline any comedic juxtapositions you find.
■ Circle unknown words and phrases.

Essay

i've got a few pet peeves about sea creatures

by Dave Barry

1 Pets are good, because they teach children important lessons about life, the main one being that, sooner or later, life kicks the bucket.

2 With me, it was sooner. When I was a boy, my dad, who worked in New York City, would periodically bring home a turtle in a little plastic tank that had a little plastic island with a little plastic palm tree, as is so often found in natural turtle habitats. I was excited about having a pet, and I'd give the turtle a fun pet name like Scooter. But my excitement was not shared by Scooter, who, despite residing in a tropical paradise, never did anything except mope around.

3 Actually, he didn't even mope "around": He moped in one place without moving, or even blinking, for days on end, displaying basically the same vital signs as an ashtray. Eventually I would realize—it wasn't easy to tell—that Scooter had passed on to that Big Pond in the Sky, and I'd bury him in the garden, where he'd decompose and become food for the zucchini, which in turn would be eaten by my dad, who would in turn go to New York City, where, compelled by powerful instincts that even he did not understand, he would buy me another moping death turtle. And so the cycle of life would repeat.

4 I say all this to explain why I recently bought fish for my 4-year-old daughter, Sophie. My wife and I realized how badly she wanted an animal when she found a beetle on the patio and declared that it was a pet, named Marvin. She put Marvin into a Tupperware container, where, under Sophie's loving care and feeding, he thrived for maybe nine seconds before expiring like a little six-legged parking meter. Fortunately, we

have a beetle-intensive patio, so, unbeknownst to Sophie, we were able to replace Marvin with a parade of stand-ins of various sizes ("Look! Marvin has grown bigger!" "Wow! Today Marvin has grown smaller!"). But it gets to be tedious, going out early every morning to wrangle patio beetles. So we decided to go with fish.

5 I had fish of my own, years ago, and it did not go well. They got some disease like Mongolian Fin Rot, which left them basically just little pooping torsos. But I figured that today, with all the technological advances we have such as cellular phones and "digital" things and carbohydrate-free toothpaste, modern fish would be more reliable.

6 So we got an aquarium and prepared it with special water and special gravel and special fake plants and a special scenic rock so the fish would be intellectually stimulated and get into a decent college. When everything was ready I went to the aquarium store to buy fish, my only criteria being that they should be 1) hardy digital fish; and 2) fish that looked a LOT like other fish, in case God forbid we had to Marvinize them. This is when I discovered how complex fish society is. I'd point to some colorful fish and say, "What about these?" And the aquarium guy would say, "Those are great fish but they do get aggressive when they mate." And I'd say, "Like, how aggressive?" And he'd say, "They'll kill all the other fish."

7 This was a recurring theme. I'd point to some fish, and the aquarium guy would inform me that these fish could become aggressive if there were fewer than four of them, or an odd number of them, or it was a month containing the letter "R," or they heard the song "Who Let the Dogs Out." It turns out that an aquarium is a powder keg that can explode in deadly violence at any moment, just like the Middle East, or junior high school.

8 TRUE STORY: A friend of mine named David Shor told me that his kids had an aquarium containing a kind of fish called African cichlids, and one of them died. So David went to the aquarium store and picked out a replacement African cichlid, but the aquarium guy said he couldn't buy that one, and David asked why, and the guy said: "Because that one is from a different lake."

9 But getting back to my daughter's fish: After much thought, the aquarium guy was able to find me three totally pacifist fish–Barney Fife fish, fish so nonviolent that, in the wild, worms routinely beat them up and steal their lunch money. I brought these home, and so far they have not killed each other or died in any way. Plus, Sophie LOVES them. So everything is working out beautifully. I hope it stays that way, because I hate zucchini.

My Notes

💬 **Interact in Meaningful Ways:
Academic Collaboration**

Learning Targets

- Ask and answer questions about an essay in collaborative conversations.

- Express and support opinions of an essay in conversation.

Turn to your partner or small group to discuss each question about "I've got a few pet peeves about sea creatures." After you have discussed a question, write notes about your answer before going on to the next question.

1. What are the author's basic pet peeves with "sea creatures" (pet turtles and fish)?

> The author finds it annoying that pet turtles _____ and fish_____.

2. In paragraph 2, how does the author use repetition and juxtaposition of ideas to create a comic effect?

> The author repeats the phrase _____.

3. How is the author's tone toward his and his daughter's pets irreverent?

> The author's tone is irreverent in that_____.

4. In paragraph 7, how does the author combine a simile and juxtaposition of ideas to create humor?

> I think it's funny when the author compares_____.

Asking Questions

The jokes and funny lines in "I've got a few pet peeves about sea creatures" are almost nonstop. So it's hard to appreciate them all. What jokes or lines in the essay did you *not* understand or find funny? Write one question about this joke or line to share with the whole class.

_____

_____

Interact in Meaningful Ways: Comic Syntax

Learning Targets

- Expand noun phrases to enrich the meaning of sentences and add details.
- Express ideas on familiar topics by asking and answering questions.
- Support opinions and persuade others in conversations.
- Analyze how language choices have different effects on audiences.

Comic Syntax

"I've got a few pet peeves about sea creatures" uses a variety of techniques to create a humorous effect. These techniques include colorful descriptions, juxtaposition of ideas, and repetition.

Skim through "I've got a few pet peeves about sea creatures" looking for examples of comic syntax. Write a few examples of each technique in the chart below. Use the definitions in the Language Resources chart for support.

Colorful Descriptions	Juxtaposition of Ideas	Repetition

Language Resources

Comic Syntax

description: the type of writing that creates a colorful, exact picture of a person, place, object, or event

juxtaposition: a writing technique that places words, phrases, and ideas that normally wouldn't go together next to each other for effect

repetition: the repeated use of the same words or phrases for effect

syntax: the relationships among the words, phrases, and clauses in sentences; sentence structure

💬 Quick Conversation

● Share your chart with a partner. Read aloud some of the examples you found and tell how they illustrate the technique. Discuss whether you think the examples are funny or not, and why. Finally choose one example that is your favorite and explain why you like it so much. Record notes from your discussion.

> In my opinion, this description is colorful because_____.

> Did the juxtaposition of _____ and_____ make you laugh?

> I think my favorite sentence might be_____ because_____.

Write an Expository Paragraph

Now write a paragraph about the example of comic syntax you like best. First quote the line or lines from the essay. Then tell why you think it is funny. Finally explain how Barry used comic syntax to achieve this humor.

_____

_____

_____

_____

_____

_____

_____

_____

Interact in Meaningful Ways:
Analyze Vivid Verbs and Adjectives

Learning Target
- Analyze and explain in conversation and writing how vivid verbs and adjectives produce effects on the reader.

Vivid Verbs and Adjectives

Dave Barry, the author of the comedic essay, uses vivid verbs and adjectives. These colorful words help the reader see the action and events not just clearly, but often in an unusual way. As a result, the vivid word choices add to the humorous effect.

"Fortunately, we have a beetle-intensive patio ..."

The vivid adjective *beetle-intensive* helps us see the patio in a humorous way.

"But it gets to be tedious, going out early every morning to wrangle patio beetles."

The vivid verb *wrangle* is usually used to describe cow herding, so it creates a colorful picture when used to describe the action of catching beetles.

Read these sentences from "I've got a few pet peeves about sea creatures." Circle any adjectives or verbs in each sentence that create a vivid image in your mind.

1. "But my excitement was not shared by Scooter, who, despite residing in a tropical paradise, never did anything except mope around."

2. "She put Marvin into a Tupperware container, where, under Sophie's loving care and feeding, he thrived for maybe nine seconds before expiring like a little six-legged parking meter."

3. "When everything was ready I went to the aquarium store to buy fish, my only criteria being that they should be 1) hardy digital fish; and 2) fish that looked a LOT like other fish, in case God forbid we had to Marvinize them."

4. "After much thought, the aquarium guy was able to find me three totally pacifist fish—Barney Fife fish, fish so nonviolent that, in the wild, worms routinely beat them up and steal their lunch money."

Language Resources
Literary Terms
Verb: a word that expresses action or a state of being
Adjective: a word that modifies a noun or pronoun
Vivid: forming or giving a clear picture in the mind

Language Resources
Connotation
Denotation is a word's dictionary meaning. Connotation is a word's emotional overtones, the effects it has on you. The words *thrifty* and *stingy*, for example, have similar denotations—"tending to save money." *Thrifty*, however, has a positive connotation while *stingy* has negative emotional overtones.

Choose one word from each sentence to add to the chart. List the word, its meaning, and its connotations. Finally tell why you think the word is humorous.

Verb or Adjective	Meaning of Word	Connotations	Why It Is Funny
1.			
2.			
3.			
4.			

Quick Conversation

- Share your work with a partner. Take turns identifying the vivid words you chose, their meanings and connotations, and why you think they are funny. Discuss whether your partner agrees or disagrees with your choices and why they are funny. Record notes from your discussion.

> In my opinion, this adjective is _____ funny because _____.

> I think Dave Barry made up the verb _____ in order to _____.

> Do you agree that the connotation of _____ is _____?

Write a Short Description

After analyzing and evaluating the vivid verbs and adjectives in "I've got a few pet peeves about sea creatures" you might be inspired to write a short description of a pet or animal that you are familiar with. Try to use a vivid verb or vivid adjective in each sentence of your description. Before writing, read the model short description provided. Try to structure your description in a similar way.

_____

_____

_____

_____

_____

_____

_____

_____

MODEL: SHORT DESCRIPTION

For a half-pint puppy, Fritzi had a werewolf appetite. Every night, he ogled Dad's newspaper as if it were a USDA-certified sirloin steak. Whenever he could, he wolfed it down, releasing only an editorial burp or two afterwards. He also awarded Mom' slippers blue-ribbon status, snacking on a pair a week. Worst of all, my action toys qualified as five-star fare, and he polished them off until they qualified as an endangered species.

Interact in Meaningful Ways: Writing an Expository Essay

Learning Targets

- Express and justify opinions about an essay by providing text evidence or relevant background knowledge.

- Write a description of an essay, analyzing the author's motivation and intended audience.

Dave Barry is known for his irreverent humor. He tends not to show reverence, or respect, for things that his audience usually holds in high regard, such as the lives of their pets.

Think about some things you have heard or read recently that seemed irreverent to you. List examples on the chart.

Language Resources

irreverent: unconventional; lacking respect for that which is usually respected

audience: the type of reader or readers for whom a piece of writing is intended

What I Saw or Heard	Why It Seemed Irreverent

💬 Quick Conversation

- Share your work with your partner. Discuss the events you heard or saw and why they seemed irreverent. Try to decide what the serious issue behind the event was. Also, discuss who the audience was for the event. Then tell how the audience seemed to react. Record notes from your discussion.

> I think this event or incident was irreverent because _____.

> I disagree that the serious issue behind this was _____.

> I think the audience for this event was _____.

> It sounds like the audience reacted _____.

Planning an Essay

Now plan a brief essay about one of the irreverent events you listed. Or, if you prefer, you can write about "I've got a few pet peeves about sea creatures." Before you begin to write your essay, jot down answers to these questions:

What were the key details? _____

What serious issue was raised? _____

Who was the intended audience? _____

How did the audience react? _____

Expository Writing Prompt

Write a draft of your expository essay. Be sure to:

- Start with a short description of the event (or Dave Barry's essay).
- Discuss the serious issue that was raised.
- Identify the intended audience and the audience's reaction.
- Use vivid verbs and adjectives to describe actions and events.

Selecting Language Resources

Learning Targets

- Develop language resources to use while speaking and writing about drama.
- Use an expanded set of words to speak and write precisely.
- Adjust language choices to suit the academic setting.

The chart presents words and phrases you will use in discussion and writing. Think about each word or phrase. Circle Q, H, or T to indicate how well you know it. Work with a partner, asking your partner to explain each word or phrase. Listen closely to the explanation, and then write your partner's name in the In Our Own Words column along with his or her condensed idea.

WORD CONNECTIONS

Etymology

The Latin word *scriptum*, meaning *"writing,"* gives us many English words. In addition to *script*, *describe*, *prescription*, and *scripture* all come from this root.

Rating	Q	H	T
	I have seen this word or phrase, but I have **questions** about its meaning.	I have **heard** this word or phrase but do not know it well.	I know this word or phrase so well that I could **teach** it to someone else.

Word or Phrase	Definition	In Our Own Words
script Rating Q H T	a copy of a play used by those putting it on	
act Rating Q H T	one of the main divisions of a play	
scene Rating Q H T	a separate part of an act in a play	
gesturing Rating Q H T	moving some part of the body, usually the arms and hands, to show some idea or feeling	
visualize Rating Q H T	to form a picture of something in the mind	
insult Rating Q H T	to say or do something on purpose that hurts a person's feelings or pride	
quarrel Rating Q H T	an argument or disagreement, especially an angry one	

Academic and Social Language Preview

Learning Target
- Develop knowledge of a growing set of academic and social vocabulary to create precise shades of meaning in reading, speaking, and writing.

VOCABULARY PREVIEW

cowardice: (noun) lack of courage

esteem: (noun) respect; high regard

fie: (interjection) shame on you! for shame!

mock: (verb) make fun of; tease

modesty: (noun) shyness; simplicity; decency

perceive: (verb) observe; to take in through the mind

personage: (noun) a person, especially a famous or important person

shrewishness: (noun) the tendency to scold in a bad-tempered way

stature: (noun) the height of a person; high rank or position

Vocabulary Practice
Use the definitions in the Vocabulary Preview or a dictionary to support your work.

Practice 1. Circle the word or phrase whose meaning is closest to the meaning of the vocabulary word.

Vocabulary Word	Words or Phrases to Choose From
mock	be nice to make fun of pay no attention to
stature	height width length
esteem	disrespect uncertainty admiration
perceive	ignore notice criticize

Practice 2. Complete each sentence, paying attention to the **bold** vocabulary word.

1. My grandmother said **Fie!** when she learned I had _____

2. As an example of my aunt's **shrewishness,** she often _____

3. One soldier, charged with **cowardice,** had _____

Practice 3. Write the vocabulary word that best matches each set of traits.

modesty   personage

1. _____ booming voice   flashy clothing   overpowering manner

2. _____ quiet voice   simple clothing   gentle manner

Interpret the Text Using Close Reading

Learning Targets
- Apply understanding of how dramatic scripts are structured to comprehend the text.
- Read closely and annotate the text to find the language resources an author uses to establish character, setting, and incident.

Read and Annotate

Read the passage as a group. Annotate the text as you read.

- Use the My Notes area to write questions or ideas you have about the story.
- Underline the insults the women give.
- Put stars next to words and phrases that help you "hear" the speaker.
- Circle unknown words and phrases.

Drama Excerpt

from a midsummer night's dream

Act 3, Scene 2, Lines 282–306

by William Shakespeare

HERMIA	Oh me! you juggler! you canker-blossom!
	You thief of love! What, have you come by night
	And stolen my love's heart from him?
HELENA	Fine, i'faith!
285	Have you no modesty, no maiden shame,
	No touch of bashfulness? What, will you tear
	Impatient answers from my gentle tongue?
	Fie, fie! you counterfeit, you puppet, you!
HERMIA	Puppet? Why so? Ay, that way goes the game.
290	Now, I perceive that she hath made compare
	Between our statures; she hath urged her height;
	And with her personage, her tall personage,
	Her height, **forsooth**, she hath prevail'd with him.
	And are you grown so high in his esteem;
295	Because I am so dwarfish and so low?
	How low am I, thou painted maypole? speak;
	How low am I? I am not yet so low
	But that my nails can reach unto thine eyes.

forsooth: indeed; used to express surprise or indignation

Interpret the Text Using Close Reading

HELENA	I pray you, though you mock me, gentlemen,	
300	Let her not hurt me: I was never curst;	
	I have no gift at all in shrewishness;	
	I am a right maid for my cowardice:	
	Let her not strike me. You perhaps may think,	
	Because she is something lower than myself,	
305	That I can match her.	
HERMIA	Lower! hark, again.	

My Notes

Interact in Meaningful Ways: Academic Collaboration

Learning Targets
● Ask and answer questions about a dramatic scene in collaborative conversations, demonstrating active listening, and drawing upon an expanding pool of language resources for discussing literature.

● Express and support opinions of a dramatic scene in conversation.

Turn to your partner or small group to discuss each question about the scene from *A Midsummer Night's Dream*. After you have discussed a question, write notes about your answer before going on to the next question.

1. As the scene opens, what does Hermia accuse Helena of coming to do? Explain in your own words.

> Hermia accuses Helena of coming to _____.

2. In what key physical way must the actors who play Hermia and Helena differ from one another? How does Hermia seem to feel about this difference?

> Compared to Hermia, Helena must be _____.

3. How does Helena react when Hermia threatens physical violence?

> When Hermia threatens Helena with violence, Helena _____.

4. How do the multiple meanings of *high* and *lower* add to the humor of the scene?

> It's funny when Helena says Hermia is lower because _____.

Asking Questions

Much of this scene from *A Midsummer Night's Dream* is a series of insults exchanged between Hermia and Helena. With your partner or small group, skim through the scene and list some of the insults you find. In your own words try to explain what the insults mean. Write one question about an insult you don't understand to share with the whole class.

_____

_____

**How English Works:
Exclamations and Written Verbal Language**

Learning Objectives

- Analyze how dramatic scripts are structured to comprehend the text.
- Engage in short written exchanges with peers and collaborate on simple written texts.
- Explain how phrasing or different common words with similar meanings produce different effects on the audience.
- Write brief summaries of texts and experiences using complete sentences and key words.

Exclamations

The scene from *A Midsummer Night's Dream* was written to be performed on stage by actors who use their voices and bodies to express meaning. Seeing and hearing the scene performed would be very different from reading it. In a live production, you would see the actors express feelings by gesturing with their arms and hands. You would also hear their feelings in how they said their lines. And some lines, especially exclamations, have more meaning when spoken than written.

Skim through the scene from *A Midsummer Night's Dream*. Look for words and phrases that the characters use to express strong feelings. (These words will have more meaning when spoken than when written.) Write some examples in the chart and tell what you think they mean.

> **Language Resources
> Exclamations and Written Verbal Language**
> An **exclamation** or exclamatory sentence expresses strong feelings. An exclamation is usually followed by exclamation point.
>
> > What an amazing drama this is!
>
> An **interjection** is a word that expresses emotion. It has no grammatical relation to other words in the sentence,
> > Wow! Ugh! Aha!

Words and Phrases	Meaning
Oh, me (l. 281)	I can't believe it.

Quick Conversation

- Share your work with a partner. Read aloud the words and phrases you listed and what you think they mean. Discuss how you think Hermia and Helena would say these words and phrases to express their feelings. Talk about how they might gesture with their hands and arms to make their feelings even clearer. Record notes from your discussion.

> In my opinion, the interjection i' faith means ____.

> Do you think Hermia would use a ____ tone to say ____?

> Helena might gesture by ____.

Write a Short Analysis

Now work in small groups to read the scene. Focus on the words and phrases that express strong feelings. As you read, experiment with different tones of voice and hand gestures. Decide which tones and gestures seem most expressive.

Write a short analysis of your findings. Explain why you think Shakespeare included these words and phrases in this scene. Then tell whether or not they are effective, and why.

_____

_____

_____

_____

_____

_____

_____

_____

Interact in Meaningful Ways: Modifying and Creating Nouns with Affixes

Learning Targets
- Use knowledge of affixes to determine the meaning of words.
- Use knowledge of morphology to appropriately select affixes in basic ways.

Modifying and Creating Nouns with Affixes

One reason English has so many words is affixes. Affixes are syllables added to base words to create new words. Becoming familiar with the meanings of affixes will help you understand these new words. In this activity, you will identify and analyze how suffixes can be used to form nouns from other parts of speech.

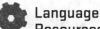
Language Resources

Literary Terms
affix: a prefix or suffix
base word: a word with no affixes
prefix: a word part added to the beginning of a base word to change its meaning
suffix: a word part added to the ending of a base word to change its meaning

Language Resources: Noun-Forming Suffixes

Suffix	Meaning of Suffix	Example	Meaning of New Noun
-er or -r	one who	paint + -er = painter	one who paints
-hood	state of being	hardy + -hood = hardihood	state of being hardy
-ice	state of being	just + -ice = justice	state of being just
-ment	act or result of	improve + -ment = improvement	result of improving
-ness	state of being	good + -ness = goodness	state of being good
-y	state of being	villain + -y = villainy	state of being a villain

The chart below lists lines from the scene from *A Midsummer's Night Dream*. Circle a word in each line that is a noun formed with a suffix. Then briefly note how the noun was formed. Finally write the meaning of the suffixed noun. Use the examples in the Language Resources box to help you.

Noun Formed with a Suffix	How the Noun Was Formed	Meaning of Noun with Suffix
Oh me! you juggler! you canker-blossom!	the suffix -r is added to the verb juggle	"one who juggles"
Have you no modesty, no maiden shame,		
No touch of bashfulness?		
I have no gift at all in shrewishness;		
I am a right maid for my cowardice:		

Quick Conversation

- Share your work with a partner. Take turns explaining your analysis of the nouns formed from suffixes. Discuss whether your partner agrees or disagrees with your choices. Record notes from your discussion.

_____

_____

> In my opinion, the noun _____ means _____.

> What other nouns can be formed from this suffix?

> I agree with your choice because _____.

> Can you think of other suffixes that form nouns?

Write a Short Explanation

After analyzing how certain nouns can be formed with suffixes, you have enough information to explain how some longer nouns are formed with two or more suffixes. Take, for example, the word *shrewishness* in this line from *A Midsummer's Night Dream*.

I have no gift at all in shrewishness

The model paragraph below explains how this noun was formed. Write a similar explanation of how one of these nouns was formed.

joyfulness   cheeriness

Try to structure your explanation in the same way the model paragraph does.

_____

_____

_____

_____

MODEL: SHORT EXPLANATION

The noun *shrewishness* is an example of a noun with two suffixes. The base word is *shrew*, a noun that names a small animal. The suffix *-ish* is added to *shrew* to form *shrewish*, an adjective that means "like a shrew." Finally the suffix *-ness* is added to the adjective *shrewish* to form *shrewishness*. This is a noun meaning "the condition of acting like a shrew."

Creating and Presenting a Comic Dialogue
Creative Writing and Dramatic Performance

Step 1: Introduction

In the scene from A *Midsummer Night's Dream*, William Shakespeare presented a comic dialogue between two characters. The playwright entertained his audience with a humorous exchange between Helena and Hermia.

Dialogue Writing Prompt:

In this lesson, you will create your own version of this dialogue with a partner. Your task is to rewrite the scene between Helena and Hermia in modern-day English (the speech you use every day). You'll keep Shakespeare's characters but put contemporary words in their mouths. To do this, your comic dialogue should:

- Paraphrase the original dialogue.
- Follow the original action.
- Maintain an overall humorous tone.
- Substitute modern words and phrases for old-fashioned terms.
- Use vivid verbs and adverbs to create color.
- Use comic syntax, including colorful description, juxtaposition of ideas, and repetition.
- Include exclamations, words, and phrases that express the characters' feelings.

Step 2: Brainstorming

Work with a group of classmates to discuss how you will go about creating modern-day versions of the scene. You might begin by reviewing the scene on pages 172–173 and summarizing what happens in your own words. Next, take turns paraphrasing one of the character's lines into your everyday speech. Use a classroom computer with an online dictionary or thesaurus to find synonyms for old-fashioned words and phrases. Also, choose words you think your audience will find funny. Use a chart like this to keep track of your ideas for substitutions.

Shakespeare's Text	My Modern Speech Version
Oh me! you juggler! you canker-blossom!	Unbelievable! You sneak. You little pest!

Use the sentence frames on the next page to help you brainstorm. Remember to take turns sharing your ideas and asking questions.

My Notes

Instead of "touch of bashfulness," I would say ____.

What's another way to say "thief of love"?

Instead of "Ay!" people today might exclaim ____.

Should I keep the word "puppet" or change it to "____".

For a Quickwrite, try rewriting Hermia's first three lines in modern-day English:

> Oh me! you juggler! you canker-blossom!
> You thief of love! What, have you come by night
> And stolen my love's heart from him?

As you write, keep in mind what Hermia is like and use her dialogue to show it. Then, read what you've written to a partner. Ask him or her for ideas and reactions to your word choices and ideas for how you might make the dialogue funnier.

Step 3: Prewriting/Planning

Working with your partner, reread the scene more closely, pointing out words and expressions that you think should be rewritten. Make suggestions to each other about possible replacement words and phrases. Keep in mind that the changes you make should maintain the humor of the dialogue. Also use insults to show the conflict between the two women. As you talk, jot down any ideas you get for your scene.

I think I'll keep the puns on the words "higher" and "lower" because ____.

What can I substitute for "i'faith?"

The phrase ____ sounds more modern than "made compare."

What is a "painted maypole," and why is it an insult?

Creating and Presenting a Comic Dialogue
Creative Writing and Dramatic Performance

You are working on lines 282 through 306 of Act 3, Scene 2. As you look back at this scene on pages 172–173, jot down your ideas for changes to each line on the script organizer below. Work line by line so your version follows Shakespeare's closely. Feel free to say your lines aloud to practice how they'll sound in your presentation.

Hermia: _____

_____

_____

Helena: _____

285 _____

_____

_____

_____

Hermia: _____

290 _____

_____

_____

_____

_____

295 _____

_____

_____

_____

_____

Helena: _____

300 _____

_____

_____

_____

_____

305 _____

_____

Hermia: _____

My Notes

Language Resources

Comic Syntax

Syntax, also known as sentence structure, is the relationship among the words, phrases, and clauses in sentences.

Comic syntax, the language of comedy, relies on these techniques:

description: the type of writing that creates a colorful, exact picture of a person, place, object, or event

juxtaposition: a writing technique that places words, phrases, and ideas that normally wouldn't go together next to each other for effect

repetition: the repeated use of the same words or phrases for effect.

Writing Checklist
- ☐ Review the Student Comic Dialogue Writing Rubric
- ☐ Review the Student Comic Dialogue Writing Exemplar
- ☐ Review your draft
- ☐ Participate in peer editing
- ☐ Revise
- ☐ Publish
- ☐ Present

My Notes

_____
_____
_____
_____
_____
_____
_____
_____
_____

Step 4: Drafting

Use your completed graphic organizer and brainstorming document as guides as you begin to draft your version of the scene. Remember to use the skills you practiced in Unit 3 to create your dialogue. Those skills include:

- using comic syntax, such as juxtaposition of ideas and humorous repetition.
- using diction, or word choice, to create a humorous tone.
- using vivid verbs and adjectives to create colorful and funny images.
- using exclamations and other words that convey special emotional meaning when spoken.

Before you begin the first draft, work in groups to study the scoring guide. It shows how your script will be scored. Discuss the points on the scoring guide with your classmates. As you can see, your comic dialogue should:

- follow the original scene closely.
- use modern-day language.
- express a humorous tone.
- contain examples of comic syntax

Step 5: Editing and Revising/Practicing

With your partner, practice reading aloud your draft, one student reading the lines of Hermia, the other Helena. Discuss what you might do to improve the dialogue. Then review the scoring guide again and look at the Student Comic Dialogue Text Exemplar, which you will receive from your teacher. Finally, switch drafts with another pair. Use this checklist as you read your classmates' draft.

Peer Editing Checklist

- ☐ Did the writer follow the prompt?
- ☐ Did the writer revise the scene into modern-day English?
- ☐ Did the writer use the characters and action of Shakespeare's original scene?
- ☐ Did the writer use comic syntax?
- ☐ Did the writer substitute vivid verbs and adjectives to create color?
- ☐ Did the writer use exclamations and other words and phrases to express feelings?
- ☐ Did the writer achieve an overall humorous tone?
- ☐ Did the writer use correct spelling and punctuation?

One thing I really liked about this scene is _____.

I also thought it was effective when _____.

To improve the dialogue, the writer could _____.

_____ would also make the scene funnier.

> Can you think of a funnier way to say ____.

> One other change you might make is ____.

> The verb ____ isn't very vivid.

> A better exclamation for ____ might be ____.

My Notes

Study the peer editing checklist that your classmates completed. Use it to help you revise your draft. Revise and complete your draft on a classroom computer. Check your final dialogue against the scoring guide before you submit it to your teacher.

Step 6: Performing

You will now perform your dialogue for a group of classmates. Perform your presentation with your partner, each playing one of the characters in the dialogue. Keep these points in mind as you present your scene:

Tips for Presenting

- Speak loudly and clearly.
- Maintain eye contact with the audience.
- Avoid laughing at the humor in your own script.
- Use gestures—hand and body movements—to emphasize feelings.

Tips for Listening Actively

- Pay attention and don't distract others.
- Feel free to laugh when the dialogue is funny.
- Think about how the performance contrasts with the original scene.

Use an Active Listening chart like this to record notes for each presentation.

One thing I really liked about the dialogue: _____.

One question I have about the scene: _____.

Other comments or notes: _____.

My Notes

Step 7: Feedback

Keep track of the feedback—good and bad—that you get on your comic dialogue. Use a T-chart like this.

What Went Well	What Needs Improvement

Creating and Presenting a Comic Dialogue
Creative Writing and Dramatic Performance

SCORING GUIDE

Scoring Criteria	4	3	2	1
Ideas	The dialogue • shows a deep understanding of Shakespeare's original humor.	The dialogue • shows an adequate understanding of Shakespeare's original humor.	The dialogue • shows an uneven understanding of Shakespeare's original humor.	The dialogue • shows little or no understanding of Shakespeare's original humor.
Structure	The dialogue • closely follows the action and meaning of the original dialogue.	The dialogue • largely follows the action and meaning of the original dialogue.	The dialogue • often varies from the action and meaning of the original dialogue.	The dialogue • does not follow the action and meaning of the original dialogue.
Use of Language	The dialogue • effectively substitutes apt modern-day words for old-fashioned terms. • demonstrates command of the conventions of standard English capitalization, punctuation, spelling, grammar, and usage.	The dialogue • adequately substitutes apt modern-day words for old-fashioned terms. • demonstrates adequate command of the conventions of standard English capitalization, punctuation, spelling, grammar, and usage.	The dialogue • substitutes some modern-day words for old-fashioned terms. • demonstrates partial or inconsistent command of the conventions of standard English capitalization, punctuation, spelling, grammar, and usage.	The dialogue • substitutes inaccurate words or makes no substitutions • lacks command of the conventions of standard English capitalization, punctuation, spelling, grammar, and usage; frequent errors obscure meaning.
Collaboration	Student exceeds expectations in working collaboratively with others.	Student works collaboratively with others.	Student is weak in working collaboratively with others.	Student does not work collaboratively with others.
How English Works	The dialogue • demonstrates full command of comic syntax. • Uses exclamations and other words to express feelings colorfully.	The dialogue • demonstrates good command of comic syntax. • Uses exclamations and other words to express feelings.	The dialogue • demonstrates some command of comic syntax. • Occasionally uses exclamations and other words to express feelings.	The dialogue • demonstrates little command of comic syntax. • Fails to use exclamations.
Interact in Meaningful Ways	The dialogue • shows a full command of diction that supports a humorous tone. • makes effective use of vivid verbs and adjectives.	The dialogue • uses diction that generally supports a humorous tone. • makes some use of vivid verbs and adjectives.	The dialogue • uses diction that occasionally supports a humorous tone. • makes little use of vivid verbs and adjectives.	The dialogue • uses little diction to support a humorous tone. • uses general or vague verbs and adjectives.

Reflections

Use this space to write a reflection about what you learned in this unit.

Resources

Active Listening Feedback

Presenter's name: _____

Content

What is the presenter's purpose? _____

What is the presenter's main point? _____

Do you agree with the presenter? Why or why not? _____

_____

_____

Form

Did the presenter use a clear, loud voice? ☐ yes ☐ no

Did the presenter make eye contact? ☐ yes ☐ no

One thing I really liked about the presentation:

_____

_____

_____

One question I still have:

_____

_____

_____

Other comments or notes:

Active Listening Notes

Title: _____

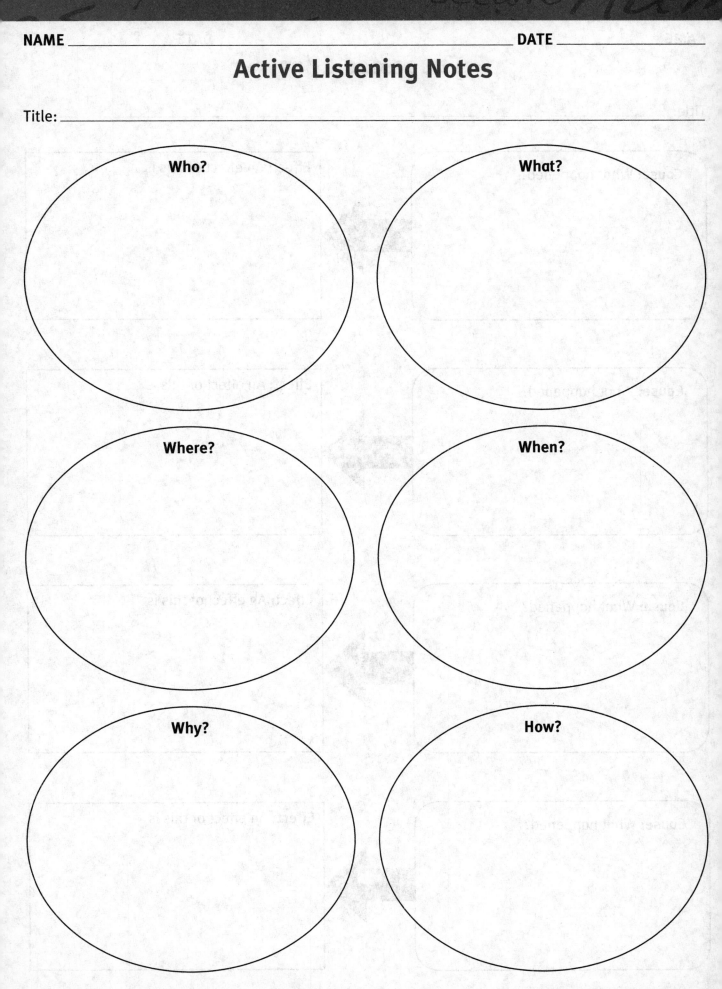

Who?

What?

Where?

When?

Why?

How?

Cause and Effect

Title: _____

<table>
<tr><td>Cause: What happened?</td><td></td><td>Effect: An effect of this is</td></tr>
</table>

Cause: What happened?   →   **Effect:** An effect of this is

Cause: What happened?   →   **Effect:** An effect of this is

Cause: What happened?   →   **Effect:** An effect of this is

Character Map

Character name: _____

What does the character look like?

How does the character act?

What do other characters say or think about the character?

Collaborative Dialogue

Title: _____

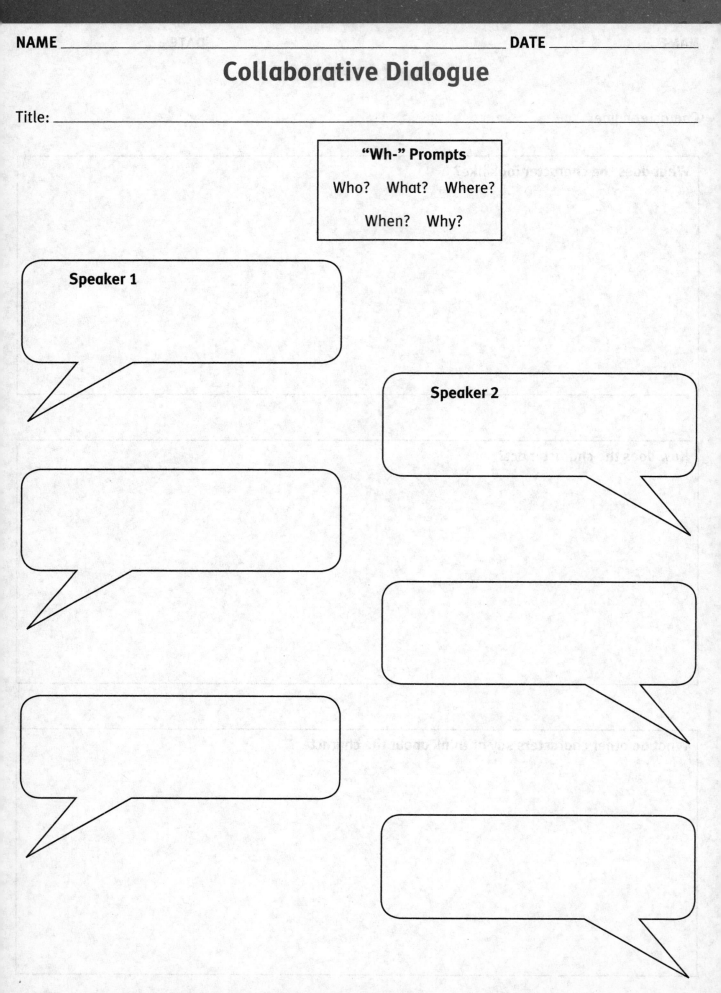

"Wh-" Prompts

Who? What? Where?

When? Why?

Speaker 1

Speaker 2

Conclusion Builder

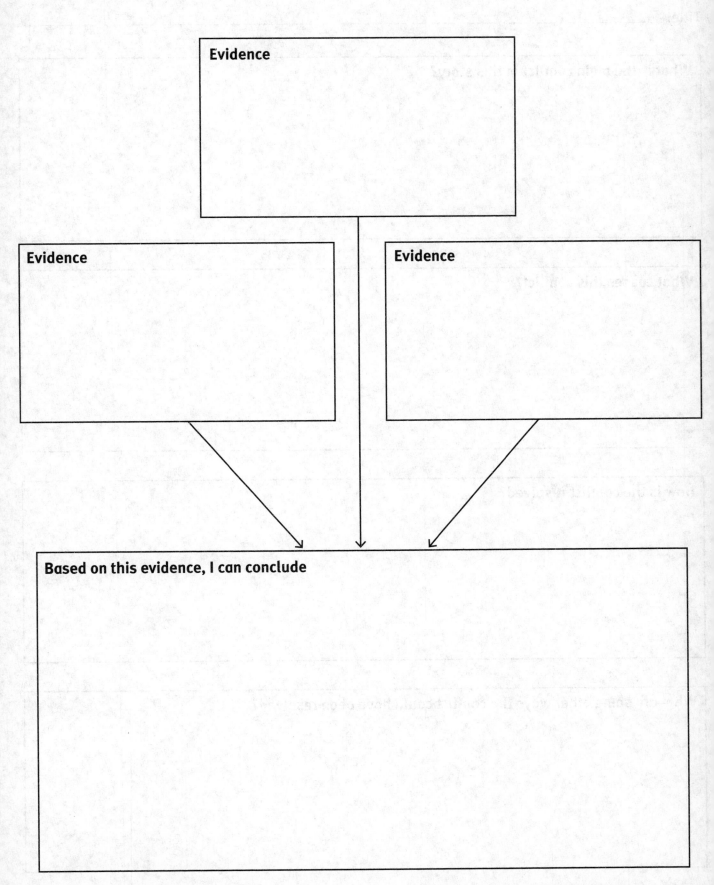

Evidence

Evidence

Evidence

Based on this evidence, I can conclude

Conflict Map

Title: _____

What is the main conflict in this story?

What causes this conflict?

How is the conflict resolved?

What are some other ways the conflict could have been resolved?

Conversation for Quickwrite

1. Turn to a partner and restate the Quickwrite in your own words.

2. Brainstorm key words to use in your Quickwrite response.

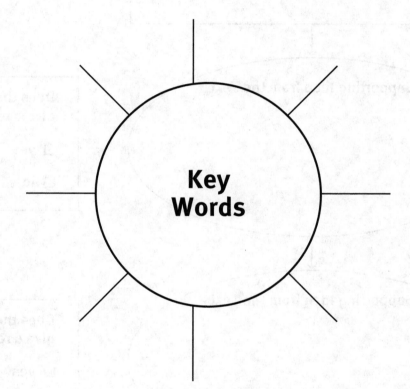

Key Words

3. Take turns explaining your Quickwrite response to your partner. Try using some of the key words.

4. On your own, write a response to the Quickwrite.

NAME _____   DATE _____

Idea and Argument Evaluator

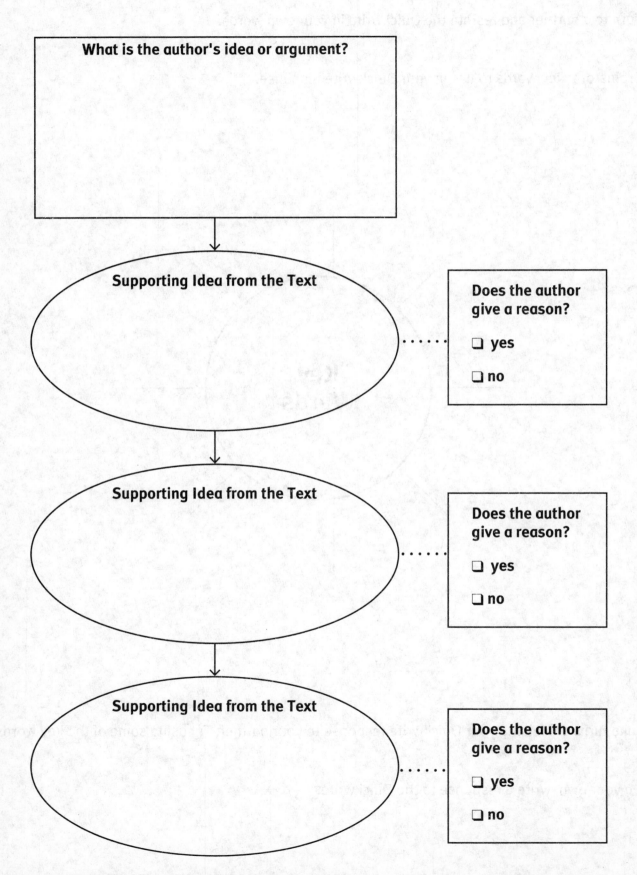

Idea Connector

Directions: Write two simple sentences about the same topic. Next, write transition words around the Idea Connector. Then, choose an appropriate word to connect ideas in the two sentences. Write your combined sentence in the space below.

Sentence One

Sentence Two

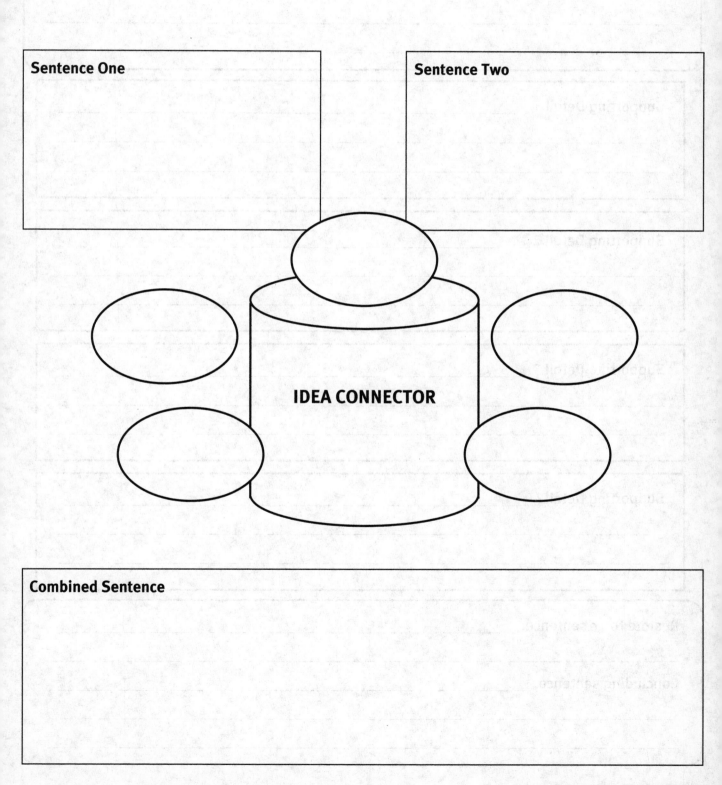

IDEA CONNECTOR

Combined Sentence

Key Idea and Details Chart

Title/Topic _____

Key Idea _____
_____
_____

Supporting Detail 1 _____
_____
_____

Supporting Detail 2 _____
_____
_____

Supporting Detail 3 _____
_____
_____

Supporting Detail 4 _____
_____
_____

Restate topic sentence. _____
_____

Concluding sentence. _____
_____
_____

Narrative Analysis and Writing

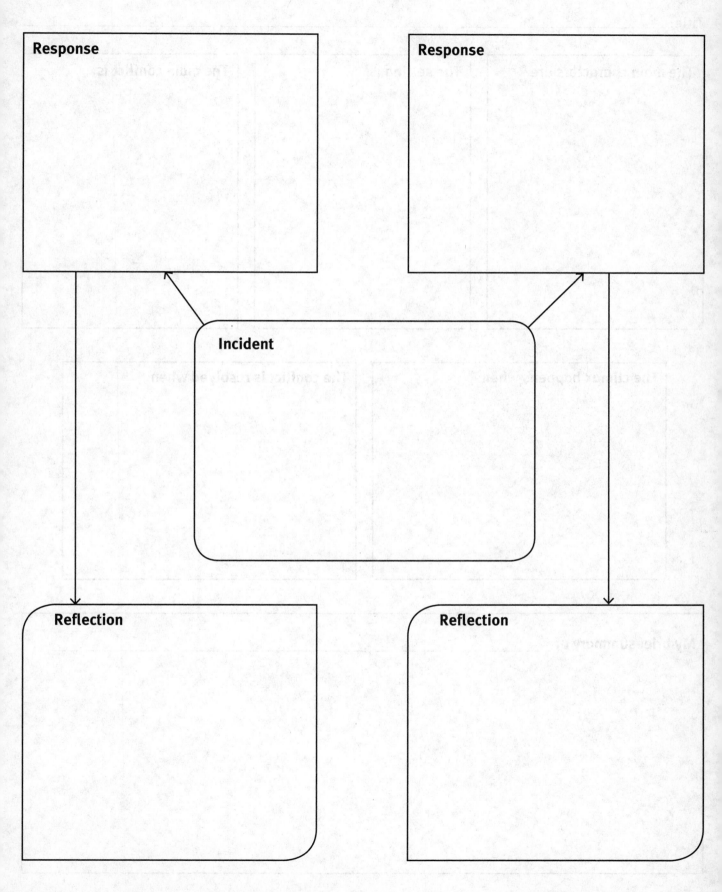

Response

Response

Incident

Reflection

Reflection

Notes for Reading Independently

Title: _____

The main characters are	The setting is	The main conflict is

The climax happens when	The conflict is resolved when

My brief summary of _____

Opinion Builder

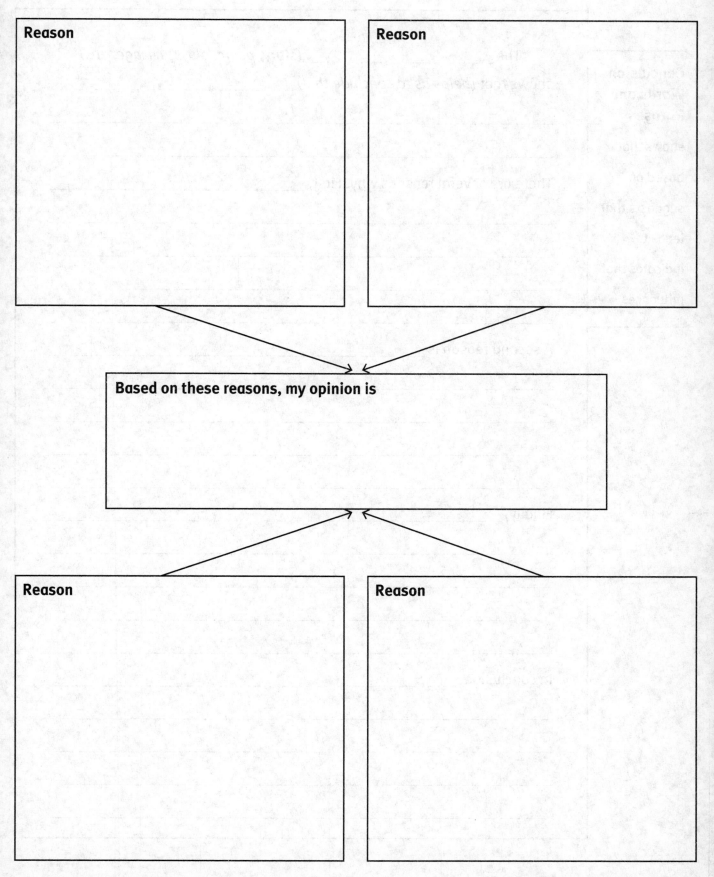

Reason

Reason

Based on these reasons, my opinion is

Reason

Reason

Paragraph Frame for Conclusions

Conclusion Words and Phrases

shows that

based on

suggests that

leads to

indicates that

influences

The _____ *(story, poem, play, passage, etc.)*
shows that *(helps us to conclude that)* _____
_____
_____

There are several reasons why. First, _____
_____
_____
_____
_____

A second reason is _____
_____
_____
_____
_____

Finally, _____
_____
_____
_____
_____

In conclusion, _____
_____
_____
_____
_____

Paragraph Frame for Sequencing

Sequence Words and Phrases

at the beginning

in the first place

as a result

later

eventually

in the end

lastly

In the _____ (story, poem, play, passage, etc.)

there are three important _____

(events, steps, directions, etc.)

First, _____

_____

_____

_____

Second, _____

_____

_____

_____

_____

Third, _____

_____

_____

_____

_____

Finally, _____

_____

_____

_____

_____

Paraphrasing Map

What does _____ say?	How can I say it in my own words?	What questions or response do I have?

Peer Editing

Writer's name: _____

Did the writer answer the prompt? ☐ yes ☐ no

Did the writer provide evidence to support his or her reasons? ☐ yes ☐ no

Is the writing organized in a way that makes sense? ☐ yes ☐ no

Did the writer vary sentence structures to make the writing more interesting? ☐ yes ☐ no

Are there any spelling or punctuation mistakes? ☐ yes ☐ no

Are there any grammar errors? ☐ yes ☐ no

Two things I really liked about the writer's story:

1. _____
   _____
   _____

2. _____
   _____
   _____

One thing I think the writer could do to improve the writing:

1. _____
   _____
   _____

Other comments or notes:

Persuasive/Argument Writing Map

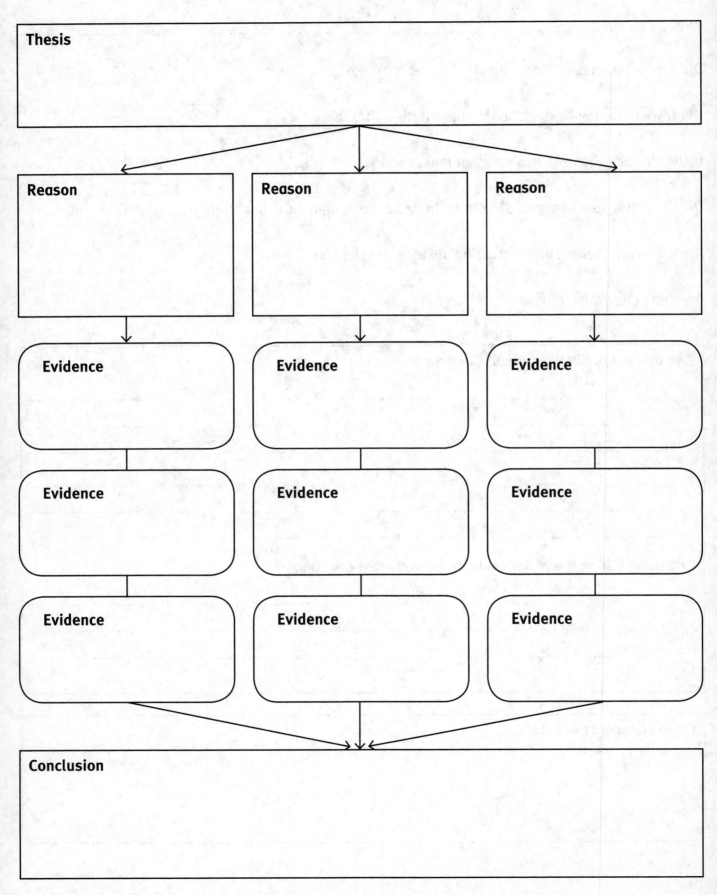

Thesis

Reason

Reason

Reason

Evidence

Evidence

Evidence

Evidence

Evidence

Evidence

Evidence

Evidence

Evidence

Conclusion

Roots and Affixes Brainstorm

Directions: Write the root or affix in the circle. Brainstorm or use a dictionary to find the meaning of the root or affix and add it to the circle. Then, find words that use that root or affix. Write one word in each box. Write a sentence for each word.

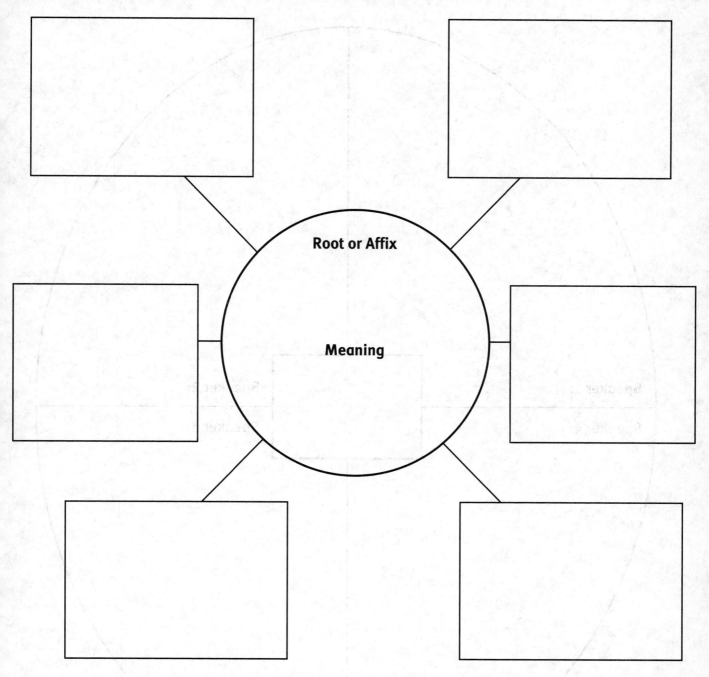

Root or Affix

Meaning

Round Table Discussion

Directions: Write the topic in the center box. One student begins by stating his or her ideas while the student to the left takes notes. Then the next student speaks while the student to his or her left takes notes, and so on.

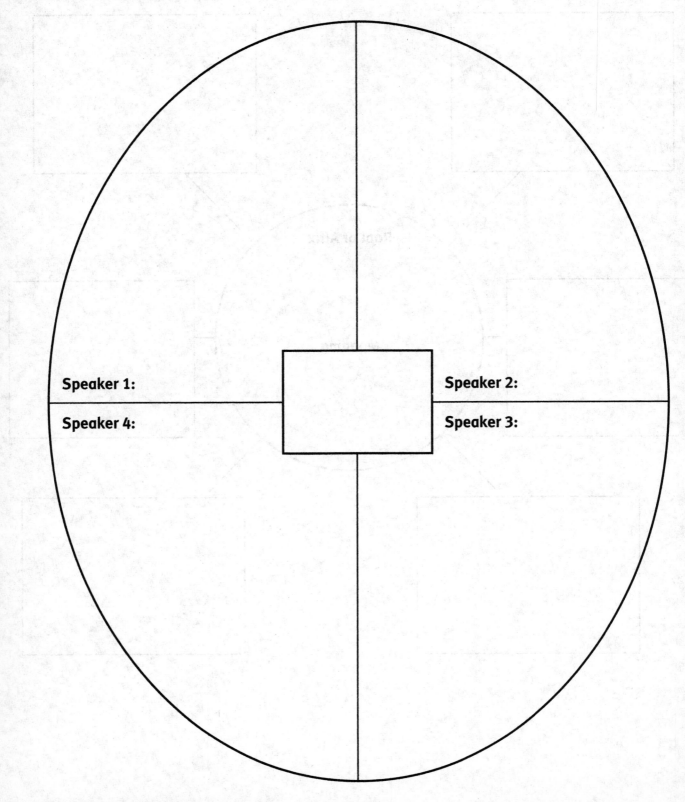

Speaker 1:

Speaker 2:

Speaker 4:

Speaker 3:

Sequence of Events Time Line

Title: _____

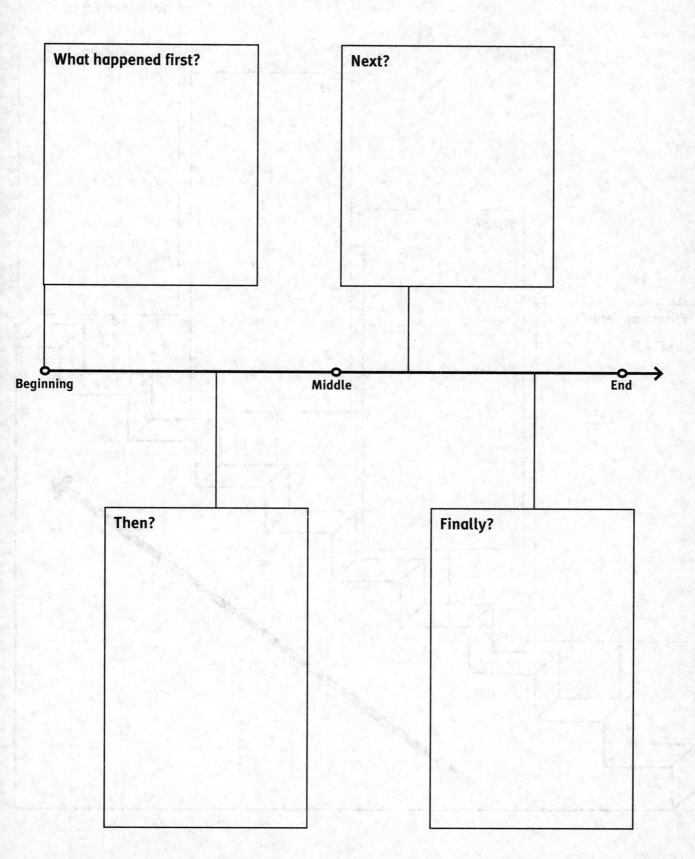

What happened first?

Next?

Beginning   Middle   End

Then?

Finally?

Text Structure Stairs

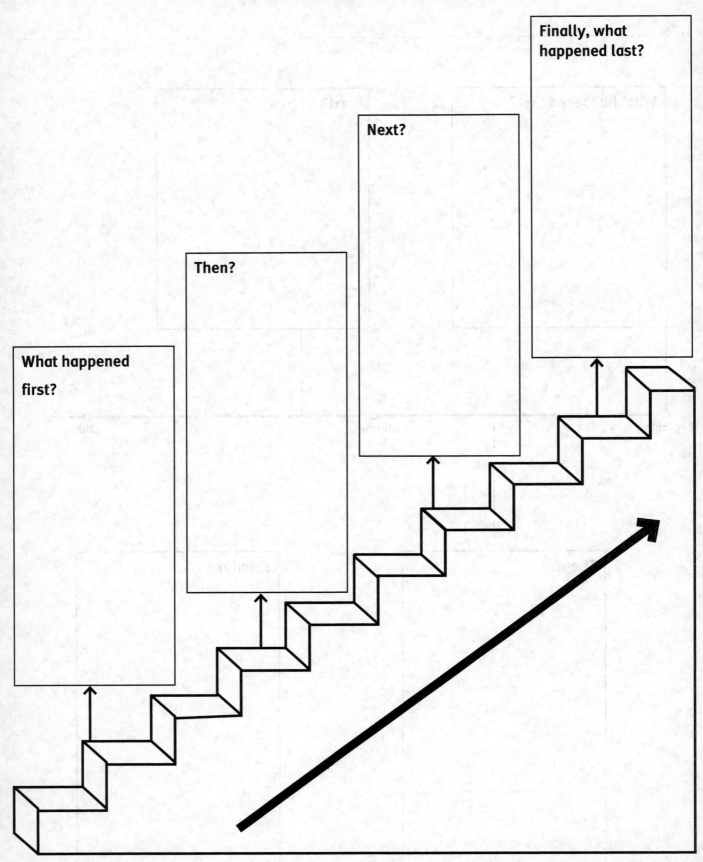

What happened first?

Then?

Next?

Finally, what happened last?

Unknown Word Solver

Unknown Word

Can you find any context clues? List them.

Do you recognize any word parts?

Prefix:

Root Word:

Suffix:

Do you know another meaning of this word that does not make sense in this context?

Does it look or sound like a word in another language?

What is the dictionary definition?

How can you define the word in your own words?

Venn Diagram for Writing a Comparison

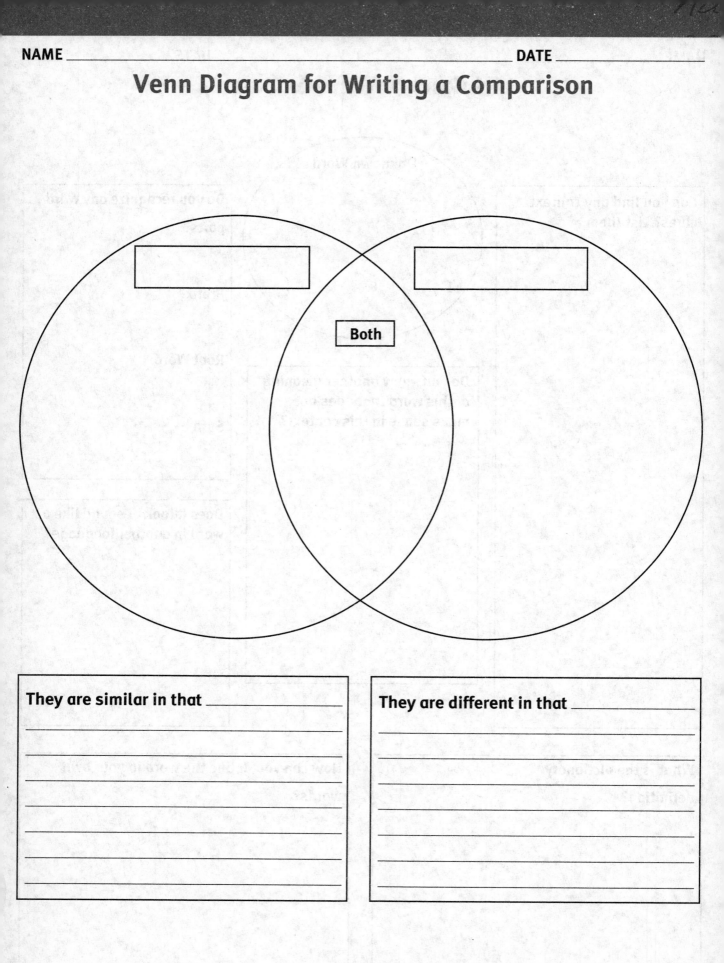

Both

They are similar in that _____

_____

_____

_____

_____

_____

They are different in that _____

_____

_____

_____

_____

_____

Word Choice Analyzer

Word or phrase from the text	What does the word or phrase mean?	What is another way to say the same thing?	What effect did the author produce by choosing these words?

Explain Your Analysis

The author uses the word or phrase _____, which means _____

Another way to say this is _____

I think the author chose these words to _____

_____

One way I can modify this sentence to add detail is to _____

_____

Phonemes Chart

PHONEMES

Phonemes are sounds. You can remember this by noticing the Greek root *phone-*, which means to *listen*. You have probably noticed this root in the words *telephone* or *microphone*.

Each letter in the alphabet has its own sound, or phoneme. When these phoneme parts are put together, they make up the sound of a word. Knowing phonemes is important because it helps you to decode words quickly as you read. Here are some ideas to help you learn phonemes:

1 Say each phoneme in the chart. Then read aloud the key words. As you say the word, pay special attention to the phonemes that are underlined. For example, for /a/, you might say: *haaaabitaaaat*. Be careful with phonemes blend sounds together, such as: *ouch*. In this example, the /ow/ sound should be focused on, not the /o/ or the /u/ alone.

2 Choose one of the phonemes and then find other words that rhyme: *brew, blew, chew, drew, crew, grew*.

3 Have you heard of tongue twisters? They are sentences that the same letters over and over. One example is: *Silly Sodhka se seashells by the sandy sea shore*. Choose one of the phonemes try to come up with your own tongue twister.

4 Work with a partner or a family member. Take turns saying words. Then try to guess which phoneme the word starts or ends with.

5 Write phonemes on many index cards. Shuffle them and pick few cards. Put them together to make new words. It's even bett they are not real words! Say the new words aloud.

Category	Phoneme	Common Graphemes	Key Words
Short Vowel Sounds	/a/	a, au	h<u>a</u>bi<u>ta</u>t, v<u>au</u>lt
	/e/	e, ea	d<u>e</u>finite, st<u>ea</u>dfast
	/i/	i	h<u>i</u>story, rel<u>i</u>c
	/o/	o, a, au, aw, ough	pl<u>o</u>t, cl<u>au</u>se
	/u/	u, o	<u>u</u>ntil, cl<u>u</u>tter
Long Vowel Sounds	/ā/	a, a_e, ay, ai, ey, ei	dec<u>ay</u>, det<u>ai</u>n, f<u>a</u>ble
	/ē/	e, e_e, ea, ee, ey, ie, y	<u>e</u>quality, refer<u>ee</u>, troll<u>ey</u>
	/ī/	i, i_e, igh, y, ie	emphas<u>i</u>ze, th<u>igh</u>, th<u>y</u>
	/ō/	o, o_e, oa, ou, ow	thor<u>ough</u>, em<u>o</u>tion, afl<u>oa</u>t
	/ū/	u, u_e, ew	br<u>ew</u>, spectac<u>u</u>lar, substit<u>u</u>te
Other Vowel Sounds	/oo/	oo, u, oul	childh<u>oo</u>d, c<u>oul</u>d, c<u>a</u>mpus
	/ō ō/	oo, u, u_e	cart<u>oo</u>n, intr<u>u</u>de, br<u>u</u>te
Vowel Diphthongs	/ow/	ow, ou, ou_e	tr<u>ow</u>el, v<u>ou</u>ch, ar<u>ou</u>se
	/oy/	oi, oy	empl<u>oy</u>, rec<u>oi</u>l, b<u>oi</u>ler
R-Controlled Vowels	/a(r)/	ar	bomb<u>ar</u>d, rad<u>ar</u>
	/ā(r)/	air, ear, are	<u>ear</u>shot, aff<u>air</u>, welf<u>are</u>
	/i(r)/	irr, ere, eer	<u>irr</u>egular, m<u>ere</u>, sh<u>eer</u>
	/o(r)/	or, ore, oor	sh<u>or</u>tage, c<u>ore</u>, m<u>oor</u>ing
	/u(r)/	ur, ir, er, ear, or, ar	p<u>ur</u>ify, reh<u>ear</u>sal, cal<u>or</u>ie

Category	Phoneme	Common Graphemes	Key Words
Consonant Sounds	/b/	b, bb	butler, hobble
	/d/	d, dd, ed	meddle, decimal, unexpected
	/f/	f, ph	curfew, phantom
	/g/	g, gg	jagged, peg
	/h/	h	habitation, herd
	/j/	j, g, ge, dge	project, outrage, judge
	/k/	c, k, ck, ch, cc, que	arc, slack, technical, unique
	/l/	l, ll	ballad, ruthless
	/m/	m, mm, mb	recommend, ambassador
	/n/	n, nn, kn, gn	annoy, knead, reign, nun
	/p/	p, pp	appease, policy
	/r/	r, rr, wr	wrath, barren, poetry
	/s/	s, se, ss, c, ce, sc	recede, assault, relapse
	/t/	t, tt, ed	antler, putty
	/v/	v, ve	eaves, pave
	/w/	w	winter, dwell
	/y/	y, i	yacht, union
	/z/	z, zz, ze, s, se, x	xylophone, grizzly, immerse
Consonant Digraphs	/th/ (not voiced)	th	blacksmith, sheath, breadth
	/th/ (voiced)	th	ruthless, athlete, sympathetic
	/ng/	ng, n	boomerang, bankrupt
	/sh/	sh, ss, ch, ti, ci	ashore, caution, assure
	/ch/	ch, tch	research, twitch
	/j/	ge, s	camouflage, version
	/wh/ (with breath)	wh	wheeze, whim, whimper

Glossary/Glosario

A

act: one of the main divisions of a play
acto: una de las secciones principales de una obra de teatro

action: an event that takes place in a literary work
acción: un suceso en una obra literaria

active voice: writing in which the subject of the sentence does the action of the verb
voz activa: tipo de escritura en la cual el sujeto de la oración realiza la acción del verbo

adjectival clause: a sentence part that tells who, what, which one, what kind, and begins with a relative pronoun
cláusula adjetival: parte de la oración que indica quién, qué, cuál, de qué tipo y que comienza con un pronombre relativo

adjective: a word that modifies a noun or pronoun
adjetivo: palabra que modifica a un sustantivo o pronombre

adverb: a word that describes a verb, an adjective, or another adverb; often shows time, manner, place, or degree
adverbio: palabra que describe a un verbo, adjetivo u otro adverbio y que con frecuencia indica tiempo, modo, lugar o grado

adverbial clause: a group of words that act like an adverb, complete with a subject and a verb
cláusula adverbial: grupo de palabras, con sujeto y verbo propio, que actúa como adverbio

affix: a word part that, when added to the beginning or end of a root or word, changes the word's meaning. A prefix is an affix added to the beginning of a word; a suffix is an affix added to the end of a word.
afijo: parte de una palabra que cambia el significado de la palabra cuando se coloca al principio o al final de la raíz de la palabra. El prefijo es un tipo de afijo que se coloca al principio de la palabra, mientras que el sufijo es un tipo de afijo que se coloca al final de la palabra.

allegory: a story or poem that uses an extended metaphor to create two levels of meaning, the surface or literal story, and what the characters, events, and objects symbolize outside the literal story
alegoría: cuento o poema que usa una metáfora extendida para crear dos niveles de significado: el significado superficial o literal de la historia y el significado de lo que los personajes, sucesos y objetos simbolizan más allá de la historia literal

allusion: an indirect mention of a person, place, or event
alusión: referencia indirecta a una persona, lugar o suceso

analogy: a comparison to similar situation or of the similarity of two things
analogía: comparación a una situación similar o de la semejanza de dos cosas

appeals to logos: appeals to reason
apelaciones al logos: apelaciones a la razón

appeals to pathos: appeals to emotions
apelaciones al pathos: apelaciones a las emociones

archetype: a character, symbol, story pattern, or other element that is common to human experiences across cultures
arquetipo: personaje, símbolo, patrón de un cuento u otro elemento común a la experiencia humana entre culturas

argument: a set of reasons given to persuade others that an idea or action is right or wrong; an argument is stronger if it supported by evidence
argumento: conjunto de razones usado para persuadir a otros de que cierta idea o acción es correcta o incorrecta; los argumentos más solidos usan evidencia como apoyo

argumentation: the act of giving reasons for or against something
argumentación: acción de proporcionar razones a favor o en contra de algo

attitude: a way of thinking about something
actitud: manera de pensar sobre algo

audience: the people who will read a text, listen to a speech, or view a performance
público: las personas que leerán un texto, escucharán un discurso o acudirán a una presentación

author's purpose: the reason that the author is writing a work: to inform, to entertain, or to persuade
propósito del autor: la razón por la cual el autor escribe una obra, como informar, entretener o persuadir

B

base word: a word with no prefix or suffix
base de la palabra: palabra sin prefijo o sufijo

Beginning of the Adventure stage: the part of the Hero's Journey archetype in which the hero begins the adventure, leaving safety to go into an unknown and dangerous world
Comienzo de la aventura (fase): la parte del arquetipo del Viaje del héroe en donde el héroe comienza su aventura, abandonando la seguridad para dirigirse a un mundo desconocido y peligroso

C

call to action: in an argument, the statement that makes clear what the writer or speaker wants the audience to think or do
llamado a la acción: en un argumento, la declaración que indica qué es lo que el escritor o hablante quiere que el público piense o haga

Call to Adventure, The: part of the first stage of the Hero's Journey archetype, in which the potential hero is first given notice that his or her life is going to change
El llamado a la aventura: parte de la primera fase del arquetipo del Viaje del héroe en donde se le informa al posible héroe que su vida está por cambiar

central idea: the theme or most important message in a literary work
idea central: el tema o mensaje más importante en una obra literaria

character: a person, animal, or imaginary being that takes part in the action of a story
personaje: persona, animal o ser imaginario que forma parte de la acción de un cuento

characterization: the way an author develops a story's characters, by describing their appearance, actions, words, and thoughts
caracterización: métodos que usa un autor para desarrollar los personajes de un cuento al describir su apariencia, acciones, palabras y pensamientos

citation: a quote of or reference to a source of evidence
cita: referencia a una fuente de información o evidencia

claim: an assertion of something as true, real, or factual; to say something is true
declaración: aseveración de que algo es cierto, real o fáctico

clause: a group of words with a subject and a verb that may or may not form a complete sentence
cláusula: grupo de palabras, con sujeto y verbo propio, que podría o no formar una oración completa

cognates: words in different languages that are formed from the same original word or root
cognados: palabras que comparten la misma raíz en diferentes idiomas

cohesion: the use of conjunctions and other parts of speech to make connections and create logic and flow in writing
cohesión: cualidad de un escrito lógico cuya consistencia es el resultado de usar conjunciones y otras categorías gramaticales para hacer conexiones consistentes

combined clause: a sentence that contains two or more clauses
oración coordinada: oración con dos o más cláusulas

comic syntax: a variety of techniques used to create humorous effects in writing. These techniques include colorful descriptions, juxtaposition of ideas, and repetition.
sintaxis cómica: variedad de técnicas para crear efectos humorísticos en un escrito, como descripciones coloridas, yuxtaposición de ideas y repetición

compound sentence: a sentence with two independent clauses joined by a semicolon or comma and a coordinating conjunction such as and, or, but, not, or so
oración compuesta: oración con dos cláusulas independientes unidas por un punto y coma o coma y por una conjunción coordinante, como lo son y, pero, no, así que

conclusion: the ending of a paragraph, essay, or story, which brings it to a close and leaves an impression with the reader
conclusión: fin de un párrafo, ensayo o cuento corto que lo lleva a su término y que deja una impresión en el lector

conditional mood: verbs that express something that hasn't happened or something that can happen if a certain condition is met
modo condicional: verbos que expresan algo que no ha sucedido o que podría suceder si se cumple cierta condición

conflict: a problem or struggle that a character faces; a struggle between opposing forces, either internal or external; also called central conflict
conflicto: los problemas o la lucha de un personaje; una lucha entre fuerzas opuestas, ya sean internas o externas; también se conoce como conflicto central

conflicting perspectives: attitudes or beliefs that disagree or conflict with each other; can be between two people or groups, or between a person and society
perspectivas en conflicto: comportamientos o creencias en conflicto; dicho desacuerdo puede suceder entre dos personas o grupos, o entre una persona y la sociedad

connotation: the feeling or association that a word carries, separate from its literal definition
connotación: significado o sensación de una palabra independientemente de su definición literal

connotative diction: emotions and feelings connected to a word
dicción connotativa: emociones y sensaciones vinculadas a una palabra

context clue: information in words and phrases surrounding an unfamiliar word that hint at the meaning of the unfamiliar word
clave de contexto: información en las palabras y frases que rodean una palabra no conocida y que dan una pista acerca del significado de esa palabra

contraction: the combining of two words (one is normally a verb) to make one word, with an apostrophe in place of the missing letters
contracción: la combinación de dos palabras (una de ellas usualmente un verbo) para formar una palabra nueva; en inglés, la palabra nueva usa un apóstrofe para reemplazar las letras eliminadas

coordinating conjunction: a word that joins two simple sentences or independent clauses to form a compound sentence—but, or and so

conjunción coordinante: palabra que une dos oraciones simples o dos cláusulas independientes para formar una oración compuesta como pero, o, así que

counterclaim/counterargument: in argument, a claim based on knowledge of the other side of a controversial issue; used to demonstrate understanding of the audience, expertise in the subject, and credibility

contraargumento: en un argumento, declaración basada en el conocimiento de la posición contraria en un asunto polémico; las personas lo usan para demostrar su conocimiento del público, su experiencia en cierto campo y su credibilidad

credible source: a reliable and verifiable source of information

fuente confiable: fuente de información confiable y comprobable

D

debatable: having two or more sides or opinions that can be argued

debatible: que tiene dos o más perspectivas u opiniones para pueden ser discutidas

definition essay: a type of expository writing that explains, or defines, what a topic means

ensayo de definición: tipo de escrito expositivo que explica o define el significado de un tema

denotation: a word's dictionary meaning

denotación: significado de una palabra tal como aparece en el diccionario

description: the type of writing or speech that creates a colorful, exact picture of a person, place, object, or event

descripción: tipo de escrito o discurso que genera una imagen precisa y colorida de una persona, lugar, objeto o suceso

descriptive language: the type of writing or speech that creates a colorful, exact picture of a person, place, object, or event

descripción: tipo de escrito o discurso que genera una imagen precisa y colorida de una persona, lugar, objeto o suceso

detail: evidence (facts, statistics, examples) that supports the topic sentence

detalle: evidencia (hechos, estadística, ejemplos) que apoya a la oración principal

device: something designed to bring about a certain result

recurso: algo que sirve para generar cierto resultado

dialogue: the words spoken by a character in a story, film, or play; in written texts, dialogue is set inside quotation marks

diálogo: las palabras que forman el diálogo de un personaje en un cuento, película u obra de teatro; en los escritos, el diálogo va ente comillas

dialogue tag: the words that indicate which character is speaking and how the words are spoken

acotación de diálogo: palabras que describen al personaje que habla y que explican cómo habla el personaje

diction: the way in which a writer uses words in speech and writing; word choice

dicción: método que usa un escritor para seleccionar palabras para sus escritos y discursos

dystopia: a community or society, usually fictional, that is undesirable or fright

distopía: comunidad o sociedad, generalmente ficticia, en donde las condiciones de vida son repugnantes o desagradables

E

epic: a long poem that tells the story about the deeds of a hero or gods

epopeya: poema narrativo largo acerca de las proezas de héroes o dioses

essay: a short literary composition on a single subject

ensayo: composición literaria corta acerca de un solo tema

ethos: persuading by using the author's or speaker's credibility

etos: apelación retórica que se basa en la credibilidad del orador para convencer

etymology: the study of words and their origins

etimología: el estudio del origen de las palabras

event: something that happens in a story or sequence

suceso: algo que sucede en un cuento o secuencia

evidence: the facts, details, and information that support the reasons for a claim

evidencia: los hechos, detalles e información que apoyan el razonamiento en una declaración

exaggeration: the act of making something larger than it is in reality

exageración: hacer que algo parezca más grande de lo que es en realidad

excerpt: a short part of a longer text

fragmento: pequeña parte de un texto mayor

exclamation mark: a punctuation mark (!) indicating a command or exciting statement

signo de exclamación: signo de puntuación (!) al final de una oración para enfatizar una orden o emoción

exclamation/exclamatory sentence: a statement or an expression of strong feelings
oración exclamativa: declaración o expresión de sentimientos fuertes

expert testimony: statements or details from experts or authorities
testimonio de la autoridad: declaraciones o detalles proporcionados por expertos o por alguna autoridad

explanatory essay: an essay that makes an assertion and explains it with details, reasons, textual evidence, and commentary
ensayo explicativo: ensayo que hace una afirmación y luego proporciona detalles, razones, evidencia textual y comentarios para explicarla

exposition: the part of a story that introduces background information about the characters and setting
exposición: parte de un cuento que presenta información de fondo sobre los personajes y el ambiente

expository: meant to explain something; explanatory
expositivo: que explica algo

F–G

fact: information that is true, that can be proven
hecho: información que es cierta, que puede demostrarse

figurative language: imaginative language that is not meant to be interpreted literally, but to create an effect on the reader
lenguaje figurativo: lenguaje imaginativo que no pretende ser interpretado literalmente, sino crear un efecto en el lector

gesturing: moving some part of the body, usually the arms and hands, to show some idea or feeling
gesticular: usar las partes del cuerpo, como las manos y los brazos, para comunicar una idea o sentimiento

H

Hero's Journey archetype: a plot pattern that shows the development of a hero through three major stages Departure, Initiation, and Return
arquetipo del Viaje del héroe: patrón de trama que muestra el desarrollo de un héroe a lo largo de tres etapas principales: Salida, Iniciación y Retorno

heroic characteristics: the actions, words, feelings and thoughts that show how strong, fast, brave, or smart the hero is
características heroicas: las acciones, palabras, sentimientos y pensamientos que muestran cuán fuerte, veloz, valiente o astuto es el héroe

humor: the quality of being comical or amusing
humor: cualidad de ser cómico o divertido

I

imagery: the use of words to create mental pictures; word pictures created by descriptive, sensory, or figurative language
imaginería: el uso de palabras para crear imágenes mentales; la imaginería es creada a través de lenguaje descriptivo, sensorial o figurativo

imperative mood: verbs that express a command or request
modo imperativo: verbos que expresan una orden o solicitud

independent clause: a group of words that expresses a complete thought and can stand by itself as a simple sentence
cláusula independiente: grupo de palabras que expresa un pensamiento completo y que puede funcionar como oración simple

indicative mood: verbs that indicate a fact or opinion
modo indicativo: verbos que indican hechos u opiniones

inference: a logical conclusion or guess based on textual evidence, prior experience, or observation
inferencia: conjetura o conclusión lógica basada en la observación, experiencias anteriores o evidencia textual

insult: to say or do something on purpose that hurts a person's feelings or pride
insultar: decir o hacer algo intencionalmente para lastimar los sentimientos o dañar el orgullo de alguien

interjection: a word that expresses emotion but has no grammatical relation to other words in the sentence
interjección: palabra que expresa emoción pero que no está gramaticalmente relacionada a otras palabras en una oración

internal conflict: when a character is torn by two feelings, decisions, or values
conflicto interno: cuando un personaje está divido entre dos sentimientos, decisiones o valores

interrogative mood: verbs that ask a question
modo interrogativo: verbos que hacen una pregunta

ironic: indicating a contrast between what is expected and what actually happens
irónico: que resalta el contraste entre expectativa y realidad

irreverent: unconventional; lacking respect for that which is usually respected
irreverente: no convencional; faltar el respeto debido

issue: an important subject or topic that people are talking or thinking about
asunto: tema importante del que hablan o en el que piensan las personas

J–L

juxtaposition: a writing technique that places words, phrases, and ideas that normally wouldn't be used together next to each other for effect
yuxtaposición: técnica de escritura que junta palabras, frases e ideas que normalmente no van juntas para generar efecto

lead-in: to introduce the context or background for the quote
introducción para una cita: texto que proporciona información de fondo o contexto para una cita venidera

logo: a symbol created or adopted by an individual or organization to aid and promote public recognition
logotipo: símbolo creado o adoptado por individuos u organizaciones para promover su imagen públicamente

logos: a rhetorical appeal that uses logical reasoning and evidence
logos: apelación retórica que usa razonamiento lógico y evidencia

M

mood: the overall emotional quality of a work, such as sad or exciting, that is created by the author's language and tone and the subject matter
carácter: la calidad emocional general de una obra (como melancólica o emocionante) que es creada por el lenguaje y tono del autor y por el tema

morphology: the study of the forms of words
morfología: el estudio de las formas de las palabras

multimedia campaign: the use of multiple forms of media (text, graphics, video, etc.) to reach an audience
campaña de multimedios: el uso de diversos tipos de medios (como textos, ilustraciones y videos) para alcanzar al público

multiple-meaning word: a word that has more than one meaning or can be used as more than one part of speech
palabra con múltiples significados: palabra que tiene más de un significado o que puede funcionar como varias categorías gramaticales

N

narrative: writing that tells a story or describes a sequence of events in an incident
narrativa: tipo de escrito que cuenta un cuento o que describe una secuencia de sucesos

narrative description: details in a story or other narrative to describe the characters, setting, and events
descripción narrativa: los detalles en un cuento o narrativa que proporcionan una descripción de los personajes, el ambiente y los sucesos

narrative techniques: literary techniques, such as the use of description, dialogue, pacing, and so on, to tell an effective story
técnicas narrativas: técnicas literarias (como la descripción, el diálogo y el ritmo) para relatar una historia de manera eficaz

narrator: the character or person telling a story or poem
narrador: el personaje o persona que relata un cuento o poema

novel: a work of literature that tells a long fictional story
novela: tipo de género literario que cuenta una historia ficticia larga

O

occasion: a special event or time
ocasión: un suceso o tiempo especial

opinion: a belief or idea that can be debated
opinión: perspectiva o creencia debatible

oral argument: a spoken presentation of one's opinions and reasons about a particular topic
argumento oral: presentación hablada que ofrece las opiniones y razonamientos de una persona

P

pacing: the varying speed at which the events of a story are described
ritmo de un cuento: las diferentes velocidades usadas para describir diferentes sucesos en un cuento

paraphrase: to restate something in your own words
parafrasear: reformular algo usando tus propias palabras

passive voice: narrative voice that emphasizes the person or thing receiving the action rather than the one performing the action
voz pasiva: voz narrativa que pone énfasis en la persona o cosa que recibe la acción en lugar de aquellas que realizan la acción

pathos: a rhetorical appeal to the reader's or listener's feelings
pathos: apelación retórica a los sentidos o emociones del lector u oyente

period: punctuation mark that indicates the end of a complete thought (.)
punto: signo de puntuación (.) que señala el fin de un pensamiento completo

personal narrative: a story based on one's own life and told in the first person point of view; describes an incident, and includes a response and a reflection on the incident
narrativa personal: cuento con base en la vida propia, relatado en primera persona, que describe un acontecimiento y que incluye una reflexión acerca del acontecimiento

perspective: a writer's or character's attitude, beliefs, or point of view toward something
perspectiva: el carácter, las creencias o puntos de vista de un escritor o personaje

persuasive appeals: convincing arguments an author or speaker uses to appeal to a reader's or listener's logic, ethics, and emotion
apelaciones persuasivas: los argumentos convincentes que usan los autores y oradores para apelar a las emociones, los valores o razonamientos lógicos del público

phrase: a group of words that express an idea but do not form a complete sentence
frase: grupo de palabras que expresa una idea pero no forma una oración completa

poem: a composition in verse
poema: una composición escrita en verso

point of view: the perspective from which a story is told
punto de vista: perspectiva desde la cual se cuenta una historia

precise: exact, specific
preciso: exacto, específico

prefix: an affix, or word part, added to the beginning of a base word to change the word's meaning
prefijo: afijo o parte de la palabra que se coloca antes de la palabra base y que cambia el significado de la palabra

present progressive tense: the form of a verb used to describe an ongoing action
presente progresivo: tiempo verbal que describe una acción continua

presentation: delivery of a formal reading, talk, or performance
presentación: lectura, charla o representación formal

presentation tools: tools such as Prezi or PowerPoint that help organize and present a multimedia campaign
herramientas de presentación: herramientas como Prezi y PowerPoint que sirven para organizar y mostrar campañas de multimedios

pronoun: a part of speech that takes the place of a noun, or refers back to a noun
pronombre: categoría gramatical que toma el lugar de un sustantivo o que hace referencia a algún sustantivo ya pasado

pronoun antecedent: the object or person to which a pronoun refers
antecedente del pronombre: el objeto o persona al cual hace referencia un pronombre

protagonist: the hero or main character in a story
protagonista: el héroe o personaje principal en un cuento

pun: a simple joke that plays off the sound, rather than the meaning, of a word
juego de palabras: chiste sencillo que juega con el sonido, en lugar del significado, de una palabra

purpose: the reason something is done
propósito: razón para hacer algo

Q

quarrel: an argument or disagreement, especially an angry one
disputa: pelea o desacuerdo, sobre todo en tono enojado

question mark: punctuation mark (?) that indicates the preceding sentence is a question
signo de interrogación: en inglés, signo de puntuación (?) al final de una oración que señala que la oración es una pregunta

quote/quotation: the exact words from a text or speech, set within quotation marks
cita: las palabras exactas de un texto o discurso que van entre comillas

R

reason: an explanation of one's thinking, belief, or opinion
razón: explicación sobre los pensamientos, creencias u opiniones de una persona

reasoning: in argument, logical conclusions, judgments, or inferences based on evidence
razonamiento: en un argumento, las conclusiones lógicas, los juicios o las inferencias que usan evidencia como base

references: details from history, religious texts, and classic literature
referencias: detalles obtenidos de datos históricos, textos religiosos y literatura clásica

reflection: thinking and writing that seriously explores the significance of an experience, idea, or observation
reflexión: tipo de pensamiento y escritura que explora seriamente la importancia de una experiencia, idea u observación

relative pronoun: specific words that connect an adjectival clause to the word or words the clause modifies or describes—that, which, who, whom, whose
pronombre relativo: palabras específicas que conectan una cláusula adverbial con la palabra o las palabras que son modificadas o descritas por dicha cláusula, como que, al que, al cual, la cual

repetition: the repeated use of the same words or phrases for effect
repetición: repetición de las mismas palabras o frases para crear efecto

represent: to be a sign or example of something
representación: signo o muestra de algo

resolution: the point at the end of the story when the conflict is resolved and the theme is revealed; the conclusion
resolución: la parte final de un cuento en donde se resuelve el conflicto y se revela el tema; la conclusión

Road of Trials: the stage in the Hero's Journey archetype when the hero faces mental and physical challenges he must overcome
sendero de pruebas: la parte del arquetipo del Viaje del héroe en donde el héroe enfrenta retos físicos y psicológicos

root: a basic unit of language, such as word or word part, that is the basis for other words

raíz: unidad básica del lenguaje que funciona como base para otras palabras

S

satire: a form of comedy that uses humor, irony, or exaggeration to expose and criticize issues in society or people's weaknesses

sátira: tipo de comedia que usa el humor, la ironía o la exageración para revelar y criticar los problemas o debilidades de un individuo o una sociedad

scene: a short section of a story, film, or play

escena: sección corta de un cuento, película u obra de teatro

science fiction: a genre of fiction that tells stories usually set in the future, about the effects of new or possible scientific discoveries

ciencia ficción: género de ficción que presenta historias generalmente basadas en el futuro y que muestra los posibles efectos de descubrimientos científicos

script: a copy of a play used by the actors performing it

guión: la copia del texto de una obra de teatro que los autores usan para ensayar

search term: words typed into an online search engine to locate information about a particular topic

término de búsqueda: las palabras entradas en un motor de búsqueda en línea para investigar algo

sentence fragment: an incomplete sentence that lacks a subject or a predicate, and is normally incorrect

fragmento de oración: oración incompleta que no tiene sujeto o predicado y que normalmente es incorrecta

setting: the time and place in which a story takes place

ambiente: tiempo y lugar en que ocurre un relato

shades of meaning: definitions of words with similar meanings

matices de significado: la variación en las definiciones de palabras con significados similares

shifting perspectives: attitudes or beliefs on something that change over time

cambio de perspectiva: comportamientos o creencias que cambian con el tiempo

short story: a short work of fiction; plot structure includes rising action, climax, falling action, and resolution

cuento corto: obra de ficción que es corta y cuya estructura presenta una trama con acción ascendente, clímax, acción descendente y resolución

simile: a kind of figurative language in which a phrase describes something by comparing it to something else, using the words "like" or "as"

símil: tipo de lenguaje figurativo que hace descripciones usando frases para comparar dos cosas usando las palabras "como" o "tan"

simple sentence: a sentence with one independent clause (contains a subject and verb)

oración simple: oración con una sola cláusula independiente que lleva un sujeto y un verbo

slogan: a memorable phrase or motto used to identify or promote a product or group

eslogan: frase o consigna fácil de recordar que promueve o distingue a un producto o agrupación

Socratic: referring to the ancient philosopher Socrates, who used questions to help followers discover truth

socrático: en referencia al antiguo filósofo Sócrates, quien usaba preguntas para ayudar a sus seguidores a descubrir la verdad

source: a person, book, publication, or Website that gives information about a topic

fuente: persona, libro, publicación o sitio en línea que proporciona información sobre un tema

speaker: the voice that communicates with the reader of a poem; the person giving an oral presentation

hablante: la voz que se comunica con el lector de un poema; la persona que hace una presentación oral

specific/supporting details: carefully chosen details, facts, and other information from a text or other source to support the ideas in an analysis, argument, or expository essay

detalles de apoyo: hechos, detalles e información cuidadosamente seleccionada de un texto o fuente con el propósito de apoyar las declaraciones de un análisis, argumento o ensayo expositivo

stage: a part of a journey; a phase of development

etapa: parte de un viaje; fase de desarrollo

stanza: a group of lines in a poem, usually similar in length and pattern

estrofa: grupo de versos, normalmente similares en longitud y patrón, que forman una unidad dentro de un poema

statistics: numerical facts that can be verified

estadísticas: hechos numéricos que pueden verificarse

subject: a person or thing that performs an action and is often followed by a verb; the person, idea, or topic that a piece of writing is about

sujeto: persona u objeto que realiza una acción y que con frecuencia precede al verbo; la persona, idea o tópico sobre el cual trata un escrito

subjunctive mood: verbs that describe a state that is uncertain or contrary to fact

modo subjuntivo: verbos que describen un estado incierto o contrario a los hechos

subordinating conjunctions: specific words that connect an adverbial clause to the word or words the clause modifies or describes—although, because, that, when, while, whenever, as long as
conjunciones subordinadas: palabras específicas que conectan una cláusula adverbial con la palabra o las palabras que son modificadas o descritas por dicha cláusula

suffix: a word part added to the ending of a base word to change the word's meaning
sufijo: parte de una palabra que cambia el significado de la palabra cuando se coloca al final de la raíz de la palabra

summarize: to briefly restate the main ideas of a piece of writing
resumir: replantear de manera breve las ideas principales de un escrito

summary: a short restatement of the main points of a text
resumen: una declaración breve sobre los puntos principales de un texto

supporting visuals/visual aids: videos, slideshows, projections, illustrations, graphics, and so on that strengthen the effectiveness of a speech and create interest for the audience
recursos visuales: videos, presentaciones de diapositivas, proyecciones, ilustraciones, gráficas y otros elementos visuales que apoyan y fortalecen un discurso y aumentan el interés de la audiencia

symbol: an object, a person, or a place that represents something else or expresses an idea
símbolo: objeto, persona o lugar que representa otra cosa o que expresa una idea

synonym: a word that has the same or a very similar definition as another word
sinónimos: palabras con significados iguales o semejantes

syntax: the relationships among the words, phrases, and clauses in sentences; sentence structure
sintaxis: las relaciones entre palabras, frases y cláusulas en las oraciones; la estructura de las oraciones

T

target audience: a group at which a book, speech, or movie is aimed
público objetivo: grupo de personas a quienes se dirigen los libros, los discursos y las películas

technique: a method used by an author to provide readers with a deeper understanding
técnica: método usado por un autor para facilitar la comprensión profunda del lector

text structure: the organization of ideas in writing, for example narrative structure, compare-contrast structure, problem-solution structure, and cause-effect structure
estructura textual: la organización de ideas en un escrito, por ejemplo: la estructura narrativa, la estructura de comparar y contrastar, la estructura de problema-solución y la estructura de causa y efecto

textual evidence: facts, details, quotations, summaries, or paraphrases from text passages to support a position
evidencia textual: hechos, detalles, citas, resúmenes o paráfrasis de pasajes de texto que apoyan una postura

theme: the central message or insight about life that a piece of literature portrays through its characters, plot, imagery, and other details
tema: el mensaje central o percepción sobre la vida que una obra literaria representa a través de los personajes, la trama, la imaginería y otros detalles

theory: an explanation of how or why something happens
teoría: explicación de cómo o por qué algo sucede

thesaurus: a book that lists synonyms, or words that have similar meanings, together
tesauro: libro que contiene una lista de sinónimos, o palabras que tienen significados semejantes

thesis: a sentence in the introduction of an essay that states the writer's position or opinion on the topic of the essay
tesis: oración en la introducción de un ensayo que declara la postura u opinión del autor sobre el tópico del ensayo

TLQC: a format to embed direct quotations—transitions, lead-ins, quotes, citations
TLQC: formato para integrar citas usando transiciones, introducciones, citas, y referencias

tone: the attitude that a writer or speaker displays toward his or her subject
tono: actitud de un escritor u orador hacia un tema

transition words: words or phrases that connect ideas, details, or events in writing
palabras de transición: palabras o frases que conectan ideas, detalles o sucesos de un escrito

U–V

utopia: an ideal or perfect community or society, whether real or imagined
utopía: lugar ideal o perfecto

verb: a word that expresses action or a state of being
verbo: palabra que expresa acción o estado anímico

verbal mood: the particular form of a verb that tells the manner or way in which the verb's action is expressed, such as through a statement, a question, or a command.
modo verbal: la forma particular de un verbo que dice la manera en la cual la acción del verbo se expresa, por ejemplo: por medio de una declaración, una pregunta o una orden

visualize: to form a picture of something in the mind
visualizar: formar una imagen de algo en la mente

vivid verbs: specific verbs that describe action in clear detail and add excitement
verbos vívidos: verbos específicos que describen una acción a detalle y que añaden emoción

Index

Index of Authors and Titles

Credits

"The Drummer Boy of Shiloh" from *Bradbury Stories: 100 of the Most Celebrated Tales* by Ray Bradbury. Copyright © 1960 by the Curtis Publishing Company, renewed 1980 by Ray Bradbury. Reprinted by permission of Don Congdon Associates, Inc.

From *The Odyssey* by Homer, translated by A. S. Kline. Reprinted by permission of A. S. Kline.

"Harrison Bergeron" from *Welcome to the Monkey House* by Kurt Vonnegut, © 1968 by Kurt Vonnegut Jr. Used by permission of Dell Publishing, an imprint of Random House, a division of Random House LLC. All rights reserved. Any third party use of this material, outside of this publication, is prohibited. Interested parties must apply directly to Random House LLC for permission.

From "The Giver," by Lois Lowry, ©1993. Houghton Mifflin, Boston.

"Cellphones and Driving: As Dangerous As We Think?" by Matthew Walburg, *Chicago Tribune*, www.chicagotribune.com, March 26, 2012. © 2012 Chicago Tribune. All rights reserved. Used by permission and protected by the Copyright Laws of the United States. The printing, copying, redistribution, or retransmission of this content without express written permission is prohibited.

From "Chapter Twelve: Shmuel Thinks of an Answer to Bruno's Question" from *The Boy in the Striped Pajamas* by John Boyne, copyright © 2006 by John Boyne. Used by permission of David Fickling Books, an imprint of Random House Children's Books, a division of Random House LLC. All rights reserved. Any third party use of this material, outside of this publication, is prohibited. Interested parties must apply directly to Random House LLC for permission.

From The Nobel Acceptance Speech delivered by Elie Wiesel in Oslo on December 10, 1986, www.nobelprize.org. Copyright © The Nobel Foundation, 1986. Reprinted by permission of Nobel Media AB.

Address by Cesar Chavez, President United Farm Workers of America, AFL-CIO, at Pacific Lutheran University, March 1989, Tacoma, Washington.

From "Made You Laugh" by Marc Tyler Nobleman. Published in *READ*, April 1, 2005. Copyright © 2005 by Weekly Reader Corporation. Reprinted by permission of Scholastic Inc.

"Take a Walk on the Wild Side" by Dave Barry, *The Miami Herald*, July 11, 2004. Copyright © 2004 by Dave Barry, Herald columnist. Reprinted by permission of Dave Barry.